World

lliburton

The
Romantic World
of
Richard Halliburton

❖

BY RICHARD HALLIBURTON

❖

THE **BOBBS-MERRILL** COMPANY, INC.
A SUBSIDIARY OF HOWARD W. SAMS & CO., INC.
Publishers · INDIANAPOLIS · NEW YORK

CONTENTS

ILLUSTRATIONS

Introduction

✳   After thirty-seven years my first meeting with Richard Halliburton remains vivid in memory. I had chanced to read in the *Princeton Alumni Weekly* that this member of the class of 1920, recently returned from a European adventure, would speak at the Princeton Club of New York on a certain evening. Something about the wording of the notice aroused my publisher's curiosity.

Then unexpected business took me to New York from Indianapolis on that very day. The business finally dispatched, I hurried around to Thirty-ninth Street.

There, in a room on the first floor of the old club crowded with alumni and their friends, I found young Halliburton going great guns in the final period of his extempore talk. He looked like an Apollo. His light hair made an aureole around his face. His eyes flashed. He was on fire with enthusiasm. Impetuous words, full of life and color, poured from his lips. The effect was electric. His breathless enthusiasm was contagious.

Then and there, my curiosity was satisfied. I felt positive of a popular book in the romantic adventures of Richard Halliburton. My confidence was not shaken when he told me quite frankly that he had a manuscript but it had been declined by an old-line house.

He was in a mood to consider editorial suggestions and went to work like the most eager of beavers to use them to advantage. The book that resulted was *The Royal Road to Romance,* some chapters of which are included in this volume.

I was to learn that Dick came legitimately by his gifts. His charming, intelligent mother, Nellie Halliburton, took groups of girls abroad and served as their inspiring guide. His father, the redoubtable Wesley Halliburton, an "Egyptian" of Memphis, Tennessee, went part way with Richard when he sought New Worlds to Conquer. There is a picture of them together on the slopes of Popocatepetl. Now in his nineties, Wesley in the past few years has flown to Iceland and to Peru without a companion. Richard had implicit faith in his father's taste and judgment. No copy could be finally passed into print without Wesley's stamp of approval.

The distribution of *The Royal Road* began slowly, gained momentum, rolled on and on. Because of its octavo size and many illustrations it became necessary to price it at five dollars. There were not many five-dollar best-sellers in those days.

The Royal Road created a demand for Richard's lectures all over the country. That he made a great hit on the platform did not surprise me at all after the taste I had had at the Princeton Club. And, in turn, his lectures sold his book. Everywhere he went there would be window displays and autographing parties in bookstores and department stores. He loved to inscribe a saucy message for a lively youngster.

Whenever he visited the office a gala holiday was spontaneously declared. All work was off. Everybody crowded about him, laughing and shouting.

Soon after *The Royal Road to Romance* came *The Glorious Adventure,* in which he retraced the voyages of Ulysses after the Trojan War. That delightful twentieth-century Odyssey well deserves the space given it in the ensuing pages. It may be counted Halliburton at his best.

Into the next decade he crowded ventures and adventures that led to three more popular books, and wrote a *Book of Marvels* for children that remains a prime favorite.

Richard's first three expeditions were made by almost every available mode of conveyance. As the dollars rolled in from books and lectures, the time came when he might have his own small plane, the gold-and-scarlet "Flying Carpet." Then he could speed on wings of the wind or with Seven-League Boots to the far goals of his ardent desire.

After they had run a long, happy course in original editions, his five books of hazardous travel were counted the best reprint property in the publishing range.

Richard Halliburton's influence on his generation, that "lost" generation between two world wars, was astonishing. He created in Young America a yearning "for to admire and for to see, for to behold this world so wide." And imitating, would-be authors sprang up by the dozens. His publishers were inundated with manuscripts by ambitious souls, each fancying himself a "new Halliburton." Most of them were very, very bad; a very, very few were worthy of the mark. Toward able followers, Richard showed warmest generosity, welcoming their efforts with friendly praise and encouragement.

Of course, there were scoffers and detractors. Exuberance always invites them, and who could have been more exuberant than R.H.? A peevish fellow who had once been a friend declared loudly that it was ridiculous for him to pretend that he had bathed in the alabaster pool at the Taj Mahal. So Dick made the long trip and did it again, with a photographer to catch him in the act.

I came to have complete confidence in his asserted feats of hazard. Perhaps Irvine's jest on top of the Matterhorn might have been an afterthought. But when Richard said he had climbed the mountain, it was so.

The larking spirit that pervades this anthology could not last unabated.

Time came when his letters showed alternations of severe depression. But he never let a trace of gloom appear in anything he wrote for publication. There he was always the buoyant young Ulysses, gaily intent "to strive, to seek, to find, and not to yield."

When it came to the last, the tragic adventure, he recognized the faulty construction of the *Sea Dragon,* the shining junk he built on the Asian coast and, after a trial trip, did his best to correct it. If some lingering doubt of its security remained and he sensed the risk in sailing it across the broad Pacific to San Francisco, he could not, would not give up. Undismayed, he bade his fellow mariners smite the sounding furrows. His purpose held to sail beyond the sunrise. One may not count his death unhappy. It was in the spirit of his life.

As the decades roll by what remains of pleasure and purport in the work of Richard Halliburton? You are invited now to a ready answer. I think your answer will be "Much."

Great indeed has the prospect altered since his day and further changes loom. The Parthenon itself has been singled out for threatened destruction. Vast areas where Richard might have roamed at will are blocked off by an iron or a yellow curtain. To far points in lands that remain open jets now carry travelers in short days or shorter hours—points that took him arduous weeks to reach. Ease and speed of journeying have made a host of Americans cosmopolites.

Still, our shrunken globe invites the adventurous. Only two years ago boys at Nerja in Spain wandered into a subterranean wonderland and saw cave paintings possibly twenty thousand years old. Only this year climbers have scaled the tallest peak in North America and the last, most difficult Himalayan height. And the boundless universe beckons. Now scientists plot with assurance the conquest of the moon . . . of Mars.

With all the stupendous changes in scene and outlook, still the Halliburton story holds an ineluctable interest and charm. One may still adventure happily with him, still see through his eager eyes what myth and legend, archaeology and history, epic and lyric have consecrated. Time, Richard would say, may alter or destroy other things, but Romance abides and holds fast its fascination.

On my office wall hangs an old cartoon from the *Des Moines Register* in which a bedraggled tramp of the '20s is saying to me fiercely, "Youse is lettin' a second Halliburton slip t'ru yer fingers." Beside it is a picture of the gold-and-scarlet *Sea Dragon* in full sail.

—D. Laurance Chambers

Editor's Note

✳   Richard Halliburton demonstrates the truth of the Biblical injunction: "Seek and ye shall find." No doubt the world he saw and knew so well at first hand had as many troubles as our own, but he sought instead its beauties and he found what is most beautiful of all, a great romance. His descriptions of his adventures survive the passing years superbly, because the troubles fade (or are displaced by new ones), whereas the beauties he saw remain. This new edition of his writings may encourage travelers to discover the romantic world for themselves, through the eyes of a young man of the early twentieth century or, better, by traveling to see what he saw for themselves.

He may serve as a model for later American travelers. He was not one who, no matter how far he went, never left home. He endured the fiercest heat of the Sahara, the frigid winds of Siberian December, the fatigue of traversing high passes of the Himalayas and the hard work of a seaman at sea; but if he ever had complaints about the service, he did not write them down. He did not travel to Bali to tell the citizens there how much better things are ordered in Tennessee, U.S.A. He went forth to meet the world, to discover what it was really like, and to praise its most admirable features.

Perhaps not all of his experiences were imitable, like sliding for an instant helpless off a face of the Jungfrau, or freezing, alone, atop Fujiyama in mid-winter. Others should not be encouraged to defraud, as he did, the Indian railways by traveling first class on a third-class ticket, or no ticket at all. Yet, although he does not tell us this, we must draw the inference that when he did exceed his bounds—when he was insolent to the Governor of Gibraltar after photographing the fortifications, or when he intruded upon the privacy of a Balinese family—he did so with such grace that he was forthwith understood and forgiven, and invited to stay for a week or two, or as long as he would.

In the relatively few brief years since he experienced the adventures and witnessed the scenes here described there have been many changes in the world. The world was an interlude between wars when he visited it, and it had time to pause, enjoy, and compare notes with a foot-loose young man. Come with him then to a world which is gone, but still remains.

PART ONE

THROUGH ROSE-COLORED GLASSES

1

Humiliating the Matterhorn

✳ Our families, thinking it was travel we wanted, offered us a de luxe trip around the world as a graduation present. But we had gone abroad *that* way before, and now wanted something less prosaic. So we scorned the *Olympic* and, with only the proceeds from the sale of our dormitory room furnishings in our pockets, struck out to look for work on a freighter.

To break into the aristocracy of labor was by no means as easy as we had believed. Somewhat to our dismay we found that wafting Princeton Bachelor of Arts degrees under the noses of deck agents was not a very effective way of arousing their interest in our cause. In desperation Irvine and I attempted a new method of attack. We gave each other a "soup bowl" haircut, arrayed ourselves in green flannel shirts, and talking as salty as possible descended on the captain of the *Ipswich,* a small cargo boat, with the story that this was the first time in twenty-one years we'd ever been on land. The skipper was a bit suspicious, but our haircuts saved the day. He "signed us on"—and may as well have since we had a peremptory letter in our pocket from the president of the shipping company instructing him to do so.

And so at last on a July morning as our little *Ipswich* sailed out of New York Harbor for Hamburg I waved gratefully at Lady Liberty. But she did not notice me. She does not flirt with ordinary seamen.

Hamburg was by no means a prearranged destination. Our adventures would have begun at Lisbon or Manila had the *Ipswich* happened to dock at these places. The point of embarkation upon our road to Romance was entirely unimportant. We had hoisted our sails to catch whatever winds might blow, and the winds from the west had blown us into Germany.

After squandering seven of the fifteen dollars earned at sea (part of the expenditure being for "Otto" and "Ophelia," twin bicycles on which we planned to explore Europe), we decided we had spent enough money in Hamburg and that it would not be fair to the rest of the Continent unless we scattered it impartially.

Irvine wanted to ride straight to Paris; my mind was set on Rome. In order to avoid a conflict we agreed to gamble on our next destination. Irvine closed his eyes and revolving three times before a map of Europe, struck it blindly with his index finger. On opening his eyes he found he had half covered Rotterdam—and Rotterdam it was!

Burdened with only our two-pound knapsacks, we rode first to Berlin, and then turning west rolled along so leisurely from village to village that it took us fifteen days to reach the gate with "Deutschland" painted on one side and "Nederland" on the other. Satisfied we were not escaping convicts, the officials allowed us to pass, and to pedal through Amsterdam, The Hague and so on into Rotterdam.

And now whither? Once more we disinterred our map and cast about for a new destination. Half furtively, half intuitively, my own eyes slipped south to Switzerland, and to the mountain on the Italian border marked in tiny letters: "Matterhorn." Here my heart lay, had lain ever since a picture of the regal peak had been hung in my schoolboy study at Lawrenceville to dominate and stimulate everyone who entered the room. Even now I had only to close my eyes and its glittering, beckoning pinnacle floated before me like the vision of swords and angels before Joan of Arc. Its majesty, its imperious sweep into the blue heavens, its romance and tragedies, fired my imagination anew until any possible substitute expedition became drab and insipid. A consuming desire rose within me to plant my foot upon this most notoriously murderous mountain in Europe. What if it had killed more people than any other? All the more reason to climb. Youth! Youth! Here was a magnificent chance to realize it. Here was a new and rare sensation worth almost any price—something beautiful, joyous and romantic all in one. We must attack the dragon now while we were responsive enough to sense its challenge. True, we had no equipment and could not afford such luxuries, but neither had Moses equipment when he climbed Mount Sinai, and neither had Noah when he descended Ararat from the Ark. However if the adventure was to be considered seriously Irvine must be won over, and imbued with my own Matterhorn madness.

Before I could decide on the most strategic method of attack he spoke to me: "Dick, I'd like to make a suggestion. I suppose it's out of the question though—too expensive—too dangerous—and all that, but it's something I've wanted to do ever since you hung that picture in our room. It's to—well—climb the Matterhorn."

To the astonishment of everyone in the hotel lobby, not excepting Irvine, I gave him a furious hug accompanied by three wild cheers.

It was by now the twentieth of September, and we knew that the Matterhorn climbing season would be very shortly closed, if indeed it had not been already. There was no time to lose. "Otto" and "Ophelia" were sold, and on the proceeds we got to Cologne, turning without delay up the Rhine. Our race against inclement weather in the Alps left us little time to enjoy the river journey, but even then, in an effort to get into training for the Matterhorn assault we tarried a few days along the way to climb the towers of Cologne and Strasbourg cathedrals, the soaring fortress of Ehrenbreitstein overlooking Coblenz, the famous Lorelei cliffs, the steep paths that led to half a dozen crag-topping Rhineland castles and, as a final exercise, a number of pine-clad mountains in the Alsatian Vosges through which range we tramped during a hundred-mile ramble from Strasbourg to the Swiss border.

And so, when we finally arrived at Zermatt, the village at the base of our mountain, we were prepared for the great conquest, at least to the extent of blistered heels and excruciatingly painful muscles. But neither Irvine nor I was in the least disheartened. Guides were found and negotiations begun.

"Of course you have climbed other mountains," said Adolph, one of the prospective pilots, who spoke excellent English.

We did not dare tell him that a flight of steps was our only recommendation to the Alpine Club, for it was two weeks past the end of the season, and we were afraid he would not take us.

"Oh, many," we admitted modestly, and enumerated vanquished pinnacles all the way from the Palisades to Popocatepetl.

While they had never heard of the Palisades, this sounded very difficult, and being duly impressed they agreed to make the ascent as soon as the fog and

17

The Matterhorn, seen from the village of Findelen, near Zermatt

snowstorms on the heights above permitted. They despaired of us, however, when they learned that our equipment consisted of one toothbrush (each) and a safety razor.

"But you must have cleated mountain shoes, and socks, and leggings, and mittens, and a wool helmet, and an ice ax, etc., etc., etc. You are not climbing the Mount of Olives, you know. It will be bitter cold, and, since you have come out of season, a struggle all the way."

Irvine and I looked at each other in utter dejection. If we had to buy all these articles we would have nothing left with which to pay the guides. When we explained our predicament they responded with immediate sympathy, and outfitted us de luxe from their own equipment.

All this time because of continued fog, we had not enjoyed even the faintest glimpse of our spectacular mountain, but during the fourth night a storm broke upon the valley, and torrential rain cleared the atmosphere. On waking next morning we rushed to our window, and there aflame in the early sunshine, scorning the earth and holding itself haughtily aloof from other Alps, soared in dazzling whiteness—the Matterhorn.

At noon, with the air like wine, and the sky cloudless, Adolph and André took courage and, laden with ropes, food and equipment, led Irvine and me up the valley from Zermatt into the paws of the crouching tiger, which the Matterhorn greatly resembles when seen from a certain position.

Right away our guides began to tell us of the mountain's evil reputation and to relate harrowing stories of its numerous victims. With more conscientiousness than tact they took us to the roadside cemetery and pointed out a number of graves of interest to prospective climbers. Standing before them we read in thoughtful silence:

"C. H. and R. H.—Perished on the Matterhorn, 1865."

"W. K. W.—Fell to his death from the Matterhorn, 1870."

"B. R. B.—With two guides on June 10th, 1891, slipped from the shoulder of the Matterhorn and fell 3,000 feet."

The near-by museum was equally encouraging. It contained the ice axes and clothes of the immortal young English climbers, Hudson, Hadow and

Lord Douglas, who along with a Mr. Whymper and three guides came to Zermatt in 1865 looking for new crags to conquer. The Swiss had always considered the Matterhorn absolutely unscalable and informed the sportsmen of the fact.

In our own climb we marveled a dozen times that they, as the first party, ever gained the summit. But the Matterhorn revenged herself for the humiliation of being at last conquered by man. On the descent, just below the "shoulder," where there is a steep snowbank up which one is now helped by a secured chain, Mr. Hadow, a Cambridge undergraduate and the youngest member of the party, slipped on the ice, and as all seven were roped together, dragged one member after another into the abyss, until only Whymper and two of the guides were left. They threw their weight in desperation against the drag of their falling companions; and the rush was checked with the men dangling four thousand feet above the glacier. For a moment the rope remained taut, then, unable to bear the strain, it broke, and let four of the seven daring vanquishers of this haughty mountain fall to a tragic death.

It was with our thoughts on the graves and the story of the Whymper party that Irvine and I began the ascent.

After following the zigzag path for several hours we halted at the top of a promontory, and looked back down the canyon that leads to the Rhone and civilization. We could not stop long, for we had twenty-five hundred feet more of steep and, on that day, ice-covered trail to ascend before we reached the Hut, our destination for the first afternoon. Another two hours of steady climbing brought us breathless to this shelter, which overlooked the sea of glaciers stretching like fingers in five directions from the summit of Monte Rosa, glistening in the sunset, to the winding narrowing wrist, two thousand feet below, from which an icy torrent roared on down the valley. The gigantic semicircle of snow-sparkling crags loomed about us, with the mile-high precipice of the overhanging Matterhorn glowering and towering above, tossing its head defiantly into the face of the waning sun, where it became a brand of fire reflecting glowing rays of light that formed a fitting diadem for the autocrat of the Alps. The storm of the night before had covered the entire amphitheater with a glittering canopy which, intensified by a cloudless sky, made one's eyes ache from its unbroken whiteness.

A stove and bunks awaited us inside the shelter. About three hours after midnight we were up again, in order to complete as much of the climb as possible before the sun rose to melt the ice and make it treacherous. Roped, each man to a guide, we braved the freezing air and bumped our heads against the planets. The Milky Way, sweeping overhead, challenged in brilliance the last effort of the early October moon, which shone into the clear blue night, contorting the surrounding crags and illuminating the sphinxlike Matterhorn as it soared in majesty among the stars.

Feeling very much like a pet poodle being led by a chain, I barked in response to Adolph's call, and Irvine in response to André's. The first hour, our ropes dangled uselessly between us, as we were both fresh, and, by using our arms to lift ourselves from rock to rock, managed with average agility to follow at the heels of our guides. A narrow ridge was the general course of the climb all the way up. At a distance the edge looks sharp—nor does proximity disillusion one—even on the lower slopes one must crawl up and down sawteeth not more than twenty inches in width, with not less than three thousand feet to fall. For a stretch of one thousand feet or more, we had to leave the ridge and climb up the sheer rock face. Here ascent was very difficult. The snow and ice had filled every hollow, making it necessary for Adolph to pick them free with his ax before we could find a footing. The almost perpendicular cliffs, from six to fifteen feet in height, began to grow higher and occur more frequently as we labored upward, so that we had to use elbows and knees and teeth and toes as well as hand and feet to gain every yard.

The guides would see that we were safely ensconced in some crevice, whereupon they would scale the rock wall to a point twenty or thirty feet above. Then, giving us the signal to start climbing, they would begin to draw on the ropes attached to our shoulders, and with the aid of this tugging from above we were able to raise ourselves from crack to crack with a very satisfactory sense of security.

In surmounting a particularly difficult cliff, a large stone which I had seized as a support became loosened from its bed as I pulled on it. With nothing else to hold to I immediately lost my footing, and in an avalanche of snow and rocks began to glissade down the nicheless, ice-covered right wall of the Matterhorn.

"Adolph! Adolph!" I cried in desperation.

Immediately the rope tightened and I was stopped with a jerk, before I had fallen eight feet, to swing in the breeze like a sack of cement, until, mainly by the effort of the guide, I was dragged over the difficulty. From that point on to the "hang-over" the rope never slacked its tautness.

Our pilots soon saw we were not the chamois goats we had pretended to be in Zermatt, as we dropped on a ledge, blind from altitude, trembling with weariness and wondering which glacier below we were going to fall on.

And our difficulties had only begun. The passage of the ice-bound shoulder instituted a new reign of terror. The wind blew with increasing violence as we crossed the thirteen-thousand-foot line and struck with enough force to blow us off the edge had we not clung like glue to the rock face.

Beginning at the shoulder, ropes attached at the upper end to embedded iron spikes dangled downward, and only by pulling one's self hand over hand up these ice-covered cables was the ascent possible. However, even with these indispensable aids, the last six hundred feet was not a pleasure in which I would care to indulge each morning before breakfast. The rarefied air made exertion exceedingly exhausting; the wind, whipping swirls of snow into our faces, stung like needles. Our arms ached from rope climbing and our hearts, unused to such a prolonged strain, palpitated in our chests.

The notorious "hang-over," halfway between the shoulder and the summit, where the top of the cliff protrudes over the bottom, found me almost spent, and only pride and the biting wind drove me on. I made one great effort to draw myself up the twenty-five feet of free-hanging cable, but halfway was my maximum. The wind caught me as I clutched the rope, blew me like a pendulum away from the cliff and over the sheer five-thousand-foot precipice. My eyes went blind; my arms ceased to exist; my head swam in half-consciousness. Once again Adolph had to come to the rescue. Having surmounted the "hang-over" with a score of parties as inexperienced as ourselves, he anticipated my predicament and heaving away at the attached line dragged me more dead than alive to his own level. Once Irvine was safe over the ledge we stretched our breathless lengths in the snow until we were refreshed. Then only did we notice that it was broad daylight, and realize that in the intensity of our assault we had forgotten to observe what must have been one of the world's most sublime pictures—sunrise from the Matterhorn.

The last hundred feet were like a stepladder, rough-surfaced and deep in snow into which we sank above our ankles at each step. Struggling doggedly on, looking nowhere but straight ahead, I noticed Adolph suddenly extend his hand to me.

"We're here," he said. "I congratulate you."

Indeed, we were on top—fourteen thousand, seven hundred and eighty feet, with all of Switzerland stretched out before us. In the cloudless air we could see nearly every mountain in the Alps. Mont Blanc loomed large and white to the west, and the Jungfrau, perpetually snow-blanketed, could be seen to the north. Italy with her lakes and haze faded into the south, and the Monte

22

Rosa group, rising even above our soaring ridge, dominated the east. Crouching on the supreme ledge of snow we ate our breakfast, with the wind trying to tear us to pieces for presuming to enter her private domain. Savage as they were, we forgot the aroused elements in our exultation over the humiliation of the Matterhorn. In that fierce moment of intense living we felt our blood surge within us. The terrors and struggles of the climb were forgotten. The abyss beneath us, the bewildering panorama about us, cast a spell that awed me to silence. I began to believe it awed Irvine too, for I saw him clasp his hands and look out over the six-thousand-foot chasm with an expression that assured me he was in tune with the Infinite.

"Oh, Dick," he whispered in such unusually solemn tones that I awaited some great inspired utterance about the sublimity of nature and the glory of God.

Breathlessly, tremblingly, I listened.

"At last," he continued in a far-away voice, "after talking about it and dreaming about it all these years, at last, I can *actually* SPIT A MILE!"

Only the guides restrained me from pushing him off.

No sooner had I recovered from this blow than he began to lament the fact that he had forgotten to bring along his ten-pound iron dumbbell exerciser that he had lugged all the way from Berlin and so would miss his regular morning calisthenics. I suggested curtly that he go back and fetch it.

He was equally disgusted with me when I, clinging to the wooden cross that marks the Swiss-Italian border and digging into the snow to keep from being blown away, got out my inseparable notebook, and with frozen fingers laboriously inscribed a thought or two on the wind-whipped page.

"If you fell from here to Zermatt," he snapped impatiently, "you'd write scenic impressions in that confounded notebook on the way down."

As I looked over the edge and saw how far such a fall would be I concluded one might write quite a lengthy document before contact with the earth jolted the pencil out of one's hand.

"That would be one way of getting my literary efforts read, Irvine, judging from the collection of fallen objects in the museum. If you want your old clothes or notebooks immortalized and preserved under glass to awe future generations, just jump off the Matterhorn."

The summit of this incorrigible mountain is commonly thought to be known only to a very favored few. This is a mistaken idea, for each season a number of parties beard the old lion and return to earth content and proud, with a vow, however, of "never again." There is not a mountain left in all

Switzerland that has not been scaled, so that the joy of being the first to stand on some formidable peak which only the eagles knew before, has passed forever. But there is almost as much joy in being the tenth or the hundredth. Familiarity can never breed contempt for such vast and beautiful peaks and valleys as these. The rivers bound over the rocks with just the same abandon now as a thousand years ago. The winelike air from the snow and pines is not less exhilarating. The charm of the Alps will never die; for where else may one find nature as spectacular, yet as serene, as in these, her favorite mountains?

It is charm below the snow line; it is fierce joy above, fierce joy to stand at dawn on the supremacy of some soaring crag and see the amber clearness of the jagged eastern horizon grow in intensity, to scale such peaks as the Matterhorn, surrounded by a sea of mountains, with nothing to indicate that you are in the heart of civilized Europe rather than some Greenland waste. One finds a stimulation here unknown elsewhere—a feeling of having attained unto another, higher life, unto another world, a world made not of land and sea, but of crystal air, and sky, and snow, and space. It all sent a surge through our hearts. It had been a new sensation of awful power, a new element conquered, a supreme response to the hunger for exhilaration, for motion and danger and intensity of sensation. We had achieved one of the great ambitions of our young lives. We would never be haunted now by the memory of this exquisite temptation to which we had not had the courage to yield. In future years our limbs would fail, our hearts and lungs decay. But it would not matter. There would be no vain regrets. We had realized our youth while we had it. We had climbed the Matterhorn!

Ten o'clock was approaching before we could drag ourselves away from this Alpine throne and begin the precipitous homeward journey. We wondered on coming to several of the steepest and most nicheless cliffs how we would ever get down them, and once down, it was beyond our comprehension how we ever got up. The guides followed now, lowering us from rock to rock by a slow and steady extension of rope. I shall refrain from giving the details of our descent. The complete disappearance of the seats of our corduroy pants tells eloquently enough how we really came home to Zermatt.

2

Spanish Dancing

✳ In Paris the greatest catastrophe of my story came to pass. Irvine, the wit, the optimist, unexpectedly and unwillingly was forced to hurry off to Italy, leaving me to carry on disconsolately alone. Piety and I escorted him to the station, bade him through tears as cheerful a farewell as possible, and glumly watched the train take him away. I had no idea what the next step would be. Having by now run into the ocean at St. Nazaire it was necessary to make up my mind on this subject—a very simple thing for me to do with Spain so alluring and so near. True I had little more than fifty dollars left, but what of that? Where was poverty a more popular institution than in Spain! Out came my disintegrating map of Europe. Upon the Iberian peninsula my eyes came to rest. Barcelona! Alhambra! Toledo! Gibraltar! That's where I'd go—and to make it doubly beautiful and joyous and romantic I'd climb the Pyrenees on the way. But I must make haste. Already snow was piling deep in the mountain passes.

It was an extraordinary introduction. I had gone to bed on Friday night in a Barcelona pension, more dead than alive from the three devastating days of travel by foot and train from Andorra, and by Sunday morning was still sleeping off Pyrenean fatigue when the piercing nasal whine and drumbeats of an Algerian orchestra, beginning suddenly to rend the heavens in a near-by square, brought me back to consciousness. Before I was fully awake the lilt and wild rhythm of the Oriental bagpipes had set my toes to dancing. Such

25

A medieval palace, Casa de los Canonigos, in Barcelona

stirring music was irresistible. I waltzed out of bed, hornpiped to my bath, boleroed into my clothes, fandangoed to breakfast, cancanned out the front door, and mazurkaed down the street in search of those mad, mad pipes. I found them playing furiously on a platform in the Plaza de la Paz, surrounded by circles of Spanish idiots doing the most ridiculous dance I'd ever seen. A circle consisted of from three to thirty dancers, holding hands shoulder-high, and revolving with a slight dip of the knee four steps to the left and then four steps back again. The groups moved with perfect unity, every member reversing direction on the same note, and bobbing up and down at the same instant. I laughed out loud at such an inane spectacle. Nevertheless something must be done about that tantalizing music. I simply couldn't stand still, so, looking furtively around to be sure there was no other American on hand, I jumped into a stepping sextet and soon caught the simple movement.

It was a most ludicrous sensation. The very seriousness of the dancers was absurd. There was not a word spoken or a smile smiled as the thousand people, not a twentieth of them women, stepped and dipped to the right, stepped and dipped to the left, with oppressive solemn dignity. Entire circles, including my own, were made up of men, all holding hands and all wearing their hats. Although I was continually uneasy for fear someone I knew should catch me doing this, I was as disappointed as any when the music stopped.

As my circle broke up, I saw the young man next to me reach into his pocket and pull out a fiery red English edition of Baedeker's *Spain and Portugal*. Minerva's owl! What was a dancing Barcelonan doing with *that!* The horrible truth dawned upon me—he was not a Barcelonan; he was an American examining his guidebook.

"Didn't you feel silly doing that fool dance?" I asked him abruptly.

He almost dropped his Baedeker.

"Why—why, of course," he said, looking unutterably sheepish. Then with an afterthought, he added: "But see here, my lad, you were doing it *too!"*

We agreed never to tell.

"Name and occupation?" he demanded with mock officiousness.

"Halliburton—horizon chaser. Yours?"

"Paul McGrath—Chicago—architecture student."

Evening found the architecture student and the horizon chaser celebrating their Terpsichorean meeting, appropriately in a music hall, and shouting "bravo" at Gracia, and showering her with centime pieces and coffee spoons. Gracia! Never was a girl named so appropriately—Grace. Never did a girl

27

dance with such joyousness. She was about seventeen, a true rose from Andalusia, seemingly unspoiled and uncoarsened by her Barcelona music-hall environment. When she first walked before the footlights there was supreme indifference and aloofness in her manner, as if to say: "I do not know whether I shall condescend to dance or not." A noisy ovation from the pit encouraged her. Yes, perhaps she would. Her castanets were adjusted; she stamped the floor scornfully with her heels. There was a burst of music, and Gracia threw herself into the wildest, most spirited dance abandon ever seen on the Iberian peninsula including Portugal. Her flashing black eyes and superbly agile limbs would have melted a slug of pig iron. This young Spanish flower took the music hall by storm. Everyone cheered and applauded and showered her, as is the Spanish custom, with coins, caps, cigarettes, coffee spoons, while one man from a box above, in a delirium of delight, took off his coat and dropped it at her feet as if he had been Sir Walter Raleigh and she Queen Elizabeth. We had never before seen so electrifying a dancer. Perhaps she was Salome come back to life—at least we could find out by visiting the adjoining ballroom, where after the entertainment was over, she acted as one of the hostesses.

She was there, but, oh, how changed. Her glistening black hair had been freshly frizzed. She wore a severe tailored suit becoming a woman of fifty. A stiff ugly hat, pulled low over her forehead, completely hid her expressive eyes. We groaned to see our Rose of Andalusia turned into a would-be-chic Parisian. We were to groan many times again during our succeeding six weeks in this country as the Spain of our dreams was brutally supplanted by the Spain of reality. I had thought of Spain as a land filled with art, lilting music and romantic adventure—the Spain that used to be. Disillusionment began with this first glimpse of Gracia in a Sears, Roebuck street dress.

But we could not surrender our first impression of her without a struggle. The music-hall proprietor introduced us and by the closing hour we had learned that her sophistication was only costume-deep. She was really as naïve and ingenuous in manner as we had hoped. She spoke not a word of English, and while Paul chatted away in the most fluent Castilian, I was confined to expressions out of my "How-to-Speak-Spanish-in-Five-Minutes" book.

The next afternoon it was agreed that if she would leave her Paris hat at home and wear a mantilla—oh, yes, and her castanets—we would take her for a drive in the park.

Afternoons such as that happen only once in a lifetime. We three had a victoria open to the sky and sunshine. Paul brought his mandolin (which,

28

like Irvine's dumbbell exerciser, he carried everywhere), and I a basket supper from my pension. We found a shady spot in the municipal park and dismissed the carriage. Gracia was in the gayest humor: she sang all the songs she knew, while Paul supplied the music, playing everything from Chinese hymns of the second century to Irving Berlin's latest jazz time. She spent an hour teaching me castanet technique, and ended by contributing her own clickers to the cause of my musical education. Once I had mastered them our artistic unity was complete. Gracia danced, Paul played, I clicked. We grew more and more confident as darkness began to hide us from amazed spectators. Gracia gave an imitation of a coloratura soprano, Paul stood on his head and I juggled three lemons. It was unanimously agreed that we should form a company and become wandering minstrels, and perhaps we should have, had Gracia not suddenly remembered that she was due at the music hall in ten minutes.

Depositing our charming friend at her dressing room, we bade her a sad farewell, went to the railway station, and, to compensate for the victoria extravagance, bought our tickets for Valencia third-class.

One who has not traveled third-class in Spain has yet to experience the uttermost depth in discomfort. The twelve hours' ride on the galloping, oscillating coach would have proved fatal to both of us had Paul not had his inseparable mandolin and I my castanets. All through the weary night he tinkled away his variegated repertoire while I accompanied him with the clickers.

Valencia is the very breath of Spain. The view from the bell tower of the huge cathedral makes one forget the mud and decadence in the streets. Here December is a brilliant month. There is never a wisp of cloud to be seen. Close about us the ancient white walls glittered, nestled beneath the myriads of exquisite towers, red and gold and gray. Acres of green orange and olive trees stretched to the blue Mediterranean, breaking on the Gibraltar-like Cape of St. Antoine, which rose behind the fleets of white specks sparkling and scudding before the southern breeze.

The glitter of forty Madrids could not have lured Paul away from his golden towers, and so, as I was impatient to visit the capital, I had to go on alone, planning to meet him later at Granada. Twenty-two hours more of third-class travel had to be endured, and without any Paul to while them away on his mandolin. However, my fellow passengers were not bad substitutes. For a part of the journey, a father and his three daughters, aged four, ten and twelve, sat across the aisle and supplied me with a three-ring circus.

29

The tower of Valencia's fourteenth-century cathedral

Getting out the "Five-Minutes" Spanish book I made an attempt at conversation with these chatterboxes, and thanks to my amazing mispronunciations, succeeded.

"Que preciosos son los aretes que Usted ostenta" (What beautiful earrings you are wearing) was the initial attack, having first looked it up.

"Black Eyes," the eldest sister, put her dainty hand to her bobbing gold pendants and naïvely admitted the fact.

"Usted es también muy bella, Señorita" (You are very beautiful yourself, Señorita).

"Creo que tengo el cabello bonito" (I think I have pretty hair), she replied artlessly.

"Le daría una peseta por él" (I'll give you a peseta for it). My offer was not accepted, but it made us fast friends.

Then we explored my camera, and since it was empty they could wiggle everything to their heart's content. Remembering the castanets, I dug them from my knapsack, whereupon ten-year-old "Brown Eyes" clapped her hands in delight, slipped the strings over her fingers, and, unable to resist the stimulation of their click, jumped into the aisle. Father and I began to stamp the proper rhythm, and daughter, with a broad grin on her face, threw back her curls and fandangoed and boleroed till she was out of breath. Here was another Gracia in the making. She twirled and swayed; her castanets rolled and syncopated. She had not had a lesson in her life, but what sense of rhythm she had not inherited from centuries of fandangoing forebears she had assimilated from ten years of association. Such grace deserved recognition. I gave her the clickers, Gracia's clickers—and had the pleasure of seeing before me the happiest child in Spain.

"Adios, Princesita," I said to her, as she led Butter-Ball off the train at their station.

"Adios, Señor Americano."

Then as they disappeared across the platform they turned and waved, and from that hour their country was to me a new place. I rode on into the capital in my frightful third-class coach with a light heart. I had fallen in love with Spain.

3

The Jails of Gibraltar

✳ Were this a guidebook, which it is not, or were it a travel book, which it is only incidentally, the author would state that anyone traveling in Spain who did not visit Gibraltar would miss the last word in interesting places; because among other things, it is a British colony, the headquarters of the Ninth Army Corps, an important fortress, lies opposite Algeciras, is the seat of an archbishopric, has an indifferent harbor, and consists of jurassic limestone overgrown with cactus and infested with monkeys.

Strange to say, it was none of these intriguing facts that aroused my intense interest in the Rock. I sought it for less prosaic reasons. When the road to romance crossed the Pyrenees, Gibraltar was its ultimate goal—Gibraltar, the ancients' "Pillars of Hercules," beyond which they dared not sail lest they come to the edge of the world and fall off; Gibraltar, the place where Tarik, the first Moorish chieftain, landed for the invasion of Spain, and the point from which the last of his race returned to Africa, seven hundred years later; Gibraltar, the scene of fourteen dramatic sieges dating from Phoenician times to the Napoleonic wars; Gibraltar, the Lion of Rock, the impregnable lord of the Mediterranean, the universal symbol of indomitability; Gibraltar the *romantic*.

For three days in Cadiz, whence we had come to recuperate from Seville, I poured its praises into Paul's ears. He heard none of it, so captivated was

33

he by the once queenly city's decaying but still seductive architecture. Unable to restrain my impatience longer, I embarked alone on the Gibraltar boat, having first wrung from my stubborn companion a sacred promise to follow within a week's time.

That same afternoon we approached the Bay of Algeciras, and there before me, rising abruptly across the water, I saw the majestic Rock, entirely devoid, to my great disappointment, of the Prudential Life Insurance advertisement I had always seen emblazoned upon it in pictures.

As I ferried across the bay just at twilight what should rise serenely from behind the massive head of the Lion but a full moon. Pale and mysterious, it seemed to roll for a few moments caressingly along Gibraltar's ridge, and then gently take flight into the fading heavens. I began to wonder if here, in such moonlight, on one of the world's most dramatic stages, some delightfully indiscreet adventure was not awaiting me. Prophetic instinct whispered that there was.

The Gibraltar air seemed unusually inviting that January night. Having located inexpensive quarters on the top floor of a hotel obscure enough to satisfy my dwindling funds, I ate a late dinner and strolled out into Main Street, leaving my hat and topcoat behind. Not meaning to wander far away, I started climbing aimlessly along the drive that zigzags up the town side of the Rock. There was an unusual clarity of vision that night, for the winter moon had been developing brilliance with every passing hour, and now, high above, it eliminated the conflict between the marshaled myriads of stars and the thick cluster of the colored lanterns hanging from invisible tug and battleship that dotted the Bay of Algeciras. This exquisite view of sea and city fulfilled every expectation, and made me glad that for it I had braved the elements. My purpose accomplished, I was on the point of yielding to the cold and lateness, and turning back, but on such a night there was madness in the moonlight . . . a sudden and intense desire to reach the sacrosanct summit of the Rock took hold of me.

My suspicion that strangers were not allowed to wander about the upper reaches after dark was confirmed when I bumped into an iron-spike fence fifteen feet high, that said in very eloquent terms: "Thus far, stranger, and no farther. Below this point there is only an international seaport; above— the greatest and most significant fortress in the world." The gate through which the road entered forbidden ground was guarded by a sentry box and a small hut, where a light shining through the window gave evidence of a guard. However, the gate was wide open, and I walked up to it. The box

34

Gibraltar, watchdog of the Mediterranean

was empty, but I could see the British soldiers in the hut through the open door. It was a tense moment. Should I try to slip by, or should I do the timid commonplace thing and wait until tomorrow for official passes? While I debated the subject, the moon poured its evil gleam upon me. "Yield! Yield to this exquisite temptation," it whispered.

I plunged. There was no challenge. I was safe inside. With my heart pounding in my chest I raced up the winding road until it came to a branch path before which there was a faintly legible sign: "Positively forbidden except on call of duty." Surely *this* path led to something interesting! I followed it as it climbed another five hundred feet, and led me, breathless from exercise and suspense, to the very flagstaff atop Rockgun Point, the northern peak, one thousand three hundred and sixty feet above the sparkling Mediterranean. In this soaring eagle's nest I found a camouflaged nine-inch fieldpiece. I jumped upon it, stood on tiptoe at its muzzle, and reached up into the star-strewn sky, feeling that I needed only to leap out into space in order to sail away as the moon had sailed at twilight from this very pinnacle. I wanted to give a wild intoxicated shout. The winter wind swept angrily against my hatless head. But the wind—the wind—let it blow! It filled my lungs; it drove me to deride a force so contemptible. Was I not enthroned on the very symbol of invincibility? Was I not dominating two oceans and two continents, and consorting with the planets in the sky? For those moments of ecstasy I was no longer an earthly vagabond—no, no—I was almighty Jove, commanding the universe from the summit of this British Mount Olympus.

And oh, what a glorious universe—Africa and Europe and the Atlantic and the Mediterranean flooded in starlight at my feet—the tiny blazing ships far below creeping east to Suez—the sleeping, sloping city on one side; on the other a sheer precipice from the top of which I could drop a stone into the phosphorescent breakers nearly one thousand four hundred feet below—northward was Spain and the Sierras, southward the jagged crest of this wonderful Rock as it sagged and rose once more to a point even higher than my own. The Straits of Gibraltar were turned to silver by the moon. The African Pillar of Hercules, so clear and so close, rose yet another one thousand feet above me. The stars in the heavens met the stars in the harbor. It was Paradise now even without the jug of wine.

The temptress moon had counseled me wisely for, after all, what did prison matter now? Unable longer to endure the cold, I hurried down the forbidden path, and arriving at the gate found the sentry not in his box but leaning comfortably against the doorpost of the guardhouse. I posted myself in a shadow and waited patiently for over an hour for him to disappear inside. At last about two o'clock, the unsuspicious soldier became restless, paced idly up and down, and presently sauntered into his hut, giving me an opportunity to escape. Once I slipped stealthily through the wide-open gate, feeling sure at last of a fact long suspected—that I was the devil's pet protégé.

Next day, armed with a pass, I retraced my steps of the evening before, was duly halted at the gate, and after much signing, stamping and checking, was allowed to visit the galleries with a military guide.

"Is a stranger ever allowed up here after the evening gun?" I asked my companion, still unable to fathom my experience of the previous evening.

"Indeed not!" was the emphatic reply. "This is a fortress, you know, and the military authorities are very strict. It's a pity, too, for the view from Rockgun Point in the evening is wonderful."

"It must be," I said noncommittally. "But what would happen if one *were* caught on top at night without a pass?

"Oh, he would never get by the sentries."

The wonderful pictures made by the views of land and ocean very quickly caught the eye of one as interested in photography as myself, and then and there the germ of rebellion against the anticamera law was born, a rebellion which led to an adventure such as few American visitors in Gibraltar have ever been so ill-starred as to experience.

Of course I knew that photography on the Rock was rigorously forbidden. Nevertheless I wanted illustrations for the story I meant to write about my midnight adventure, and as it was impossible to buy them, the only alternative was to take them with my own camera.

Hidden in my raincoat pocket, it was a simple matter to smuggle the infernal machine past the sentries, dispense with a guide and enter the galleries, where I took pictures to my heart's content. Finding St. George's Hall, hewn out of solid rock, deserted, I maneuvered for a time exposure and photographed whole rows of cannon. Hurrying out again and up the forbidden path to the top of Rockgun Point, I saw in my finder reflections that would have delighted the heart of any amateur photographer, and needless to say quickly used up my stock of films.

The sentinel was wholly unaware, as I surrendered my pass and rushed out again, how eager I was to get to the developer's and learn if the camera had done its duty. Long before the negatives were dry, I was back to inquire after their health, and found, to my delight, that all eighteen were models of what photographs should be.

Next morning I went back for more pictures, but finding the sun obscured, abandoned photography for the moment and paid a visit to the signal station on the ridge. The officer in charge greeted me with the greatest hospitality, and over a cup of tea talked to me for an hour about the Rock, its history, and its significance. As he escorted me to the door, I pointed to the abandoned harbor 'way below us seen through a rift in the pine trees, and remarked what a fine photograph it would make.

"Yes, it would," he replied, "but I fear it never will, for, as you know, photography above all things is forbidden. It is the unpardonable crime in Gibraltar—and heaven help the person caught at it!"

I turned a bit pale. I had a roll of photographed cannon in my pocket that very moment.

How many successes are plunged into failure by not letting well enough alone! That weakling policy of "just one more" all but wrecked my quest for romance and all but led me to an inglorious end. With thirty splendid photographs taken from every possible point, I returned for just one more expedition. Climbing up to a position near the signal station I was on the point of opening my camera, saying to myself that after this picture I would pay my respects to the commander and bid him good-by, when I looked up to find that gentleman standing about thirty feet behind me with a look of indignation on his face.

"Young man," he said coldly, "I can't understand how one who has been warned so repeatedly against the act you are committing could be so stupid as to commit it. I hope you will understand that it is my duty to arrest you."

To deny that I had taken the picture would have been contemptible, and only half true, for others had been taken. So all I said or could say was: "Yes, sir, I understand."

More curious than fearful of the consequences of my indiscretion, I descended the road unaccompanied, and, to my surprise, was not detained by the sentries. However, I suspected that this was only the calm before the storm. On reaching my lodginghouse, I thought the situation over and decided that if I met the charges in a straightforward way the authorities might consider the affair of small importance and allow me to make the freight boat, which, sailing the next day, was to take me to Marseilles. Had I foreseen the harsh temper of the Gibraltar courts, I should not have been so optimistic. Photographs I knew would be demanded and my room searched. I could not deny having any pictures for the proprietress of the shop was sure to be questioned. But only I knew of the two undeveloped rolls and they could be secreted without involving anyone. These, under the cover of darkness, were placed in the gutter which ran along the eaves near my window. The eighteen negatives I left carelessly on the bureau.

Not till next morning did the inspectors call. They had delayed, thinking perhaps I might try to make a break for safety, and thus compromise myself by being arrested at the military border attempting to escape with the pictures. But I was not so foolish. Without any preliminaries they quietly seized all my belongings—including the conspicuous negatives—and invited me to accompany them to the police station. Here I faced a very blustering but thick-witted chief whose mind had already been made up for him by the excited military authorities that I was a German spy and that my United States passport, two marine passports and two seamen's discharge papers were all forgeries made in Berlin. As a trap one of the English officers addressed me in German, assuming, I suppose, that in my surprise I would forget my role and lapse into my native tongue. The officer, stumbling and blundering, asked me to tell him in that same language how I got the passports. So I did, floundering even more awkwardly than the officer, until our conversation became a burlesque and the entire court broke down in a roar of laughter because everyone knew that no German on earth could have spoken his language as badly as I.

I answered the thousand foolish questions that were asked and made every effort to clarify my case, sticking to all the truth except that I did not mention the two rolls in my hotel gutter. Naturally I said nothing about the midnight expedition through the open gate to Rockgun Point for fear the shock would be too much for the officers and the court-martial too much for the accommodating sentry.

They sent me up before the judge that afternoon at six. When I heard the military representatives begin to describe me as an arch spy and a suspicious character who "traveled with only one small brown knapsack," I began to get alarmed. The prosecution asked for a four-day postponement of the trial in order that they might collect more evidence. The judge granted it, and I, realizing that my social career was blasted, was led away to jail in the old Moorish keep.

The warden was ordered to take every precaution in guarding the prisoner who, while harmless-looking, was really very dangerous. My clothes were minutely searched; I was weighed, numbered and conducted to a six-by-six cell, lavishly furnished with a mattress of the Queene Anne period in one corner and a canned-tomato packing box, Louis Quatorze, in the other. A guard brought me two semiwashed sheets and tossed them at me. "Get to bed—lights out in ten minutes!" he said curtly, as he walked away.

"But wait a minute, guard," I called after him through the bars. "I've had no lunch and no dinner. How do you expect me to live till my trial?"

"Oh, you'll get food tomorrow," he said consolingly.

Next morning before daybreak an electric bell awoke me with such suddenness that at first, unable to comprehend what I was doing in a cell, I began to wonder if I'd lost my mind and murdered someone. In a moment the much less interesting truth dawned. Presently an inspector came into my apartment and nearly expired when he found it was still disheveled.

"The maid is out this morning so you will have to tidy up your own bed," he said with withering sarcasm.

"But I do not know how this prison wishes it done," I replied truthfully.

"*This* prison! And how many prisons are you acquainted with?"

"Oh, many."

"What for?"

Realizing I was on the downward path, I decided to make a good story of it, and confess to really interesting crimes.

"Train robberies and bigamy."

From that moment his respect for me was profound. However, that did not keep him from ordering me to do so many disagreeable things that I finally went to the warden with my indignation.

"I have been found guilty of no crime; no sentence has been passed on me. I am merely here in your keeping until found guilty or innocent, and I refuse to be treated as a convict." My harangue had instant effect.

"You are quite right, my boy. You will not have to work till you come back after your next trial." This was rather an ominous statement.

Before breakfast, about thirty of us were lined up and made to walk an hour about the circular path in the courtyard. The morning had dawned crystal clear, and as the sun and pedal exercise thawed my half-frozen limbs, I began to whistle as though God was really in His heaven and all was right with the world, whereupon the slavedriver told me to "shut up."

"Shut up what?" I asked.

"Shut up whistling."

"May I sing?"

"No! Can't whistle, can't sing, can't laugh, can't talk, can't do anything. You're in the *jib,* son."

"Oh—that's right!" I said, straightway forgetting the fourth prohibition.

As the morning wore on, the warden, on learning that this was my twenty-second birthday, granted me more and more privileges. In response to a request for something to read he opened up the "library," a shelf containing some twoscore of dusty books, and invited me to help myself. The first volume I picked up was *Lives of the Saints.* The next was *Moses. Catholic Theology* proved the prize and pride of the collection, for it was bound in red leather. There were nearly a dozen Bibles in both English and Spanish, and had there been an essay on excommunication or transubstantiation the library would have been the most perfect illustration of inexcusable stupidity ever perpetrated against a prison full of helpless convicts. I resolved then and there that if I ever got free again I was going to send these fellow sufferers the sort of literature that would make them glad they were in jail—the *Police Gazette,* or my first book, for example.

There was just one little volume in the collection, *Short History of Gibraltar,* that attracted my attention. It contained a splendid picture of my cell, so, desiring a souvenir to remind me of this penal experience, I pocketed the volume; and when I departed from the prison, the *Short History of Gibraltar* departed with me.

By this time Paul had arrived at Cadiz. After a prolonged search, he found me, much to his surprise, enjoying the hospitality of the city, and had the audacity, on peering at me through the iron bars, to laugh. He came at a very opportune time, for I was growing uneasy about the fate of the two gutter-hidden rolls of negatives, and needed him to report whether or not they had been discovered by the police. Positive of their safety, I could stand firmly by my defense. Paul promised to establish himself in my old room, if possible, to search the gutter, and to greet me as I entered the courtroom with a smile if the rolls were safe, but with a frown if missing.

On the fourth day the police called for me. I was more than willing to go, for the novelty of cell-dwelling had worn off and this life of passivity become a bore. The warden bade me farewell and wished me success in my trial.

Meanwhile Paul had played his role with great skill. He met me in the corridor, and there was a smile on his face that reached from ear to ear. There was no mistaking its meaning—the films were safe. I was immensely relieved.

After much swearing on all sides to tell all and nothing but the truth, the trial began with a rehearsal of facts by the military authorities, who accused me of magic powers because I had slipped past their infallible sentries with my camera; of designs against the safety of their fortress, as my pictures of the fortifications which they had so cleverly seized (all but the rolls hidden in the gutter) showed; of being an insidious character in general because a small *brown* knapsack was my only baggage. So they advocated a heavy sentence in punishment of my great crimes.

Having no counsel, I was allowed to defend myself.

"I plead guilty, Your Honor, of taking photographs. They were merely to illustrate a magazine article about the Rock. I have surrendered my pictures. (How bold I could be with Paul's smile to back me up!) You found from the shop that developed them that eighteen were left there. All eighteen are in your hands. The American Consul has assured you that my five passports are authentic. I admit I knew photography was forbidden in Gibraltar, but seeing *five* supply shops doing a thriving business, I concluded the law was not to be taken seriously. As to my suspicious small *brown* knapsack, I am surprised that my accuser (whose powers of criminal analysis are so penetrating) should find the color and diminutive size of my baggage proof that I am a German, when four days' growth of beard on my face argues so much more eloquently that I am a Bolshevik!"

Then the judge had his turn.

"Young man, this court is no place for your ironies. They are quite inappropriate, coming from one in your dangerous position. I am convinced you are not a spy, but I think it dishonorable of you to have taken photographs when you knew so well that they are forbidden."

"But there is a utilitarian side to this question, sir," I replied. "The publication of these pictures, taken against your law, would in no way have harmed your fortress, but would have interested thousands of readers who have not had the pleasure of visiting Gibraltar."

"I do not agree with you." The judge was emphatic. "And as a warning to all others who have your contempt for the law, I sentence you to a fine of ten pounds *or* a month in *jail*."

I gasped at the weight of the sentence. Thirty days more among that undernourished gang of rogues was unthinkable, yet at that moment I could have paid a fine of fifty thousand dollars as easily as fifty dollars. The English officers then showed what gentlemen and good sports they were, for the very man with whom I had held the brilliant German conversation, learning that I did not have the amount of the fine on hand, *was the first to offer me whatever sum I needed.* It was not necessary, however, to accept this favor, for Paul came to the rescue and provided me with the necessary funds.

The fine paid and felicitations exchanged, I left the courtroom somewhat purged of my photographic ardor, yet not entirely. It would never do to leave Gibraltar without a picture of my dungeon, so, I seized my camera, which the authorities had returned to me, and climbed the familiar trail to the old Moorish keep. Gaining admission, I persuaded its friendly warden to pose before the door of the very cell that had caged the notorious German spy.

"You'll come to a bad end yet, young man, unless you throw away that camera," he admonished paternally.

He grinned into its finder nevertheless.

That night, under cover of darkness, I rescued my gutter-hidden films and fled to Algeciras, armed to the teeth with a first-class Spanish railroad mileage book, a seven-hundred-mile remnant of which had been given to me in Gibraltar by a philanthropically inclined American woman who was leaving Spain and had no further use for it. Paul's skillful fingers steamed off the donor's photograph and substituted my own. With it I traveled de luxe to the French border, and, aided by a loan from Paul, reached Marseilles.

Shortly after, I sat in a café, smiling triumphantly over the copy of a letter that I had sent to the Gibraltar Military Censor:

"My dear Sir: You may remember the case of an itinerant American journalist who was arrested and tried at Gibraltar a week ago for espionage. I am he, and as a memento to the tempest you raised over this teapot affair, I am enclosing twelve excellent photographs of your picturesque fortress, the negatives of which I saved from the gentle treatment accorded their companions. Realizing how rare such pictures as these are, I am sending one duplicate set, autographed, to the jail warden, whose considerate treatment I appreciate; and another set, artistically mounted on cardboard, to the judge for courtroom decorations.

"Please do not concern yourself with any letter of acknowledgment. I know how busy you are apprehending spies. Anyway my address is very uncertain. Kindly present my compliments to the detective force and my homage to the Rock,

Very cordially yours,

RICHARD HALLIBURTON."

4

The Garden of Immortality

✳ It was almost night, and the first shy breeze we had felt that day came from Jumna. Across the river, through the twilight haze, a huge and swelling dome could be dimly distinguished from the dark sky behind. Soaring from the treetops into a bank of clouds, it seemed a Maxfield Parrish picture come to life.

"What's that?" I asked of Ahmed, my Punjabi companion.

"That the Taj Mahal."

Had it been the post office or the mission church he could not have spoken with less enthusiasm, yet it would be impossible to describe how deeply I was stirred by this casual reply. It was as if Columbus on his first voyage had asked Roderigo: "What's the dark line over there?" and Roderigo had answered: "Oh, that? That's land."

The Taj Mahal had been deified in my mind ever since that childhood day when I had first looked at an oil painting of the fairy tomb and read the immortal story of its creation. It had always been a dream castle to me, something so fabulous it would not have dimensions and weight and location; something so lovely it could not exist outside of picture books. Poring for hours at a time over these very books I had come to revere this building above all others, and had made a divinity out of Arjemand, the Mogul princess who became the Empress Mumtaz-i-Mahal, whose beauty and perfection it commemorates. All my adventures in India up to this time I had known to be only preludes to the great final adventure —the actual sight and touch of the Taj.

Facts and legends came to me now in a jumbled mass, as I stood in the fortress tower and watched the great dome disappear into the night. The follies of the Emperor Shah Jahan, who built the Taj, were forgotten; what mattered the number of his crimes?—his genius as a builder, his fame as the greatest lover in history, were more worthy of memory. In the marble poetry of the Taj this greatest lover has immortalized the object of his passion. Arjemand, favorite among a thousand wives, is embodied in its stones; her chastity is carved into its spotless walls; her exquisiteness reproduced in every delicate line; her majesty reflected in the aerial grace of dome and minaret that floated and faded there above the riverside.

We had been silent for some moments, enjoying the coolness of the night that now had blotted out the distance. Ahmed was the first to speak:
"You know Shah Jahan?"

"Yes," I said, "I 'know' him."

"He die here in balcony."

"What! You mean this is the *Jasmine Tower!*"

He assured me it was, and that we were treading thoughtlessly on stones numbered among the most hallowed in India, for this was the point from which the emperor last saw his beloved wife's memorial. For her shrine he had squandered the wealth of an empire, until his subjects, led by his own son, revolted and imprisoned the "King of Earth" here in his own palace, on the banks of the Jumna. Dethroned, disgraced, held captive, for seven years he had only the memory of his lovely Arjemand to comfort him. At last, when he felt his end was near, the old and broken man pleaded, not in vain, to be carried at dawn to the Jasmine Tower, where his dying eyes might rest upon the distant minarets of the mausoleum. There his heart and soul already were, there he knew his body was soon to be, beside her for whom he had created the one perfect thing. Through fading eyes he watched the eastern horizon brighten with light, watched the first beam of sunrise strike the dome. Then the heavy weary gates closed forever—and the Taj passed from view.

"You stay here all night, *Sahib?*"

"No," I said, my reverie broken, "I am ready to go now."

We descended from the tower, threaded our way out of the unlit corridors, found the grim entrance gate, and hurried homeward through

India Tourist Office

The Taj Mahal

the animated streets. But I saw neither the swinging lanterns, nor the shops, nor the crowds. My thoughts were of Mumtaz-i-Mahal, whom, on the morrow, I planned to meet, at last, face to face.

Early and eagerly the next morning I set forth alone. I passed beneath the ruddy arch that commands entrance to the gardens of the Taj, and there—behold!—beyond, in the blinding summer sunshine I saw it, a miracle of sky and verdure and ivory, beckoning to me through the framing gateway. My dream castle had come to life.

I answered its call with absolute surrender, moving almost without volition down the marble pavement that led straight and glittering into its very heart. I was unaware of the fountains at my feet, or of the indigo sky above. I saw only my long-sought Taj awaiting me, harmonious as music, lovely as the face of the immortal woman it commemorates.

The entire day I remained beside the snowy temple, enchanted by its serenity, forgetful of time and self. I wandered about its polished corridors, climbed upon its roof, descended into its crypts. Attracted by a myriad of colors I drifted about the gardens that enthrone the monster pearl, tarried by the lily pools reflecting dome and minaret, and loitered along the avenue of stately cypresses.

Noon came, and afternoon. From a shaded bed of grass I looked up at the shimmering walls. Built of cold stone they are, and yet how ethereal; erected by man, yet touched by the gods. "Make it as beautiful as she was beautiful, as delicate, as graceful," commanded the grief-stricken emperor of Ustad Isa, his greatest architect. "Make it the image and the soul of her beauty." And in a dream Ustad Isa visioned a finished tomb that was as lovely yet withal as majestic as the moon-faced empress. Though two hundred and fourscore years have passed since this dream was realized and Mumtaz-i-Mahal laid to rest, today the Taj appears to have been built but yesterday. There it floated above me, not only a symbol of matchless feminine beauty but an expression of the adoration the Shah-in-Shah felt for his chosen favorite of all the palace. Even in building, it was marked by the passion that distinguished the idyllic union of the emperor and the Lady Arjemand, for he spent upon it not only his treasures, but his grief and his tears. Thus it has come to pass that the sepulcher has a soul, which, so legends tell, has been known to manifest itself on summer nights, and in the image of the queen emerge in radiance from the tomb, dissolved to mist by moonbeams.

Twilight came, and the wind ceased. The tropical dark-blue background of all this beauty was fading into night. About me the deserted gardens were hushed except for the faint splash of falling water. Twilight faded into starlight. Still I clung to my veiled Taj, and no duty or need could lure me away from this glimpse into Paradise.

The summer moon had reached its zenith a week before, and now, rapidly waning, rose nearer the hour of dawn than darkness. Yet at midnight every visitor must depart from the gardens, so I would have to leave without seeing the palace melt beneath the flood of moonlight. Already guards were closing the tower gates; sentries were gathering before the threshold of the tomb. A few belated stragglers were being hurried to their waiting *gharries,* and as I saw them go the thought came to me: "Why not try to stay? Then I could possess the Taj by myself alone!" The romantic possibilities of such an adventure captivated my fancy. Quickly I hid in a darkened grove. The watchmen, carrying their lamps, came close to me—but passed on. Not for a kingdom would I have surrendered, with this opportunity before me to remain through the night by the side of my marble mistress.

Then from the entrance I heard the ponderous iron-bound doors groan as they were swung laboriously into place. I heard the clank of fastening chains, and their ominous echo, reverberating from wall to wall across the breathless garden, filled me with sudden dread, for I, a mortal, was now imprisoned with a pale pearl ghost—I was alone with the Taj Mahal.

For an hour, and an hour more, waiting for the moon, I lingered patiently beneath my willow grove, enraptured by the dim beauty of this dreamland and by its hovering mystery. Then with the tolling of two the shroud was lifted from the sky, as the moon glinted through the boughs upon the sleeping garden.

Utter silence had reigned till now; but all at once from a topmost branch came the herald hooting of a sentinel owl, commanding the myriad invisible inhabitants of the garden to awake from bush and vine and flower, to acclaim their lady of the night. Straightway a cricket orchestra began to chirrup forth its homage; flying foxes tumbled through the air. From flame-of-the-forest and banyan bough, from clematis vine and honeysuckle tangles, came stirs and flutters of awakened doves and the faint woodnote of the hoopee. Only the guardsmen at the gateway slumbered on.

Then, as I watched, the moon floated upward from the trees to commune in secret with the phantom Taj, while all earthly worshipers were

The pools of the Taj Mahal

far away and the union safe from the disenchanting gaze of mortals. Silvered, the mausoleum emerged from shadow, and hypnotic in new radiance beckoned to me once more. Heedless of consequences I crept from my green grotto; there was no sound. On tiptoe I mounted a stairway to the dais; there was no challenge, for the sentries had been touched by magic too, and slept profoundly.

Higher rose the moon; fairer gleamed the Taj, a harmonious pile of masonry in the sunshine of the morning, a specter underneath the stars, now transfigured to a gleaming gossamer, an airy bubble that might evaporate into ether while one looked at it.

Unaware of the passing moments, I watched the shadows move in the deep recesses of the façade, until, unable to resist the lure of the interior, I turned to the main portal. Stealthily I crept around the sleeping sentries, softly crossed the threshold, and entering stood beside the faint-lit tombs of the Shah-in-Shah and Arjemand. A bronze lantern hung by a chain from the obscurity of the dome above, and the light shining through its perforated sides cast fantastic shadows on the carved walls. Forgetful of sentries, I whistled a subdued note and listened to it ringing and reringing in slowly dying echoes far up in the blackness of the vault.

The fourth hour came, and found me standing pensive beside the Empress' grave. A pilgrim to her shrine, she had blessed me with protection. With sudden shame I realized I had brought no offering. Neither gold nor silver did I have, not even a flower; but in a recess of my wallet, kept for memory's sake, there withered a twig of myrtle, plucked six months past from some courtyard in the Alhambra of the Moors, amid whose storied battlements I had sought romance on such a night as this. From one Moslem monument in Spain it had come to another in India, directed perhaps by the hand of Allah. Reverently I placed these fragile leaves upon her tomb. The wind brushed gently through the vaulted corridors, and slowly swung the hanging lantern to and fro; and I was filled with happiness, fancying that her spirit had sent this murmured benediction.

No one was awake to see me creep forth into the balmy night, or to watch my shadow as it left the marble platform and moved again across the moon-blanched park. Streams of water from the Jumna flowed upon the thirsty gardens, so that a glittering film covered lawn and bed and pavement. Barefoot, I waded in the flowered ponds. How cool and refreshing was the touch of flooded grass—how far from the realities of earth I felt myself. On a marble bench I sat beside the deepest lily pool and looked at the great white blossoms drifting among the reflected stars of an Indian sky. And as I looked there seemed to come from its depths a call, the same that had twice drawn me powerless into the Taj: "Come to my caress, O mortal—bathe your body in my coolness—float upon my tranquil mirror—wash your mind of consciousness."

Only an insomniac owl watched me remove my clothes, or heard the faint ripple as I dropped into the alabaster pool. This was a page from the *Arabian Nights,* a reversion to the fabled luxury of ancient emperors —this, at last, was Romance.

It was but an hour before dawn. The moon had reached the peak of its course and was shining with unearthly brilliance. Alone, in all this supernatural beauty, resting by the pool before the phantom Taj, I felt myself transported to some previous existence that knew neither time nor space nor substance. I and all that I beheld were myth. The subconscious mind was master, linking me with previous incarnations in the dim past.

A strange ecstasy came to me. I heard myself laugh deliriously. A giant lily floated on the unruffled mirror, and as I leaned over the alabaster rim to tear it from its stem—whose eerie face peered back at me from the water, whose queer slant eyes, whose horns? In terror I leaped to my feet. Was it this that I had been in the beginning, or was it to this that I had come, distorted by some avenging spirit for profaning with my touch a sanctuary of immortality?

Caw—caw—caw! A crow in a nearby grove mocked my bewilderment. Twice startled, I glanced up to find day streaking the east. There was a rush of wind, a rustle of leaves. . . . Suddenly I was aware of being bitterly cold. Realities began to emerge before my eyes. The gardens lay about me, stark and tangible. The Taj . . . had turned again . . . to stone.

In a fever of dread and perplexity, I flung on my clothes, hurried to the tower gate, surrendering myself to the sentries, and besought them to liberate me from this realm of the supernatural.

As I passed, with a guard on either side, underneath the vaulted tower, I looked back through the arch-framed opening to find the sky in amber hues, the park dew-pearled, waking to the matin song of lark and oriole. I saw the Taj, reflecting the rose-and-gold horizon, still tenderly beautiful, still beckoning, and as I turned to her for one last farewell glimpse, the first beam of sunrise struck the dome. Then the heavy weary gates closed behind me, and the Lady of my Dreams passed from view.

5

Adventure in the Punjab

✳ Straight to the bungalow of the British superintendent I was led. He got out of bed to investigate the cause of the disturbance raised by our approach, and was in none too amiable a mood when I was marched before him.

"What were you doing in the garden at such an hour?" he asked sternly on hearing my captors' report. "It is forbidden and a punishable offense."

As at Gibraltar I pleaded my own case, explaining as frankly as possible my position, and emptying my pockets to disprove any suspicion of having stolen the Taj.

Assured that my infringement of the rules was harmless, and too sleepy to care one way or the other, he dismissed me and went back to bed.

Through the early morning I tramped back to the ugliness of Agra, beset by the depression that always follows intoxication. The terrific morning heat, the dust, the hunger, brought my thoughts brutally back to stern realities, and to the realization that with all the enchantment of the previous night I was still a frail-pursed vagabond, walking homeward from Paradise because I could not afford a vehicle.

On reaching my lodging, the English proprietress had good news for me. "Last evening, during your absence, another American, named David,

India Tourist Office

The Kartub Tower, Delhi

54

came to visit us. He's about your age and seems to be 'bumming' just as you are—and he was on the lookout for a companion and right away I thought of you. He's here now."

David proved a made-to-order comrade, globe-trotting from east to west on the proceeds of a year's work in central Alaska. He was twenty, a good sport, and a clever vagabond whose youthful appearance and manners persuaded his creditors to cancel his debts, railroad officials to wink at tickets, and chance acquaintances to supply him gratis with food and shelter.

With this companion I moved on to Rawalpindi, where we found that Srinagar, the fantastic metropolis of the Vale of Kashmir, and our goal, lay two hundred miles away and was accessible only via a single long and tortuous highroad. The price of overland transportation proved entirely beyond our capacity to pay, but that didn't stop us. All our lives we had been attracted to this poetic vale, this Paradise of Asia that had always seemed as intangible as heaven itself, and now we were too close to the realization of our dream to allow a little thing like two hundred miles to interfere. Shouldering our knapsacks we started up the Kashmir road on foot, trusting that by some means or other we would be delivered from our difficulties. As usual, we were. A heavy freight truck lumbering behind just at the outskirts of the city halted in response to our waving, and with a rupee and package of cigarettes the native driver was bribed into a state of such amiability that he made room for us on his leather seat and drove us over the famous Jhelum River highroad as it bored and writhed and bridged its way along the one hundred and sixty spectacular miles to Baramula. Here the canyon opens wide and the most beautiful valley in the world is at hand.

The year was at the spring, the day at the morn, the morning at seven, when David and I began to tramp the last forty miles to Srinagar. The walnut trees that shaded the road through Baramula shut out the sky and withheld from view the surrounding landscape. Suddenly the branches stood aside, and there, before us, stretched the Vale of Kashmir. Far and away we beheld a sea of green, the fresh lush green of sprouting rice paddies, the springtime green of waving poplar trees, the deep, dark green of pines and deodars that climbed the slopes. Green, green, green, all overflowing with water and radiant in the spring sunshine. Ten miles to each side the towering mountain walls wrapped in unbroken snow extended in parallel lines the length of the valley. Not mere Sierra Nevadas, these, not mere Mont

55

Blancs and Matterhorns, but *Himalayas*. Eighteen thousand, twenty thousand, twenty-two thousand feet, breaking the skyline as far as the eye could reach. What else could the poets through the ages have called this valley but an emerald set in pearls?

We had chosen well our season. It was May. On every hillside branches of white pear blossoms dipped into the fields of wild poppies that splashed the landscape with scarlet. The river, soon to begin its impetuous dash through the Jhelum gorge, here flowed as the gentle Avon, between banks rioting with royal iris. This brilliant flower seemed like a plague, smothering every other plant that crossed its path—every other save the belligerent wild rose, which dared defy even the iris and struggled for supremacy in a battle of pink and purple blossoms.

In our first day's tramping we stopped often to drink at bubbling springs or to climb into roadside mulberry trees to dine upon the large and luscious fruit. Greatly astonished at our lack of dignity the local population gathered around to stare into the branches at the two unconventional white *sahibs*. They were justified no doubt in their astonishment, for almost the only foreigners who visit Kashmir are British Army majors and lady missionaries, and neither is in the habit of scrambling up mulberry trees on the public highway in search of food.

These distractions came so frequently that by teatime we had progressed no farther than Petan, a picturesque hamlet less than twenty miles from Baramula. Here we sought shelter in the travelers' resthouse, a comfortable little cottage nestled in a flower garden. All that day the sun had shone with true tropical ardor, but with twilight came a drop in the temperature that made us remember the six-thousand-foot elevation and regret that khaki shirts and shorts were our only protection against the chill. On the scorching plains of India the very thought of more clothing had been unendurable. "Going to bed" had consisted simply of removing our sun helmets and lying down on the barest possible canvas cot. Such cold and stoic beds here in the mountains, at a season which by no means had blossomed into summer, made it impossible to sleep, so we commandeered the carpets and red cotton draperies in both rooms for comforters. Thus wrapped in vast bundles of red and rugs we thoroughly enjoyed the cold night, and recalled that with the exception of Simla it was the first David had experienced since China, and I since Madrid.

I wondered, on seeing occasional tourists rush past in motorcars, how they could afford to treat the vale so lightly. In time I learned. It was to get to Srinagar, for in comparison with the interest of the capital the sights of the

FPG

The Red Fort, Delhi, once the palace of Emperor Shah Jehan

country are secondary. Not only has this strange metropolis great natural beauty, but also a setting amid waterways and bridges and gardens that makes it rival Venice itself in charm. It is, in fact, a picturesque, tumbledown replica of the Queen of the Adriatic, divided by the river Jhelum, which glides under its seven bridges and bears a fleet of gondolas as graceful and swift as ever floated down the Grand Canal.

So much did the novelty of our first glimpse of this fantastic city appeal to us we blocked traffic standing on the footpath of First Bridge and looking downstream past the other six at the panorama of picturesque watercraft and quaint houses that lined the banks.

Residing in Srinagar at the time was a Mr. C of New York, a man of benevolent spirit and understanding heart. When he heard from the English agency that there were two new Americans in town, he at once invited us to dine. We called at the given address and found a palatial houseboat, with a roof garden, a gay gondola alongside, and several immaculate servants to admit us. Our host immediately became interested in our vagabond careers and insisted that we make use of his establishment and stay as long as we liked, since he had three spare bedrooms and an extra bath or two. We were very happy to accept his hospitality, and that same night were at home on the *Lucky* houseboat, feeling our craft had been well named.

The days that followed stood out in bold contrast to the days that had preceded. It was no longer necessary to appropriate the red curtains for comforters or climb mulberry trees for food. A vagabond life is the logical life to lead if one seeks the intimate knowledge of the world we were seeking, yet an occasional reversion to luxurious respectability was very welcome nevertheless. The houseboat seemed doubly delightful right on top of the long weeks of stern economy David and I had been practicing. On the *Lucky* it was necessary only to clap one's hands to have slaves rushing in all directions. One clap brought our valet; two, our bootboy; three, our bath boy; four, the gondola. Mr. C's well-stocked wardrobe was at our disposal so that we could enter into the pleasant social life the Srinagar foreign colony enjoys. Such an Occidental sport as golf was the last thing on earth I should have expected to find in the Vale of Kashmir, yet a splendid course awaited us in the heart of the capital, and we played almost daily. It was rather difficult however to keep an eye on the ball, for soaring in a ring all about one the snowy giants caught and held the attention that should have been centered on the stroke.

Golf in the midst of these peaks was a novelty; riding through the flowering

58

countryside a delight; dinner coats and club life were a welcome change; but of all the happy hours the happiest were spent in our gondola. It was a graceful little craft, lithe as a canoe, canopied with bright cretonne and cushioned with soft pillows. The three of us floated about Srinagar's waterways hours at a time. There are almost no streets in this Asiatic Venice—a network of canals serves the purpose. They wind between grassy banks and under groves of walnut trees that arch above and make cool green tunnels for the gently gliding craft to travel. Here a Hindu shrine framed in branches casts its shining image in the still mirror, and there through a rift in the foliage one sees the hoary Himalayas glittering in the sunlight of another world.

Mr. C was one of those rare individuals who, try though they may, can never spend all of their incomes. Even with our gallant assistance there was always a big surplus. On several occasions we made tours of the art shops that overhung the Jhelum River, buying for a song the most exquisitely carved furniture pieces, the rarest Oriental rugs, and Kashmir shawls so soft and flexible that they could be pulled through an ordinary finger ring. In one shop the Mohammedan proprietor as a special favor displayed to us his most prized possession—a twenty-four-foot peacock-blue Persian rug made of pure silk and of ancient weave. Here was an unmistakable masterpiece, and Mr. C immediately began negotiations to purchase it. The merchant, much to our astonishment, emphatically refused any price—an experience unique indeed in the Orient.

Finding me staring reminiscently at a picture of the Taj Mahal upon his wall our shopkeeper brought forth ivory miniature portraits of Shah Jahan and Mumtaz-i-Mahal, the very things that I had looked for and longed for ever since the romantic night I had spent within the marble mausoleum. At last I could see what the "Lady of my Dreams" looked like. The portraits, yellow with age, were so delicately beautiful I could not resist them and offered the merchant half my capital. This was not nearly enough, and I would have had to go without, had not Mr. C, realizing how *very* much I wanted the miniatures, secretly bought them for me, and left them at my breakfast plate next morning.

Our four gondoliers rarely rested. After a day spent moving up and down the Jhelum, we often turned at twilight to Dal Lake, there on cushioned ease to float till the glow of sunset faded upon the flaming water and the moon waxed above the amphitheater walls. Then down a glittering path, our gondoliers would take us on to the gates of Shalimar. I had heard songs sung about this famous garden all my life and pictured it as a little paradise. For

59

The tomb of the Emperor Humayun (1512-1584), Delhi

once there was no disillusion. Built by a Mongol emperor for his favorite queen, it combines all that is beautiful and best in nature with enchanting artifice to make a poem in verdure and falling water. It is sensuous with heavy perfumes and musical with splashing fountains. On any summer night one will find young lovers from Srinagar stealing across the lotus-covered lake to disembark upon the garden's marble shores. They are fortunate Kashmiri who have such a romantic spot as this wherein to pursue their love affairs.

6

The Magic Stones of Angkor

✳ In Cairo I met an Englishman who had see. Angkor. He spoke of it in awesome tones as if it had been a superhuman experience. Again and again in India I heard the name linked with superlative adjectives relating to its monstrous size and exquisite detail, yet always encompassed in rumor and obscurity. No one there had seen it—everyone said it was a miracle. Angkor—the murmur of its name grew as I moved eastward. *Angkor*—tales of its reputed glories were rumbling in my ears at Bangkok. ANGKOR —the wind and the jungle and the vast gray cloud of stone roared at me now as I hurried from the bungalow toward the mile-distant mystery: "Here is the superlative of industry, here the crown of human achievement. Here, here, is Angkor, the first wonder of the world, and the greatest mystery in history."

Jungle, jungle, for mile after mile on every side it smothered the earth, dense, black, consuming—and from out of it, unheralded and unbelievable, rose the gigantic, the magical temple with its tier on tier of gray-tapestried stone, acres of carving, hundreds of delicately wrought windows, miles of galleries, great lace towers—all powerful and beautiful and desolate beyond imagination.

The spectacle was so amazing, stumbled on here in the forest, I would have scarcely credited my eyesight had I not been prepared by the fleeting distant glimpse of it snatched over the treetops early that morning. To have blundered upon the Pyramids or St. Peter's suffocating in the jungle depths of

Wat Arun, the Temple of Dawn in Bangkok

this wild corner of Asia and utterly deserted but for bats and lizards would not have astonished me more—indeed not nearly so much, for Angkor, built by gods for a fabulous vanished empire, in the might of its dimensions, in artistry, in purity, in magnificence, and above all in preservation, Angkor surpasses anything Greece or Rome or Egypt has ever seen.

Whence came this superhuman monument and the even more extraordinary dead city that surrounds it, both lost for seven hundred years in the impenetrability of an Indo-China wilderness and but recently uncovered to the amazement and admiration of the world? No one knows exactly. Whither departed the Titans that piled these stones together and deluged them with incredibly lavish carvings? No one knows that either. All trace of their beginning, all records of their destruction, have been utterly lost.

For lack of a better name, history calls the mysterious race that once dwelt here the Khymers. Conjecture founds their empire in the fourth century and obliterates it in the twelfth. Except for miles and acres of bas-relief pictures of battles and mythology and common life carved on the stones of the six hundred ruined public buildings found in the space once covered by the Khymer capital, we should not know one single thing about this race, whose ability as artists and architects has rarely been approached.

It seems impossible that this masterpiece could have escaped for so long the attention it is now beginning to enjoy. However, when one sees the flood of vegetation it is buried under, and realizes in what an isolated part of the world it is hidden, one can understand why it remained unknown and unsung while archeological monuments of a far lesser magnitude were being explored and in picture and story made familiar to the whole world.

As far back as 1857 a Frenchman, urged on by the fabulous legends of an angel-built temple then within the southeast borders of Siam, fought his way through leagues of jungle to the spot, and on his return to civilization told such unbelievable stories of the size and magnificence of the ruins he had seen, obviously erected by a lost race of superbeings, that people laughed at him and thought his deprivations had weakened his brain.

No one laughs today at the first superlatives of praise that came from Angkor. To quote one recent archeological writer, it is: "The most amazing archeological site in the world. It stands, and is perhaps destined to stand, the noblest monument raised by man."

All during the latter half of the nineteenth century Angkor the inaccessible was left as it had been left since 1432, at the mercy of the elements and inhabited by wild beasts. In 1907, France, by a "treaty" with Siam, seized a large slice of the latter's eastern forest wilderness [now Cambodia] that includes the site of the ancient Khymer capital, with its fifteen square miles of magnificent ruins—ruins of palaces, libraries, gates, walls, and Angkor Vat, the mighty temple. Owing to the fact that it was the latest and most ponderously built, it stands today in all its original glory, while the other Khymer structures have fallen prey to the gourmand jungle and the assaults of time.

The Siamese [Thais], who are believed to have driven the Khymers from Angkor Vat, insist it was built by divinities, because human beings could not have been powerful enough or inspired enough to do it. You may not be inclined to believe this legend from seeing pictures or reading descriptions of Angkor; you may not believe that it took four generations of constant industry to complete, or that kings commandeered and kept occupied five hundred thousand slaves from their sixteen provinces; but when you at last look upon Angkor in reality, you believe *anything*.

The temple is in the form of a pyramid, with five hollow squares each fitting into and above the other. Each corner of the last two terraces is adorned with an elaborate tower completely covered with carvings of seven-headed cobras, medallions, deities, chains of dancers; and reaching higher and higher with each tier until the great supreme tower of lace soars two hundred feet and looks with majestic defiance over the miles of waving, waiting jungle tops that stretch unbroken on to China.

Alone, I approached the entrance, along a twelve-hundred-foot stone viaduct, forty feet wide, that led across what was once a lake. Raised well above the bed, balustraded with seven-headed nagas and deeply rutted by the passage of ancient chariot wheels, this great bridge is a fitting approach to so great a building.

I moved toward the stone mountain with a feeling half of awe and half of wonder, that I, a product of the materialistic, modern age, a vagabond, a pagan, should be granted a sight of this handiwork of the gods. In solitude I climbed the worn steps that led up to the second gallery, and found myself in the midst of the most magical array of stone tapestry on earth. It is this proximity that lends the greatest enchantment to the gigantic temple. From afar Angkor with its ascending rows of colonnaded galleries, its hundreds of elaborately barred windows, its labyrinth of roofs, steps, cupolas, towers, looks more like a mirage than a reality. Only close at hand can one fully appreciate the inconceivable intricacy and beauty of its details and ornaments. The Egyptians might have raised this vast pile of stones in place, but only the Khymers could ever have executed the carvings. Every inch of the wonderfully wrought structure is covered with finely chiseled decorations. The

The principal entrance to the temple of Angkor Vat

splay of each window, the facing of each door, is a masterpiece with an individual design unapproachable for delicacy and grace. Kings and cobras, smiling deities and dancing figures, riot over wall and tower. There is no mechanical ornamentation, but dash and reality to everything. The fancy of the decorator has been given free play, yet more perfect blending of detail could not be conceived. However, I cannot do justice to the stones of Angkor—only a Ruskin or a Chateaubriand could, and either would fill many volumes in the task.

Of the many Angkor wonders, the most wonderful is the bas-relief that stretches unbroken for a half-mile around the second terrace. Protected from the weather by a gallery, it has withstood the ravages of time, and is as vivid and fresh today as it was seven hundred years ago. One could spend weeks before this great stone picture and not see it all, since there are fully fifty thousand figures chiseled on it in such inextricable confusion one's head begins to swim from examining them.

One wall, three hundred and fifty feet long, portrays the battle scene between a Khymer king and his enemies. There are hundreds of fighters in armor with shield and sword, on foot, on horseback, hundreds more in chariots and on elephants, yet not one figure is passive. It *is* a battle. Each army sweeps against the other, and the clash in the center is terrific. Men are piled on one another, struggling in groups, in pairs, with clenched teeth, in agony, in fury, in despair, in triumph; arrows and spears fly thick and fast; the officers urge on their followers; the trumpeters sound the charge; the horses and elephants rear and tremble with excitement; the dead and dying are piled on the ground to be trampled by succeeding waves. At the rear deep ranks of reinforcements, cheering and hurrying, are marched forward into the slaughter. There is action, action, and carnage and the roar of battle. One's eyes stare at this realism; one's heart beats faster in sympathy with this mortal combat. Yet all this is in stone—cold, silent, colorless stone. Someday the artistic world will recognize the Khymers as the greatest artists that ever lived—though perhaps they never lived. Perhaps they were angels, as the Siamese insist, descended from Heaven to carve this superhuman work.

Their conception of Heaven and Hell takes up another hundred yards. They were none too prolific in their ideas about the rewards of a virtuous life, Heaven being depicted as a pleasant grove of trees filled with peacocks, where the men sat around eating and the women (off in one corner) played with their children. But ah, Hell!—that was different. The pictured Gehenna was a museum of all the physical tortures the devil himself could think of. No vagueness about the punishments of evil. Great horned demons drive in their victims, all reduced to skin and bones, and, by rings in their noses, drag them through endless diabolical torments in comparison with which drawing and quartering would be a springtime frolic.

A flight of steps worn almost to a slide leads from terrace to terrace, and into the galleries, through which one could walk all day and never retrace one's steps. They were once the scene of great activity; they are silent now except for the endless screech and whir of a million bats that swarm in the black recesses of this desolate building.

As I walked from tier to tier, from stone picture to stone picture, these repulsive creatures, disturbed by the hollow sound of footsteps, tumbled in swarms about the evil-smelling vaults, execrating me and my intrusion. For seven hundred years, Angkor Vat has been the private property of the lizards and the monkeys. Who was I to disturb their peace?

For an hour I had seen no human being. All about me was the most gorgeous architecture ever reared, and yet it was a corpse—a corpse that had maintained its complete physical being though unutterably dead. This depressing silence, this ghostly emptiness, this grim ruthless jungle that was waiting at the gates to spring again upon these god-hewn stones and devour them, all made me shiver and want to cry out against the doom that clanked beside me no matter where I turned.

What was that yellow streak—I started—that flitted like an enormous butterfly across a patch of distant sunlight? I hurried to investigate and found a Buddhist priest in his daffodil gown, wandering, even as I, along the endless corridors. He was one of an order that used this prodigious corpse for its monastery. Angkor was built as a temple to Siva, but local followers of Buddha, like mice in a deserted dwelling, have taken several corners of the pile, and established shrines by setting up battered statues of Buddha and a few miserable candles.

These imperturbable statues, so calm and mysterious, sitting and smiling in the gloom, are startling when one comes upon them unexpectedly. In one courtyard there is a Buddha morgue, where several hundred images have been stored pell-mell. They are discarded and decayed, and yet one of the few gaunt priests that are always prowling about the temple almost obliterated me when I picked up a piece of a broken Buddha from the pile, and used it as a stepladder to reach the roof where I wanted to take photographs.

These ecclesiastics, but for their bright yellow robes, would be lost in the vastness of Angkor. Nevertheless, let the trespasser beware! There is a persistent rumor current among the natives that fabulous treasures are buried in the sealed crypts beneath the central tower, and these obstructed passages are

The Bantey Sreay temple of Angkor

Ruins of the Bayon, Angkor Thom

Underwood & Underwood

guarded with special zeal by the priests. But if there is any great wealth buried here it is little used by its guardians, for more bedraggled disciples of Buddha I have never seen.

Angkor Vat, after all, is only the greatest and best preserved of a vast array of magnificent sandstone structures once enclosed in the city of Angkor Thom, which in the days of its glory had several million people and was the luxurious capital of a mighty empire. The number and dimensions of the city's ruins are staggering—and, oh, how melancholy, how indescribably desolate! How was it possible for such a race as the Khymers to disappear so absolutely? Did it happen in a day? Was this heavenly city, with its vast population, its armies, its palaces, its might and glory, surprised by its enemies and destroyed overnight by the sword? What diabolical wrath was spent upon it? No sooner had the roar of tumbling battlements died away than that insatiable fiend, the jungle, rushed upon the prostrate magnificence and suffocated all but a few of the most indomitable giants.

Of the remaining buildings the Temple of Bayon is in a class of interest by itself. Mutilated, overthrown, the lodgment for a forest of trees and vines, it is still the most original and fantastic temple in the world. Formerly it contained fifty-one towers, each faced near the top of all four sides, with a great carved countenance of Siva eight feet high. Although many of the faces are lost, a number remain, and the sight of them, looking calmly out to the four quarters of heaven as passive as Sphinxes, is weird and wonderful. The cracks and yawns in the joints of the stones upon which they are carved give each of them a different and contorted expression, some wry, some smiling, some evil. Lianas have crept across the eye of one; lichens and moss have blinded another. They peered at me from the treetops; they pursued me with their scrutiny like a bad conscience, no matter where I tried to escape. Stamped with the wisdom of a thousand years, they seemed to read my puny soul and mock the awe of them that rested there.

Slowly and wonderingly I climbed about these fabulous ruins. The sun set beyond the western jungle tops, and before I realized that day had gone twilight enveloped me. Every bird became hushed; the faintest breeze seemed to hold its breath. Not even a cricket broke the pall of silence that sank upon this mighty corpse. From the shadows, death and oblivion crept forth to seize the city from the retreating sunshine; ghosts drifted beside me as I moved and dreamed through the gathering darkness. Loneliness—loneliness—in all this stupendous graveyard of man and monument, I stood—the only living human being.

7

Dolce Far Niente in Bali

✳ A lazy haze floated over the ocean, blotting out the horizon and dulling the intensity of the equatorial sunshine. For an hour I had been lying on deck (since the deck as usual was my stateroom) absorbed in an enormous gray cloud that loomed mysteriously out of the fog and seemed to reach a hundred miles into the sky.

"Looks just like a gigantic mountain, doesn't it?" I remarked to the mate, pointing to the curious mass.

"*Looks* like a mountain?" He laughed. "It *is* a mountain. It's the Peak of Bali."

Bali! A thrill ran through me. At last I was on the threshold of this amazing island, this little paradise in the Dutch East Indies that I had come so far to visit. At Saigon (where I had emerged from the Angkor jungles after a two-day voyage down the Mekong River) I had first heard about its lure—its beautiful people—its brilliant coloring—its unspoiled naturalness. Drifting about the docks, looking for a ship that would take me away—anywhere—I ran across an old tropical tramp who had combed the beaches of New Guinea and Sumatra and knew every isle and city on which the sun of the equator blazed. *He* had been to Bali, and when he spoke of it, he might have been Adam telling Cain about the Garden of Eden. To him it was the most idyllic spot in the Pacific, chiefly because it was almost the only one not blighted by European culture and American tin cans. He assured me it was a siren isle, enslaving by its beauty and romance everyone who looked upon it.

Long before he had completed his Bali panegyrics I had decided to go there—and right away. It occurred to me just before departing that I had not the slightest idea where it was, so I extracted my map of Asia and had the beachcomber show me the tiny emerald all but touching the eastern tip of Java—two thousand miles south and east of Saigon.

By good fortune there was an American freighter about to sail for Surabaya, the Javanese port from which one embarks for Bali, and the consul placed me on it as a deck passenger. The captain, like the dipsomaniac chief engineer of the *Adamson,* was a kindhearted old piece of salt, and shared with me his meals and his canvas cots so that not for five minutes during the eight days across the equator was it necessary to descend to the deck occupied by the vulgar crew.

By only one day I missed connection for Bali and, with nearly two weeks to wait for the next boat, decided to get acquainted with Java. From the very outset this "Queen of the Indies" proved a disappointment. Though I managed to see almost every city and temple and volcano of major interest on the island, there was never a romance, never an adventure, because Java with all its gorgeous scenery, bizarre arts and picturesque swarms of natives has not a spark of personality. After Rajputana and the Punjab, the Javanese seemed like so many brown peas with about as much magnetism; after Angkor, the world-famous temple of the Borobudur in the center of the island, that makes all travel writers and archeologists jump up and down, was about as exciting as a red-brick Baptist church on a corner lot in Kansas. Java is the most beautiful dumbbell in the world. Her conventional Dutch overlords have put their own dull and ugly stamp upon a tame and passive race, and the result is painful. There is an atrocious harmlessness about the people, an utter negativity, that makes one want to stick pins into them or start a revolution. Had the boat to Bali not sailed when it did I should certainly have done one or the other.

All expectation, I landed at Boeleleng, the seacoast village on the north side of my island. The Saigon beachcomber was right. Here indeed was a little paradise, a south sea Eden, and the Eves whose beauty he had praised so highly. Erect as Dianas they moved about the streets, no more aware of their half-nude bronze bodies than the fat yellow babies that trotted at their heels.

In Bali it is considered brazen and shameless to cover the breasts, and no respectable woman would think of doing so. Considerable trouble was caused recently by a native official, who having been molded by Dutch ethics, felt it immodest for his daughter to dress in the native fashion. In order to clothe her in the conventional Dutch manner and yet protect her from reproach, he commanded that *every* woman should wear a jacket, and all being thus debased no one could condemn his daughter. The new law met with indignant opposition, and, except in Boeleleng where the few foreigners live, has never been enforced.

Long before this island expedition I had learned that the pleasure of travel increases in direct proportion to the decrease of baggage. In consequence I left behind at the Surabaya consulate even my knapsack, bringing only my camera, toothbrush, razor and soap. The small articles fitted snugly into the big breast pockets sewn on my one shirt and made from the sleeves which I had ripped at the shoulder from that same garment. I knew that to see and "learn" Bali I must walk, and to walk comfortably in such a torrid climate, one must not be burdened with nonessentials such as clothes and self-consciousness. If everybody else undressed properly for the equatorial weather, why shouldn't I? With twenty dollars (all that remained of the one hundred and twenty dollars I had when I left Calcutta), a map, a staff, a minimum Malay vocabulary—the *lingua franca* of the Indies—and a light heart, I set forth to explore the island, to follow only my nose, planning to linger where fancy dictated and advance only when the spirit moved.

I knew that the centers of population and interest lay on the south side of the mountain wall, which, running east and west, rose abruptly from the north coast. After a leisurely inspection of carefree, lazy Boeleleng, I headed for the ridge, and had ascended half a mile above the sea when evening fell, and found me standing entranced before the magic of a tropical sunset. The ball of fire was dropping straight through the crater of a sky-scraping volcano in the eastern tip of Java, inflaming the clouds above it and suffusing with amber the ocean, the jungles of palms along the coast, and the terraces of tiny rice fields which climbed with astonishing agility up the steep slopes to where I stood. That night, for the first time since crossing the Malay Isthmus, I slept on the ground. There was no monsoon to plague me now, no cobras, no flood of water—only forest solitude amid the ferns, and soft caressing wind, and heavy odors of night blossoms that carried memory back to the garden of the Taj Mahal. I broke an armful of flowered boughs from the hibiscus trees, and, spreading them on the mountainside, slept peacefully on this green and scarlet bed.

Awake with the sun, I bethought myself of breakfast. That was easy to procure, as the trail was dotted with little hamlets, at each of which a dozen bananas could be bought for a penny. In place of a morning cup of coffee I secured a green coconut, and, boring a hole, drank its refreshing milk. This draught was so satisfying that for the month I wandered about the island I never tasted water—and who would have, with this vastly superior substitute always obtainable?

The farther away from the north coast one gets, the more unsophisticated the people become, and the more superfluous they consider clothes. Having descended the ridge, the equatorial palms again made their appearance in dense jungles, and under a great cathedral arch of them the pathway led. At each village my appearance caused more excitement that had been known in months. The vast population of pariah dogs clamorously heralded my approach, and all the villagers ran out to stare as I passed. Every community had its temples, old and crumbling now, yet with all their faded appearance there were traces of chisel virtuosity that indicated the high state of artistic civilization these people of Bali once enjoyed.

The third day I reached Denpasar, the little metropolis near the southern coast, but finding it less interesting than the wilder aspects of the island, I turned to the east, tramping leisurely through terraces of rice and palm-hidden villages hedged with flaming hibiscus. For food I had coconuts, bananas and mangoes, and for a bed, the ground shaded by a grove of trees beside a stream of fresh, cool water, or a spot on the shore beneath the fronded palms that stretched out hungrily toward the blue, blue ocean.

The east coast is entirely too rugged for roads, and is therefore the most aboriginal part of Bali. The beach extends unbroken for forty miles and is the only highway. Here, if anywhere, was Bali primeval—unknown, unsung, unspoiled. The coast is in the form of a semicircle, rotating about the base of the towering Peak of Bali which rises ten thousand feet from the sea and dominates every landscape on the island. With this great mountain always on my left and the indigo ocean always on my right, I spent three weeks idling along the palm-shaded beach—the more carefree, most romantic weeks I had known since my quest began.

For a few days I lived with a hermit fisherman, sailing forth with him in his miniature outrigger canoe to set his nets. Ocean water was never so clear. One could look down into it for several fathoms and watch the roving schools of brilliant fish.

His living quarters could scarcely have been more Spartan—two poles covered with palm leaves, braced against a boulder. For myself I matted a bed of fronds and slept on the sand. In Denpasar I had bought paper and pencil, and when sunburn had put me out of the fishing business, I sprawled on the rocks of a near-by wooded promontory, and let the wind and the waves dictate to me a story for my American newspapers.

Becoming restless again, I moved on up the broad beachway. Fifteen miles brought me at sundown to a little cove where a family of salt collectors had built a very attractive hut of poles and matting in a dense grove of palms. They were bathing as I passed, father, mother, son and daughter, in a fresh-water pool close to the house, and being half broiled myself and parched with thirst, I followed their excellent example. They did not know whether to be frightened or amused at my spirit of fraternity, but on hearing my desperate effort to converse in Malay, decided to take it smilingly. The mother rubbed coconut oil on my blistered arms; the half-grown son climbed a tree to secure for me a "fresh drink." Little by little their original timidity wore away, disappearing altogether when I offered the *père* a guilder and invited myself to dine on their frugal meal of rice and fish. The night brought forth as big and round a tropical moon as I ever saw, and a desire to cling to whatever human association I could find, if only to this simple-spirited family; so I remained all night, sleeping on my usual palm bed.

It was a novel sport assisting them next day in raking the salt deposits from the hollow logs they filled with water and left in the hot sun till the moisture evaporated. By the second evening I was quite captivated by this ingenuous household, and decided to pass the time until next boat-sailing on this idyllic spot with my hospitable friends.

I soon found out that surf swimming was more pleasant than collecting salt, and spent hours each day in the ocean, hurrying for shelter from the sun the moment the protection of the water was lost. The two children, unlike the rest of the Balinese—who are not especially interested in aquatic sports—were marvelous swimmers and having been demoralized by my desertion of the salt business played truant themselves and answered their parents' scolding with shouts and splashing.

Most of all we enjoyed the twilight hour. Then the sea was still and the beach deserted. The boy and girl of our ménage had never before had so strange a companion as this curious white man, a white man who loved the water as they loved it. In consequence, darkness always found the three of us still enjoying the cool, calm sea. If hunger drove us back to the sand, Taja, the daughter, would fetch a supper from her mother's table. Then these brown children and I, speaking different languages, knowing different

The dreamy shores of Bali

worlds, would sit on the beach under the rising moon eating our meal and laughing as merrily as if we were of one race and one mind. Communication of thought soon ceased to hamper us. A common tongue is not vital to understanding when there is congeniality of spirit.

In these romantic hours I forgot the difficulties that had beset me in the search for them. I forgot all previous existence, since in my shell of coconut milk these gentle Balinese had pressed a lotus bloom that dimmed all recollection of the past and deadened the call of the future. We obeyed the behest of Rupert Brooke; we heard "the calling of the moon, and the whispering scents that strayed about the idle, warm lagoon." We hastened "down the dark, the flowered way." "Along the whiteness of the sand and in the water's soft caress," we washed our minds, "of foolishness."

A week or so after my adoption by the salt collectors, groups of gaily-dressed Balinese began to troop past our beach dwelling, all moving in the same direction. By means of gestures I asked Taja where they were going.

"Denpasar," she replied, and with more gestures she added that her entire family was likewise going and wanted me to accompany them.

"But why?"

In answer Taja danced and sang and grew very excited . . . some sort of fete or celebration evidently . . . certainly I'd go.

The next day found the five of us tramping steadily toward Denpasar. The road was lined with pilgrims like ourselves, all merry and eager over impending events. As we entered the outskirts of the town I heard the jargon of distant native orchestras, and realizing that the great volume of their sound indicated something beyond the ordinary, hurried in the direction, coming soon upon a magnificent procession before which I stood, with Taja beside me, gazing in wonder at the passing flashes of color. Long lines of women draped in vivid hues marched in single file, on their heads bearing food for a banquet. Great towering floats of tinsel and gilt were carried along by a mob of struggling coolies. The community dancing girls, painted and crowned, acted as festival queens, and were borne aloft in gilded chairs surrounded by a bodyguard of cavaliers. The *sine qua non* of the procession was the rout of savage monsters and ogres, made of paint and plaster, that roared and pranced through the crowded sidelines, scattering the shrieking spectators and being trailed by all the naked little urchins in Denpasar. Every few feet a xylophone and cymbal band vigorously executed its three-note music, but they marched so close together nothing could be heard except a terrible din that was deafening. The glittering, hilarious, noisy spectacle wound its way

79

through the village's palmy lanes and on to the temple, there to gorge itself to stupefaction.

Consumed with curiosity, I hurried to find the English-speaking Dutch commissioner and to ask him if this Mardi Gras procession was just a circus parade—or what.

"It's a *funeral*," he replied.

Seeing my astonished expression he offered more information.

"I think the greatest spectacle in the Indies is one of these Balinese cremation ceremonies. The more prominent the dead person, of course the more elaborate the funeral. You are very fortunate to be here now—a rajah died a few days ago, and this is going to be the biggest cremation fete they've had for a generation."

And all this hilarity, I learned, was only the first day of mourning, the actual cremation not taking place until the next day.

The beachcomber had been right in saying that the Balinese were a simple people; yet they have their own little vanities, one of the most peculiar of them being a love of mortuary display. When a person whose family is not rich enough to afford a triumphant cremation dies, he is embalmed and buried, and remains buried until a nobleman or plutocrat follows suit. Then amid the trumpeting and parades that distinguish the funeral of a lord, the bourgeois corpses are disinterred, and, attached to the end of the splendid procession, get full benefit of all the music and banqueting and ostentation, none of which their own small wealth could have commanded. Indeed, when a rajah shows signs of approaching death there are no cremations at all for a time as everyone postpones the ceremony in the hope that the rajah will die soon and allow the lesser dead to reap the great honor, and their families the greater glory, of participating in the funeral of a king. Then, too, when the gates of Heaven open to receive the nobleman, who knows but that a few spirits of the common clay may not slip in?

In consequence of this custom, there were over a hundred other coffins in the second day's procession, each borne in floats of various sizes all the way from the rajah's ponderous masterpiece of glass and gilt down to the crude small box of coolie's bones.

The coffins presented one of the strangest of the many strange Balinese characteristics, for in place of the conventional oblong box, the corpse was encased in a gaily-spotted hobby bull made of wood and paper, and adorned with horns, glaring teeth and upraised tail. This vicious animal is carried on top of the float, which in turn rests on the shoulders of the pallbearers, and

80

after being placed upon the pyre is burned to ashes along with the enclosed body. I could learn neither the origin nor the significance of this custom. It had always been observed—that was all they knew.

The crowds of the second day's cremation festival were even more hilarious. A circus could not have caused as much excitement as this event. When the towering hearse came into view I saw that it was borne by a mob of almost naked men, those in front pulling forward, those behind holding back—a conflict that subjected the unwieldy bull to dangerous tilting and inconstant support.

This struggle represented the reluctance of the soul to leave the body. Half the pallbearers represented the "friends of Heaven," half the "friends of Earth." The "soul" dragged the corpse to the exterminating pyre; the "body" fought against the inevitable, and strained for prolonged earthly residence. The two forces were battling over the coffin as it labored slowly and haltingly toward the flames.

The most astonishing spectacle was yet to follow. When, after a great struggle, the coffin finally reached its goal, the saddle of the rajah's bull was displaced and the corpse itself, tightly encased in bamboo, was lifted out. Then began the climax of the ceremony. Suddenly the "friends of Earth," marshaling their strength for one supreme effort, seized the mummy and with shouting began to carry it away from the very gates of eternity. The "friends of Heaven," taken by surprise, were at first overpowered, but they did not abandon the field, and soon succeeded in halting the escape. The struggle was long in doubt. Scores of fresh recruits rushed to both sides and plunged into the crushing mass of fighting humanity. The corpse was lost in a sea of brown flesh. It was the final desperate rebellion against the torch, and both sides put forth hysterical efforts to assist their cause. The solid acre of sweating, yelling, fanatical men were trampling on one another, clawing at the mummy, falling by the wayside, gasping for breath and devoid of the last shred of clothes. The yards of shrouding encasing the corpse became loosened and entangled a score of the fighters. The hundreds of spectators were as excited as the participants. They cheered on the side they favored, or, unable to restrain their zeal, rushed to join in. Simultaneously, in a great circle at the edge of the glade, the hundred lesser dead were being consumed by the flames which sent forth great columns of smoke that hung ominously overhead, and mingling together made a solid wall about the mad battle within. The final dramatic touch for this incredible picture was the musical accompaniment, for twenty native orchestras outside the wall, frenzied by the gen-

Left and above—the pastoral village of Trunjan, on Lake Batur, Bali

eral spirit of abandon, pounded wildly on their xylophones until their rolling notes could be heard even above the crackling of the hundred pyres and the shouts of the multitude. Not until both sides were utterly exhausted was the ill-used corpse dragged back to the pyre.

With Taja I stood wide-eyed on a near-by knoll and gazed on this extraordinary scene. Where on earth could it be equaled—this ruthless combat over the corpse, this swarm of garish colors, this pall of human smoke, this barbaric music, all melting together into one great savage spectacle? A wave of revulsion rushed over me. I saw instead of gentle peaceful children of Holland's island empire, mad savages stripped of their thin veneer of Dutch culture, reveling in brute instincts inherited from cannibal ancestors. To me it was desecration of the dead, the orgy of a pack of ghouls; but I realized that I had seen what so few have seen—Bali the real, the undisguised.

With the music gone, the food consumed, the pyres in ashes, it was amazing how quickly the crowds dispersed. Having five more days to wait before the Java boat sailed, I tramped back with my hospitable friends to our east coast home.

Not until the hour of departure did I fully realize how attached I was to them. Taja insisted on guiding me up the faint and precipitous trail which, climbing five thousand feet abruptly from the sea, led over the crest of Batur Mountain and on to Boeleleng. Although it was a trying and dangerous route, I knew that the reward of choosing this hardest way was worth the effort, for the beachcomber and the Denpasar commissioner had both waxed enthusiastic about the astonishing picture one beheld from the summit of this mountain.

The picture was indeed worth ten times the climb. As the girl and I neared the top a great blue void opened on the island side, and out of the void appeared two steaming volcanoes. We hurried to the summit and there stopped abruptly, for below us a sheer drop of fifteen hundred feet yawned, and before us one of the most bewildering landscapes on earth met our eyes.

On one side of the brink where I stood, the ocean a mile below glittered in the sunlight. On the other side, a thousand and five hundred feet below, the blue lake of Batur half filled the enormous crater, the abrupt wall of which is twenty-five miles in circumference and eight miles across. From its center two perfect cones of lava and sulphur emerge, pouring forth smoke, and, all too frequently, streams of molten rock.

I stood dumfounded by the sight; it was so unexpected and so awesome. I could discern tiny fishing boats on the blue mirror before me, and a sail out at sea behind. Squeezed between the precipice and the crater-lake a village appeared directly beneath, made of toy houses, while across at the foot of the volcanoes and on a part of the crater floor not covered by water there was another village, all but overwhelmed by a recent eruption.

Taja and I, to rest from our climb, sat on this wild wind-swept crater crest, looking out over the stupendous panorama. Neither of us spoke; words would have been futile. We had reached the brink at midmorning, but it was well into the afternoon before this child of Bali and I said good-bye. I have known happier moments.

Dejected and alone I descended the inside cliff by a zigzag trail, and climbed again to the rim on the far side. Just as twilight came I reached this goal and turned to look back over the gigantic picture. The lake, the dual cones, the granite walls, were symphonies in smoky blue. The great abyss was in heavy darkening shadows, even though the sun yet gilded the distant crest of the majestic Peak of Bali.

I sat in thoughtful mood on the edge of this mighty spectacle. Tomorrow I would seek my ship and depart from these hospitable, entertaining shores. I felt deeply grateful to the island for the refreshing weeks of rare happiness it had afforded me. I had found what I had been seeking these many months. I had justified what I wished to believe. I could henceforth challenge the idea that there is no novelty left on earth, and I derived great satisfaction from the thought that if my spirit of romanticism were ever endangered by the materialism and artificiality of the Western world, I could always seek refuge and rejuvenation in this far-off land of the lotus, this Eden, this idyllic little isle, this Bali.

8

Gulbeyaz

If someone were to ask me to which foreign city I most wish
to return, I would have difficulty answering. I would think of Rio de Ja-
neiro, and Athens, and Peking. I would certainly think of Fez in Morocco.
This city, so proud and mellow and medieval, never fails to captivate whoever visits it. My own capitulation was immediate and complete.

Fez, as my friend Moye Stephens and I found, has entirely escaped the invasion from the West. France has built an ugly, sanitary modern community on
the outskirts, and there the white man and the Christian carry on their tin-can
trade. But the original city itself, wrapped in its dreaming sun-splashed walls,
despises this upstart neighbor. Into its own narrow malodorous alleys, Western modernity gains no entrance. We heard there only the soft slow pad of
camels and the scrape of sandals worn on the feet of undistracted Moors . . .
and a voice from the minaret that bade us linger in this Arabian Nights town,
among the white domes and towers, the dim arched streets, the secluded gardens from which dark-eyed women, veiled and mysterious, smiled at us . . .
and, for the time, forget the Flying Carpet.

We found an ancient Moorish house right in the middle of the native city.
It was surrounded by a jumble of tortured lanes, tiny shops and cul-de-sacs, in
which I was always, to my delight, getting lost. No one knew when our
house was built—maybe in the eighteenth century, maybe in the eighth. It

was of one story and constructed around a court, with high blank walls on the outside, and a luxuriant garden inside enclosed by a gracefully arched colonnade. The tops of the arches were filled with lacelike arabesques once colored bright, now faded by generations of sun. But even in its decrepitude the old house was beautiful still—what one could see of it beneath the masses of bougainvillaea and geranium that rioted over every wall. The crumbling marble fountain cast its spray upon the blossoming pomegranate trees as gaily as it had done for countless seasons past. And now that early summer was flowering the land, the air in every court and corner seemed saturated with all the perfumes of Arabia.

We tried to make our house a refuge from the Philistines who inhabited the French city. To it only Arabs could come, and the few Europeans who enjoyed their company. Only the prettiest girls, only gay-spirited men, were welcome. The Foreign Legion had a passkey, and the spahi native cavalry, because they were devils and left fabulously beautiful white horses standing at our door. But no one who was solemn and severe was admitted.

Inside the garden, walled away from care, we slept by day in the shade of the lemon trees. By night, we hung the crescent moon of Islam in the sky and bathed in the pool and listened to our native orchestra . . . and the miseries of the world seemed very far away.

Every evening there was dancing and music—the exciting, agonized music of the Arabs, their bagpipes wailing, their tambours thumping, their one-string violins squeaking frantically. The musicians sang as they played, sang with heads thrown back, mouths open wide, shrill, nasal, delirious.

And how those Arab girls could dance! With this intoxicating rhythm vibrating in the courtyard, they would continue hour after hour—no wild leaps and bounds, but with stamping of feet and undulations of hips and torsos, as they clinked and rippled the tiny silver cymbals fastened to their finger tips.

The prettiest girl who came to our parties, the most striking personality, and by all odds the most accomplished dancer, was an Arab damsel of about eighteen, with the name of Gulbeyaz. She wore six richly carved woolen dresses indicative of her wealth and station, and enough jewels and junk to adorn a dozen gypsies. Her supreme decorations were a frieze of olive leaves tattooed in blue across her forehead, and two stunning gold front teeth (carefully substituted for good white ones) which lighted up her face when she laughed.

At first sight of her, Moye and I were both enslaved. Neither of us knew

A street in Fez, Morocco

a word of Arabic, and Gulbeyaz knew no other language. That made things difficult. Moye—who usually depended on the tall tales of his flying exploits to break feminine hearts, and usually with complete success—got nowhere with this method. And I, who after long experimentation have found that I am most irresistible when reciting love lyrics in a slightly quavering voice with a few telling gestures, made even less impression.

However, it was soon evident, to me at least, that Moye's curly hair and reserved manner were accomplishing with Gulbeyaz what his words could not. When she danced she scarcely even looked my way, but would cast those great black eyes of hers upon Moye, and smile, with her radiant teeth, like August sunshine.

Chagrined, I looked over the rest of our ballet, but there was none other who could match Gulbeyaz. If I were to win her, I must act at once or suffer complete defeat. In this crisis I remembered that once in Italy I'd had notable success—in a similar contest over an Italian girl—by buying my way into her heart: silk stockings, cheap jewelry, pastry and such things so dear to women. I got hold of Frankie, the irresponsible, undismissible little cockney Foreign Legionnaire who was always on hand (and always drunk), and gave him fifty francs with which to go out and buy for me the fanciest and pinkest frosted cake in Fez—one that could completely capture Gulbeyaz' heart.

Of course, I shouldn't have trusted Frankie with such a serious commission—or with fifty francs. He had joined the Legion—so he always said—to escape the penalty for having murdered three or four people; but I suspected he was just boasting and had joined because he was, like so many Legionnaires, too much of a dipsomaniac to thrive elsewhere. And so, as I should have anticipated, he spent thirty francs on brandy and only twenty on the love cake. Thereupon, he returned reeling home to deliver my prize, but on trying to cross the court he tumbled with a yelp and a thundering splash into the fish pond, and sank to the bottom—still clutching the elegant pastry with which I was to lure the beauteous Gulbeyaz away from Moye's sinister toils.

To my great annoyance and disappointment, he did not drown.

This disaster was no doubt intended to make it clearly evident to me that Allah was on the side of Stephens. But Allah or no Allah, I wasn't going to give in just because a drunken fool of a Legionnaire fell in a fish pond. I was still determined to persevere.

Beyond our garden walls, Fez offered endless opportunities for exploration, and almost every day Moye and I would venture out. Frankie, who had appointed himself our permanent courier, made an excellent guide, since in his progress from bar to bar he had come to know the city well. Sometimes, when the afternoon had begun to wane, he would fetch Gulbeyaz and meet us before one of the mosques, and we would wander through the bazaars and twisted streets of the town. Donkeys and camels brushed past us, dogs and brats, veiled ladies, porters, princes, Arabs, Berbers, Jews, Negroes—all in one confused tangle of traffic milling through the narrow alleyways.

Moye and I would stalk manfully ahead through the crowd, in Arab fashion, shouting *"Balaak! Balaak!*—Make way! Make way!"*—with Gulbeyaz, swathed in veil and burnoose, trotting behind. In this costume she looked just like everybody else, so we were forever losing her or speaking to the wrong outraged burnoose. Frankie brought up the rear, struggling to keep the procession intact.

We never grew tired of the bazaars. Of all the bazaars in the world, I'm sure those of Fez are first, in variety, in color, in evil and fragrant odors, in richness and age. And what a stock they offered! Paltry and useless little mosaic ornaments, ostentatious nothings, enticing yellow *darioles,* idle delights that held infinite surprise. But it seemed as though we were the only ones who ever purchased anything. Indeed, Moye and I spent our sous rather recklessly, buying trifles with which to break the heart of the ravishing Gulbeyaz. Moye would give her perfume and embroidered leather slippers; I'd give her tin bangles, hashish, and stick candy. Moye's gifts she received with extravagant gratitude, mine with a polite smile of thanks—but I continued to compete, in the hope of ultimately finding some bauble that would absolutely slay her.

Alas, I couldn't!

Having exhausted the resources of Fez itself in this fruitless pursuit, I thought perhaps some opportunity for me to outdo Moye might be found at the great fair then being held in the near-by town of Moulay Idris. For four days each year, some seventy-five thousand Moslems gather to barter and to pray at the tomb of Idris, the great saint who first brought Koran to Morocco. If one wants to behold the unalloyed essence of Morocco, to see the Moors as they were in the days of their greatest glory, this occasion is unsurpassed. For then the true spirit of the land is revived, with its barbaric vitality, its splendor and fanaticism, its filth and beauty; and one is translated for these four days of grace back into anterior times.

Gulbeyaz didn't care anything about anterior times, but she was delighted when I suggested the fair—and promptly asked Moye to come too. Three

91

being a crowd, particularly in this case, I decided to take Frankie also. All four of us managed to stow into the Flying Carpet—it was only a ten-minute flight, and we could endure discomfort that long. That is, I could—for Gulbeyaz, of course, sat in the double front cockpit with Moye, leaving Frankie and me to squeeze into the single rumble seat.

All the way there, I sulked over this latest frustration; but once the fair spread before us, with all its color and excitement, I must confess I entirely forgot about my elaborate heartaches. Gulbeyaz would be lucky if she got even a tin whistle out of me today!

There were so many diversions it was difficult to know which way to turn. Most of the action of the fair takes place on a broad field above the city. Across this field our little band struggled through the dusty, surging, good-natured crowds.

Hearing the wild howling of Arab bagpipes, we moved in that direction and found two hundred men of all ages formed in a great circle, dancing a religious dance. They were leaping up and down at a signal given by the leader in the center, yelling the name of Allah in chorus, swaying, stamping, and repeating the measures and invocations countless times, until each dancer had lashed himself into a trance, a delirium, that no longer felt exhaustion—only glory. Enchanted by the shrill savagery of the pipes, they had been leaping and shouting without a moment's pause since eight o'clock in the morning. It was now past noon. And not a single dancer, even among the oldest, had fallen dead!

Next we came to a troupe of Arab acrobats extorting coins from spectators, but their feats seemed tame after the frantic dance, so we wandered on. Snake charmers—glass-eaters—trained animals—magicians—and a hundred other forms of entertainment, each held a dense ring of pilgrims enthralled by the timeless and familiar tricks.

Gulbeyaz liked the snakes. We couldn't pull her away until she had seen the charmer swallow the cobra's head and suspend an adder by its fangs from his nose. She fell in love with the man who removed one eyeball from its socket and placed it in fetching positions about his face. Moye liked best to loop the loop dizzily on the children's homemade Ferris wheel. Frankie kept wandering around looking for the only thing not to be found—a bar.

I soon discovered what was my own favorite amusement at the fair—the fantasias, the wild, superb group-riding of the Arab horsemen.

From all over Morocco the best and most reckless riders had collected, bringing the finest Arab stallions. Wild riding is the national sport, the re-

92

lease, the joyous passion of the Moroccans. And here at Moulay Idris there were seventy-five thousand people ready and eager to applaud.

For each maneuver the horsemen line up at the end of the race course—twenty abreast, and row after row. Each rider has striven to outdo his companions in brilliance of costume and trappings. The saddles and bridles are made of vivid-hued leather, studded with gold, and covered with green and salmon silk. The linings of the burnooses also flame with color. The stallions, often pure white, rear and neigh and paw the ground in their impatience to be unleashed.

At a command the first riders drive their spurs into their horses' flanks. The beasts leap frantically forward. Down the course they flash, goaded into a terrified frenzy of speed. The riders, shouting their war cries, stand upright in their silver stirrups. White tails and manes, white burnooses, orange-colored cloaks, red and purple sashes, yellow and scarlet draperies, loosened turbans, all stream, sweep, swirl behind on the windstorm.

From out of this infernal gallop of twenty yelling demons, twenty strong bronze arms stretch forth, brandishing in the air twenty copper muskets. Upon a signal yell, at this mad career, they shout in unison, in unison twirl their guns, and in unison fire a deafening fusillade, fling their gleaming, smoking weapons into the air, leap out to catch them, and thunderously plunge on in a tempest, a fury, of dust and color and ferocity.

Wave after wave, each wave more abandoned, more savage, than the last; each superb rider is as fiercely handsome and graceful as a god. Saddles and bridles break—blood streams from the horses' flanks—the ground is shattered by the flying hoofs. The muskets explode—the insane yelling and the smell of powder fill the air—the riders and the horses go wild—and so do the spectators—and so did I!

It was late afternoon when we flew back to Fez. On our excursion, my suit for Gulbeyaz had not advanced one inch, but it had been a happy day just the same. While Frankie took the damsel home, Moye and I returned to our garden and went for a swim in the pool. Refreshed after the heat and dustiness of the day, we climbed to the terrace atop our house to watch the sun go down.

We always loved this hour. The city about us turned pale gold, and the snowy peaks of the Atlas, soaring mysteriously across the southern sky, burned with a conflagration of reflected fire. Everything seemed hushed, expectant. . . .

And then, just at sunset, it happened—a white flag fluttered up to the summit of the minaret of the Great Mosque, not far away, and on the balcony a muezzin appeared. Facing eastward, he wailed forth the evening chant, and from all the hundred other minarets of Fez a hundred voices took up the cry . . . Al-lah! Al-lah! Twelve hours before and half the world away, this call to prayers had started—in the Philippines, when it was sunset there. At a thousand miles an hour it had raced before the coming night to Java and Singapore. Then on to India, to Delhi, to be echoed from the minarets of that great Moslem capital . . . Al-lah! Through the Khyber Pass it swept, on to Isfahan, across Arabia to Mecca itself. Al-lah! On to Cairo. Al-lah! The cry rang over Tripoli—on to Tunis—into the Sahara. *Al-lah! haya il' al' falah!* now sang the muezzins from the towers of Fez, sending the invocation on toward the great ocean in the west, where, in a few moments more, the chanting would fade as the sun at length sank into the sea.

Darkness fell. Moye and I continued to sit quietly on the terrace, enjoying the coolness of the wind. At length, he broke the silence.

"Don't you think, Dick, it's time we were taking leave of Fez and traveling on? There's the rest of the world—we shouldn't become too attached to just one place."

I didn't know, at first, what answer to make. . . . I had not wanted this little paradise we were living in to come to an end . . . nor had I seen the sights of Fez half often enough . . . and Gulbeyaz—I didn't want to retreat so ignominiously while she was still scorning my overtures, still languishing for Stephens alone.

"I should say that your suggestion, Moye, shows a rank indifference on your part to Gulbeyaz' smiles."

"But it shows also a consideration for the Flying Carpet. We've got to get to Paris for an overhaul soon if you expect to continue flying."

That was a point against which I had no argument.

"All right," I said reluctantly, "but let's have one more party first."

The night before our departure we gave the party, asking into our secret garden, to say farewell, all those who had shared it with us. Tomorrow it would not be ours, but tonight . . . the Arab musicians played and sang their frantic best; Frankie, dissipating with ambrosia his sorrow over the loss of us, fell for one last time into the fishpond. All through the evening Gulbeyaz danced, danced as she had never danced before. How truly beautiful she was that night, despite her tattoo and gold teeth, how lithe and young, and how shining those great black eyes whenever Moye noticed her!

In a lonely and defeated mood, I left the joyful gathering in the courtyard, and, well after midnight, climbed up by myself to the terrace to look, once more before my departure, on the sleeping city—a city I felt at home in and had grown to love. How still I found the sky at this half-enchanted hour! Every star in the universe was shining down on Fez. The minaret of the neighboring mosque seemed cut out of slate and pasted against the dim horizon, and all about me the white ghosts of Moorish houses huddled and whispered together.

With so much loveliness, I should have been content to be alone. But I was not content. . . . Gulbeyaz—I heard her cymbals clinking down below. Why must she like Moye so much, and care so little for me? . . . Tomorrow at dawn I was going away, cheated and dejected. If I could only see her, here, for one brief moment, in this dimness and this starlight . . . to say good-by. . . .

Were my prayers being answered? Someone was coming up the steps, slowly and hesitantly. . . . I listened for the cymbals, but the music had stopped and all was quiet below. Gulbeyaz—it could only be Gulbeyaz! She had caught the glance I gave her, had seen me climbing to the roof and was coming after me, to say she was sorry for her indifference, sorry to see me go. She would ask to be forgiven. . . . "Never!" I said to myself. "At least, not at first." I wouldn't even look around. I'd be cold and aloof, adamantine, superior. . . . I'd gaze out, with folded arms, into the sky, while she pleaded with me.

The footsteps had reached the roof—she was now quite near . . . but I was determined to let her wait awhile before I looked or spoke.

And then, beside me, I heard—was it a sigh?

She was punished enough. Slowly, a little ashamed of my cruelty, I turned.

There—prostrate over the balustrade—was Frankie! And Frankie was ill.

As soon as I had recovered my own composure, I saw that he was *very* ill—so ill, indeed, that he needed prompt assistance. I loosened his collar, eased him as best I could, and tried to remember the proper antidote for too much ambrosia.

Preoccupied with my first-aid efforts, I paid no attention when another person came noiselessly onto the dark terrace and stood waiting, apparently for me.

After a moment, since I did not look up, the newcomer spoke—in Arabic, caressingly. Not until then did I recognize—*Gulbeyaz!*

But she had come too late.

"Oh, go on home," I said to her, over my shoulder. "I'm busy!"

95

9

Timbuctoo

✳ With Fez behind we were in the air again; and never had the Flying Carpet flown so fast. But fast as we flew the storm gathered faster. Sand spouts were whirling angrily about us, raising their heads like enraged cobras a hundred feet into the air and racing across the desert. Now they had mingled their smoke together in one vast pall blown furiously along by a steady blast. We struggled higher to escape it—and lost the earth completely. So we plunged back into the stratum of flying Sahara. We pitched and spun. The sand dug beneath our goggles, into our eyes, into our nostrils, mouths, lungs. There was no tiniest part of us or the motor where those frantic grains did not penetrate.

We were on our way to the oasis of Colomb-Béchar—the jumping-off-place for Timbuctoo—in the Algerian Sahara.

Back in Fez, where we had come down to earth after our flight over the Straits of Gibraltar, we had made ready to face the difficulties ahead. We had found there were two ways to reach our goal. One was to fly down the western coast of Africa for eighteen hundred miles, and then to Dakar, follow the Senegal and Niger rivers inland a thousand miles more. The other way was over the Atlas Mountains into the Sahara and sixteen hundred miles straight through the heart of the vastest, hottest, cruelest desert in he world.

We chose the second route. It offered considerably more dangers and complications, but we felt that the saving in distance would compensate for these—and anyway, the idea of tackling the Sahara with our Flying Carpet greatly appealed to us.

We had to tackle the Atlas Mountains first. Two hundred miles beyond them lay Colomb-Béchar, the first outpost of the vast sand ocean. Here we would fill our gas tanks to the brim and say good-by to the civilized world.

The moment we left Fez behind, the snowy summits of these mountains faced us. From the flying field there, at sunset the night before, we had watched the purple shadows fall across their barricades of ice. We blessed them, then, for their gleaming pure beauty, for their cold streams of water, for the protection they gave us against the furnace of the Sahara burning on the other side. But now that we must come to grips with them in the Flying Carpet, with their blasts and their cloud banks, they did not seem so amiable.

Nor were altitude and storms the only hazards. The Atlas Mountains were enjoying a lively war at the time between their bandit inhabitants and French troops. Airplanes were being extensively used to bomb the rebels, who in turn had the ill grace to shoot back at all airplanes. They were incredibly fine shots . . . and a gold and scarlet target such as the Flying Carpet would be an inspiration to their marksmen.

Their greatest hope was that the airplane crew could be brought to earth alive, for then they could enjoy sweet and slow revenge against the unassailable infidels who slaughtered their high mountaintop villages with bombs.

However, at fourteen thousand feet the Arab sharpshooters would probably miss us.

We climbed to fifteen thousand.

At this height, well above the highest peaks, we were almost torn to pieces by the wind. But our Flying Carpet was a strong little ship. We endured; we held together; and finally we struggled safely over without being annihilated by the blasts or shot down by the mountaineers.

On the north side of the Atlas the land had been deep in verdure, flowing with water, fragrant with spring. On the south side stretched the wilderness of the great Sahara. Down close to it we flew to pick up our course leading to Colomb-Béchar.

But to have escaped the mountaintops and reached the desert proved to be only a leap from one difficulty into another. We had been warned in Fez against trying to fly the Sahara at this time, for the sandstorm season was at hand. If caught by such a storm, flying carpets, magic or otherwise, could only expect disaster. During April, May and June, the scorching winds rush and rage across the unbroken wastes, churning the sand into a wild cloud and driving this cloud forward at incredible speed. No pilot can see fifty feet ahead, and no engine can function long in such a stinging yellow fog.

But however great the risk, we must go now. To wait three months for the sandstorm season to end was out of the question. We could trust to luck—and pray.

Alas, our prayers were not answered!

It was immediately evident as we struck the flat desert country that the winds we had encountered on top of the Atlas were not limited to the upper altitudes. They were blowing straight from the Sahara, and diminished not at all as we dived to lower levels to pick up the faint desert trail that was our only guide.

Moye and I noticed them at the same time—sand spouts ahead. They should have warned us. They *did* warn us, but it seemed so unreasonable —so like a storybook—for us to encounter a sandstorm the very first day, the very first moment, we saw the desert. Perhaps this wasn't the real article—just a feint, a mild sand shower. Anyway, we knew we could not get back now—dared not go back, with our fuel so nearly spent—over that range of mountains. We must face whatever lay ahead.

But all doubts about the true nature of the storm were soon swept away, when, after a few moments more, the seething fog of sand grew so dense that the daylight was turned off and twilight encompassed us. Moye forced the engine to its utmost speed. We had about fifty miles to fly to reach the Colomb-Béchar military landing field. Could we endure that long? . . . Could we hold our course through the yellow darkness?

A dozen times we had been warned that if we struck a storm of sand we must come down and land at once. But we couldn't land; we were in a gullied valley strewed with boulders. I felt myself growing more and more taut from anxiety. The handkerchief tied over my mouth and nose helped not in the least to keep out those diabolic grains which the storm flung at us in ever-increasing fury. But Moye had his jaws set, and continued to hurl us forward, grimly, relentlessly, at a hundred and twenty miles an hour. He had no intention whatsoever of landing, for landing on such ground would be no less dangerous than continuing to fly. . . . Only a few miles more should remain before we came to the oasis. We dropped still lower to watch for it—within a hundred feet of the ground—into the thick of things. . . . Where, oh, where, was Colomb-Béchar? We had to look around the windshields now, for they were completely blanketed with sand caught here, by the splattered oil. A blast of needles struck us in the face . . . but there, there, below, were palm trees bent over by the wind . . . and a fort . . . and a broad, smooth field. Gasping and exhausted, we brought the airplane down to earth. It took twenty soldiers to drag our Carpet through the onslaught of the storm into the military hangar.

For six days the sixteen hundred miles of unbroken yellow ocean that still separated us from Timbuctoo was tortured by the sand hurricanes. However, the day came when the desert was quiet once more, though for how long no one could say. We were able to start south again.

The question of fuel now had to be faced. Our capacity at best was only seven hundred miles. There was a military motor track we were supposed to follow, leading across the Sahara to the Niger River, thirteen hundred miles away. Once every fortnight from October till May a truck is driven along this track. To fuel the truck, automobile gasoline was on deposit at an oasis four hundred miles farther south, and again in a solitary unattended tank—the loneliest fuel station in the world—five hundred miles beyond that. This supply took one still another four hundred miles to a military post called Gao, on the Niger. The last three hundred miles were westward along the river to Timbuctoo.

So, provided we could follow the track from one deposit to another, we would have enough gasoline. To do this with an airplane is, under the best conditions, exceedingly difficult, so faintly is the trail marked on the desert. But now that one million square miles of sand had been charging back and forth over the track for six days it was questionable if there was any trail whatsoever remaining.

And yet one dare not lose it. For a thousand miles to either side there is absolutely and literally nothing but sand, sand, sand. At sea there is a chance for a floating wreck to be found by passing ships. But no ship ever passes here. The caravan route is hundreds of miles to the west. If our Flying Carpet lost the thread we had an area as large as all the United States east of the Mississippi to be lost in, and as barren and waterless as the moon.

If we were forced down on the trail, we had, at worst, fourteen days to wait for the truck, provided we could live that long with the thermometer at one hundred and twenty degrees for eight hours each day.

There was the possibility of missing the tank of gasoline and running out of fuel.

Another cursed sandstorm was more than likely to attack us, for the season was now well advanced.

100

However, that was the situation and we simply had to face it. We were not in the least discouraged. In fact, the very difficulties ahead gave us a certain elation. We had not expected to find the Sahara other than cruel and defiant. Had it been safe, had it been commonplace, there would have been no challenge to meet, no satisfaction in overcoming it. We felt sure that the airplane could get safely across; we needed only confidence in ourselves.

I knew it would take all of Moye's skill to get the Carpet off the ground, so heavy-laden was it with fuel and provisions—every tank overflowing, and food and water for two weeks. We found a hundred thousand square miles of flat desert adjoining the military field, and decided that if our plane wouldn't rise and fly to Timbuctoo, we'd taxi there on the ground.

But it rose, slowly, slowly, in the hot dry air, an inch at a time . . . turned . . . and faced the Sahara.

If the Sahara has a soul, that soul must have looked down, or up, with astonishment as the gold and scarlet Carpet, shining and alive, climbed into the copper sky, and sailed straight out across the infinity of sand.

Our great and immediate concern was the motor track below. Fortunately, the track had not disappeared—that is, not entirely. For long stretches the sand had covered it over completely, but by climbing to five thousand feet we could pick it up ahead or behind, and thus reorient ourselves.

At a hundred miles an hour the Sahara was sliding by, hard, dead, petrified, burning our lungs with its heated winds and our eyes with its blazing glare. As the league after league of nothingness rolled on we began to watch hungrily for relief from this monotony—monotony of topography, of color, of sky, of horizon. So delighted were we, after two hundred miles of desert emptiness, to note ahead a cluster of tiny oases, watered by wells, that we circled low over their palm tops to assure ourselves the trees were real, and not mirage.

Another hundred miles beyond, the wastes were broken by a vast island of soft yellow sand dunes, tossed into great troughs and ridges by the winds. Reaching out in desperation from the edges of this creeping sand juggernaut appeared the strangled tops of palm trees—all that remained of an oasis which these relentless dunes had buried alive.

Four hundred miles from Colomb-Béchar our disappearing-and-reappearing motor track led us to the oasis of Adrar, where another supply of truck fuel awaited us.

Adrar seemed as old as the Sahara. Its huts, built of mud, had stood a

Adrar

thousand years in this rainless, changeless land. The majority of its five hundred black-skinned Arab inhabitants had never in all their lives been a mile beyond the protection of the palm trees, nor had their fathers or grandfathers before them. This—the illimitable burning sand, the cool shadow of one grove of palms—this was the world. Rain they had scarcely ever seen; snow was undreamed of; rivers, fairy tales; an ocean, unimaginable.... One of the old village chiefs took us to the tiny trickle of brackish water his womenfolks lifted by buckets from a well. This trickle irrigated his palms and gave life to a cluster of wild iris—iris, even in the Sahara. The old chief's eyes sparkled with pride as he asked us in gestures, eloquently enough, if we had ever *seen* so much water. We told him solemnly that we never had. True, he had heard there was a little lake in Colomb-Béchar, but that was a month's journey by caravan, and he had never been able to go so far from home. We had filled our water bottles at that lake five hours before!

Next morning, assisted in our departure by every member of the village down to the smallest child, we struck out to find a tank of gasoline five hundred miles away.

The key to the tank lock we had in our pocket, as it had been given to us back in Colomb-Béchar. It was understood that we were to measure the number of gallons we took, refasten the lock and deliver the key at Gao, four hundred miles farther south. The price of gas at this extraordinary station was four dollars a gallon, so that this one refueling would cost

102

four hundred dollars. Even so, at any price, we were grateful for the Shell Oil Company's enterprise in having put it there.

On leaving Adrar, Moye and I took up another notch in our belts. This flight was to be the central span, the big effort, for our Flying Carpet. New York to Chicago, and not a hill or a house or a tree. A million square miles of blazing sun and flatness and unbroken nothing—nothing, save one half-buried tank of precious gasoline.

And we must cross this stretch. There could be no compromise. Our engine must function. There must be no sandstorms. We must not lose the piloting thread. We must not miss that tank!

Again the hours and the miles rolled by. Moye's eyes and mine were fixed grimly on the wisp of a track. We lost it—wheeled about to pick it up —lost it—found it—hide-and-seek all morning long.

The sky grew more dazzlingly, tormentingly hot as noon approached. The flat hard earth flung back its glare. Our water bottles were lifted more and more frequently to our lips.

I had pictured in my mind, in advance, what the center of the Sahara was going to be like. It was going to be gullied and scarred, crisscrossed by ranges of black and barren mountains where the lions had their dens and prowled at night about the encampments of the wandering Bedouin caravans.

Not one of my prearrangements came true. There were no black mountains, no gullies, no scars, no lions and no Bedouins—only an endless, endless, ash-yellow sea of sandy gravel in which no life, human, animal, bird, insect or vegetable, lived or could live. Nothing ever moves but the wind and the sand. Nothing ever changes the alternate light and darkness. In more than a million square miles only a streak of scarlet and its two lonely passengers broke the vacuum.

Moye and I took turns at the controls. By shifting, one of us could always give undivided attention to the nice sheet of totally blank white paper that served us as a map—blank because there was nothing for the cartographer to record except blankness.

During my idle periods I could not keep my mind off the morbid stories I'd heard in Colomb-Béchar about death on the Sahara. There was the story of the French officer who, in an attempt to get to the Mediterranean coast from the Niger River, tried to drive a small motorcar the two thousand miles to Algiers along the route we were following. He broke down in the middle of the vast waste, over four hundred miles from the nearest oasis.

He had water for two weeks. The two weeks passed, and a third, spent underneath his automobile to escape the murderous sun—alone, with a dead engine. On the twenty-first day his last drop of heroically conserved water had been drunk. He was loading his revolver, to spare himself the last hours of torture—when the trans-Saharan military truck, one week behind schedule, came by.

There was the story of the French army airplane transporting a general on a nonstop flight from Fez to the Niger. The pilot lost the motor track (nothing could be easier, as we knew) and made a forced landing. In doing so he ground-looped and stood his plane on end, breaking the general's shoulder. For some inexplicable reason, only the mechanic had a canteen of water —one canteen for three people in the middle of this inferno. The general died on the fourth day; the mechanic on the sixth; the pilot, according to the note left behind, on the seventh. A rescue squadron of military planes found the wreck and the corpses a week too late.

And on and on these stories spun, almost always with fatal endings.

We must not lose that track.

A new anxiety now began to assail us. We had expected to find the tank, according to information given us in Colomb-Béchar, about half-past eleven. It was now after twelve. Had we gone past? With each moment our uneasiness increased . . . an iron tank on the ground—so indistinguishable in color from the sand—so easily buried by a storm. . . .

My eyes were glued on the trail, directly beneath. Moye, looking ahead, presently noticed a half-dozen discarded gasoline tins beside the track. He decided to land . . . those tins might have some bearing on our fuel. On taxiing up to them we noted a curious-looking dune of sand close by. A pump handle was sticking out of it. There was our tank! A thousand eyes would never have seen it from above. Except for those suspicious tins, we would probably have gone on, still searching, until fuel exhaustion drove us down on the desert for a nice long rest.

Having dug away the ton of sand, and opened the lock with our key, we found the fuel, for all its elusiveness, intact. But transferring this precious elixir to our own tanks, one gallon at a time, proved far slower and more exhausting than we had anticipated . . . with the annihilating heat waves dancing up and down our wings, and a parching wind gleefully scattering the gasoline all over the desert. We had no time to be conscious of the fact that we were four hundred miles away from the nearest spring of water, four hundred miles from the nearest human being.

Despite our long delay, with luck we might still hope to reach Gao before nightfall. But luck, this time, deserted the Flying Carpet.

The hot desert wind, which had been dead against us all day, seemed to double the force of its resistance as we left the tank behind. We were forcing our engine well above cruising speed, but the flatness below seemed to be standing still. We began to watch the desert with growing apprehension, fearful lest the sand spouts would spring forth any moment and recommence their diabolical dance.

By five o'clock we were struggling for every mile.

By seven o'clock there was still nothing but limitless Sahara in sight. The sun had gone down in flames, and a pale moon told us night was at hand.

We must land again while there was yet enough light, and resign ourselves to spending the night wherever the Flying Carpet stopped rolling.

Again on the ground, as a precautionary measure we anchored the airplane with sacks which we filled with gravel. For supper we allowed ourselves a small ration of water and a can of beef. Then as darkness deepened and the desert moon rose higher in the sky, we uncovered our portable phonograph brought all the way from California, and had a musicale in the middle of this still, dead world.

The full moon gave us ample light, pouring its glow over the vast rotunda that was our concert hall. Schubert himself would have been moved and subdued by the melody of his "Serenade" spreading over the moonlit Sahara. The gentle, plaintive notes of the "Song of India" ceased to be wearisomely familiar. They became soaring, pure harmony, true and beautiful. We felt we'd never heard this old, old song before. We played the "Hymn to the Sun" from Le Coq d'Or. The audacity of this clear clarion chant sent chills and fevers through our blood. Its cascade of icy notes pierced the night with sweetness and reached the stars and bade them listen to the miracle of music rising from the heart of the wilderness.

Moye insisted that "Barnacle Bill the Sailor" come next. I objected violently. This was neither the time nor the place, with this peace pervading us, and the dim, far harmony still singing in the air. Moye said he couldn't hear any dim, far harmony. Let's have something snappy. But I was the more stubborn. Quarreling, we went to bed.

I say we "went to bed." We wrapped ourselves in coveralls, made pillows out of tool kits, and lay down on the hard, hard desert.

I couldn't sleep. I was too thirsty, the gravel couch too adamantine, the monkey wrenches under my head too unadjustable, and the wind, now that the sun had gone, too bitterly, biting cold. Moye and I shivered and shook, hardly able to believe that four hours previously our very lungs were burning from the intolerable heat. In four hours the temperature had dropped seventy-five degrees.

And yet, hot and cold, weary and thirsty as I had been that day, I now found myself by no means unhappy. There was a strange perverse satisfaction in this situation. Here was a new element, a new sensation—the sensation of being, except for my companion, the only thing alive in a dead world, a world that had supported no form of life since the beginning and would never support life till the end of time. I knew now what one would experience if one could visit a dead star wandering in space. There would be the same relentless progress of the murderous sun by day, and of the frozen firmament by night, in cloudless, seasonless silence. There would be the same appalling expanse of fixed, enchanted waste, without end, without change, without hope. In other deserts there is spring, but there is no spring here. No flower ever grew upon this boundless, barren ocean; on this illimitable corpse no bird or beast was ever born. When God made the world, some form of life was granted to every part of it—to every part but the Sahara's heart. The miraculous Finger never moved this way. A First Day, and a Second Day, and part of a Third, out of the Six, was all the Creation these silent moonlit sands about me ever knew.

The moment a rising sun gave us light enough to follow the motor track again, we climbed aboard the Flying Carpet and once more flew on toward Timbuctoo.

For another two hours we had to endure just such scorching heat, such dead, pitiless, ash-yellow wilderness, as the day before. For another two hours we kept our eyes glued on that will-o'-the-wisp of a trail.

At last, far off, we saw the Niger River. It seemed intrusive and out of place. Sand, sand, sand, for a thousand miles, and then, presto!—a great river with *water* in it. Water, but no trees to shade it; just a barren canal winding through the desert.

The city of our desire was still three hundred miles beyond—westward now, upstream. Having delivered the tank key at Gao, and settled our account, we turned at right angles to our southward course, flew high above the meandering undecided river, and watched for the fabulous city which we knew from our maps lay several kilometers inland from its banks.

106

Timbuctoo! Leagues away, from ten thousand feet, we saw it—the goal, the promise, of our long, long journey.

From two miles above, Timbuctoo looked like a great disk lying lost in the desert, round, flat, with close-packed houses, and a square hole—probably the market place—at the hub.

We wheeled and wheeled, lower and lower, trying to realize, after having traveled across America and the Atlantic and Europe and the Sahara, that this below was the city the Flying Carpet had set out from California to find.

At five thousand feet we could distinguish mosques and minarets, forts and garden walls, and the maze of labyrinthine streets.

At one thousand feet Timbuctoo came to life. The strings of dark specks became camels that moved. The market place flowed with white-robed natives gazing skyward at the Flying Carpet. We could see that our airplane was causing immense excitement. People were leaning out of windows, climbing on roofs, to watch the gold and scarlet airplane flying over Timbuctoo.

At five hundred feet one of the most extraordinary spectacles we were to meet on all our forty thousand miles of flying unrolled below us.

Right before our eyes Timbuctoo began to disappear—to be blanketed over and blotted out—by a vast, dark cloud that rose miraculously from the chimneys and the housetops. The cloud seemed alive. It was made of a million distinct and separate particles, each particle moving independently of its neighbors and yet managing to rotate in one sweeping circular motion around a central axis. I took off my flying goggles better to observe this phenomenon. No wonder Timbuctoo was considered a weird, mysterious town.

Then a small part of the cloud floated uncomfortably close to our propeller—and the mystery was explained. . . .

The cloud was not smoke.

It was not locusts.

It was not sand.

It was storks! Storks in countless multitudes, wheeling and flapping, in pairs, in squadrons, in regiments, over the housetops of Timbuctoo . . . storks, all bewildered, all agitated, by this roaring giant of a Fire Bird that came shooting out of nowhere into their midst. A million storks—or so it seemed—had risen from their nests to form this panic-stricken mass, this tossing sea, below.

Coming from the makeshift landing field Stephens and I, on horseback, rode grandly along the deep sand road into the celebrated city. Some ten thousand Moslem Negroes and a sprinkling of Arabs live in Timbuctoo, and most of them were out to stare at the two men from the moon who had flown on a miraculous gold and scarlet dragon here to earth. Crowds of laughing, shrieking little Negro boys, stark naked, ran at our horses' heels as we entered the crooked lanes between walls of squat mud houses. Groups of black-skinned, white-robed citizens pressed about us whenever we stopped. Above us, on each ledge and wall and roof, stood our friends the storks, recovered from their agitation and returned to their nests. Every house in Timbuctoo seemed deluged, overwhelmed, with hordes of unemployed storks. They had so little work to do—few people were ordering babies any more.

We were looking for Père Yakouba. Father Jacob is the town's chief patriarch and foremost personality. Born in France some seventy years ago, he came to Timbuctoo in 1903, on the heels of French occupation, as a Catholic missionary. And he has never gone home. Living so cut off from the world, he chose to modify his religious vows to the extent of marrying a Negress and begetting eight children. Removed from all modern distractions—there is not even a motorcar in Timbuctoo, and Paris is sixty days away by mail—he has been able to develop his scholarly interests without interruption, until he has become the great authority on native languages and native cultures in the Sudan. This rare old gentleman, with his long white robes and long white beard, stands like a beacon of light and learning in dark and savage Timbuctoo. He is the White Father, the teacher, the encyclopedia of the community, a wise and benign saint—but also a portly and a worldly saint, with an enormous black Amazon of a wife, six feet high, and the eight lusty brown children.

Père and Madame Yakouba greeted us cordially—white visitors were so few and far between, and especially the crews of Flying Carpets. Along with everybody else in town, this old couple had rushed to the housetop to watch our scarlet Carpet sailing overhead. Anticipating a visit from whoever was aboard, they had brought out their best liqueur and spread the table for tea.

The moment we sat down in Yakouba's study, a baby leopard and a monkey crawled into our hostess' ample lap. But the place was no zoo. All around were shelves covered with pamphlets, books, notes, written in and about the obscure languages of western Africa—the scholarly library of a

108

hermit-savant. Père Yakouba proved to be an extraordinary source of enlightenment. Every question Stephens and I asked—and they were countless —about the town, the people, their history and culture, Yakouba answered most patiently.

From the windows we could look out across the flat mud rooftops of the huddled town, and see nothing but ten thousand storks and a dilapidated mud minaret which rose up in the background. I exclaimed about the storks. I did not know there were so many storks on earth. Père Yakouba explained to us that the same public protection was given them here as in Europe. It was very bad form as well as bad luck to disturb them even though they drove you out of house and home.

But if I thought the storks were bad, wait till I saw the bats! Wait till night! For every stork in Timbuctoo there were a hundred bats. They lived in vast colonies in the mat ceilings of almost every room in town, squeaking and squirming all day, flying in and out of the windows all night. They were a pest, a plague, a curse, but nobody ever did anything about it. If you had ceilings, you had bats. To the native, that was one of Nature's immutable laws.

Timbuctoo makes an ideal refuge for all these winged citizens, since it is a dying community. For years, commerce—its only source of life—has been shifting to newer and more accessible French colonial centers. The dwindling population is not one-fourth what it used to be. As the houses are deserted, these bats and storks take absolute possession. Some day there will be no more people, only storks and bats, the emblems of birth and death, living in multitudes on the mud shell of the city that once was Timbuctoo.

But even then the ghost of the city, after the final demise, is going to be a proud ghost. No town in Africa has had such a history. A thousand years ago it was founded in the desert by a woman named Buctoo—Tin-Buctoo, the town of Buctoo—seven miles from the Niger. This woman was chieftainess of a tribe of Tuareg who dominated this part of Africa as do their descendants today.

The history of Timbuctoo has been a history of Tuareg. Sprung, some say, from a lost Roman legion, they have maintained their white characteristics in the heart of a black continent. They have remained virile, proud, belligerent. Besides their light color and fine features their most curious distinction is a heavy masklike veil worn by the men. Boys assume this veil on reaching manhood, and never remove it. Even intimate friends do

109

not behold the faces of one another. How many centuries ago this custom began, and why, no one seems to know.

The faces of the women, on the other hand, are as exposed as those of the men are hidden. And for that one is grateful—for prettier, gentler faces will not be found the length and breadth of Africa. Their skin is pale gold-brown, their hair fine and curly, sometimes blond. There is no fear, no furtiveness, in their eyes. They stand, tall and erect, draped in long Grecianlike robes with a scarf worn across their throats and over their heads, as perfect a picture of feminine charm as I have ever seen.

Even though this romantic and beautiful race founded Timbuctoo and for a thousand years supported it, they have never really lived in it. They are nomads and shepherds, and refuse to live in any city. They have left Timbuctoo to be peopled by the blacks. But they flow in and out constantly from their desert encampments to trade.

Up until thirty years ago, when France made a conquest of this part of the Sahara, these Tuareg did an enormous business in slaves. The central plaza was one great slave market to which buyers came all the way from Fez. Salt offered a no less profitable article of trade. Twice a year ten thousand camels made the journey across the desert to the mines, three hundred miles northward, and brought back tons of this precious mineral.

For three centuries Timbuctoo enjoyed great prosperity, reaching a climax of power during the period when America was being discovered and explored. Riches and culture from half of Africa were attracted to this thriving community. Four imposing mosques (imposing even though made of mud) raised their squat minarets above the crowded city. Arabic schools and colleges shed the light of art and science on this outpost of Islam. The name of Timbuctoo became a great name throughout the world.

But, long since, the glory has departed. Salt from Paris can be bought cheaper than the native product can be marketed. And as for slaves, while there is still surreptitious bootlegging on the side, the vast majority have become French citizens and dislike being bought and sold. The colleges have crumbled; the mosques, empty and forlorn, look down with grave reproachfuness at a city that has forgotten how to pray.

Yes, the glory has departed. The ex-slave market has been given over to the sale of sheep. Naked black children and indolent black women and dogs and camels and cows lie about in the deep sand of the crooked lanes that wind between the lines of tumble-down mud houses. Except on market

110

days, nobody seems to work, there is little sign of life. The storks stand above the fading, aging city—and wait.

Still followed by a pack of curious natives, Moye and I left Père Yakouba's house, and, guided by one of his sons, found our way to the caravansary. This turned out to be a most unprepossessing building on the town's outskirts, where visiting tradesmen could find shelter. It provided no furnishings, no attendant, no food, just a few barren mud-walled rooms. One brought one's own bed and cooked one's own meals. This place also seemed to be the head office for all the bats in Africa. They had burrowed their way beneath the ceiling mats, and there they lived by the thousand. For days on end no one entered the caravansary to disturb them. Consequently, when Stephens and I presumed to intrude, their indignant remonstrance was loud and long. After the first night, the evil, suffocating bat odor drove us onto the roof, but there the storks had built a dozen nests, and resented our presence as much as the bats. Defeated, we slept on the sand in the courtyard.

Twice a year this building is packed and bursting with guests. In March and September caravans converge at Timbuctoo from all over the Sudan, to travel to the salt mines I have mentioned. This is the only salt deposit in a million square miles of Africa. Thirty years ago, the spectacle of ten thousand camels moving as one enormous unit must have been a magnificent sight. But in recent years the demand for rock salt has so fallen off that only three thousand camels are required. Even at that, three hundred tons of salt and several thousand tradesmen are still brought into the city with each returning caravan. At these times the resthouse becomes the busiest place in town, sheltering merchants who have collected here from hundreds of miles around.

Once this brief period of activity is over, Timbuctoo sinks back into its lethargy. Only on the weekly market day does the city rouse itself. Then the central plaza is a most colorful place. Dozens of Sudanese Negresses, nude to the waist, sit beside piles of melons, fruits and fowls. Wild-looking Negro shepherds drive in their sheep and goats from the Niger flats. Savages from the brush country and the southern jungles, wearing only a loincloth, wander about unnoticed. One will see tall, hawk-faced Tuareg, veiled to the eyes and carrying huge Crusadic swords, moving across the square with a humble Negro close behind. They are bootleg slave dealers with a slave to sell. Locally made pottery of crude design is stacked in

111

bright little hillocks. Brassware and homemade weapons sparkle in the fierce sunshine. Cotton cloth woven by hand in the native homes is being bought—but not so eagerly as the bottles of gin an enterprising half-caste is selling to young Tuareg swells. A string of heavy-laden camels just in from Marakesh, a thousand miles away, kneels before the old slave block, waiting to be unloaded; and a dozen burros, almost hidden under sheep-skins they are bearing, struggle past through the dust.

Nine tenths of all this life and movement are given by the Negro traders and their petty commerce. The Tuareg give only one-tenth; but instantly, on a visit to the market, one feels the domination of this small minority. The Negroes seem subservient, oppressed, and pay obeisance in look and manner to the veiled lords of the desert. And what lords these Tuareg are! —conscious of their beauty and tall slim carriage, swaggering arrogantly from shop to shop. They look at one over their veils with fierce dark eyes that leave no doubt of the contempt in which they hold other men, or of their readiness—and ability—promptly to re-enslave Timbuctoo and all its unwarlike population the moment French machine guns are pointed some other way.

Stephens and I soon made the acquaintance of Timbuctoo's very limited white colony. It consisted of one army colonel, six young officers, and about eight French civilians including the postmaster and his extremely pretty daughter—the only French girl in town. The officers were our special friends and dined us frequently on the roofs of their barracks. There champagne flowed bountifully; and the singing of these young soldiers exiled in this desert town rang out over the housetops. "We have to drink and sing," they confessed. "Otherwise, we'd perish from the heat and monotony."

Moye was content to spend every evening with our military friends, but I sometimes grew restless and chose to wander about alone in the starlight to enjoy the metamorphosis that comes over the squalid little city after dark. From dawn to dusk the sky blazes overhead with a terrible heat, exhausting and withering the spirit of the land, and revealing the fabulous, mythical Timbuctoo to be in soul and body what it now really is—just mud. But when the darkness falls, a mysterious and truly magic spirit floats down upon the town. Then Timbuctoo becomes the dream city I had come so far to see. All the drabness disappears. The houses seem no longer made of mud, but of starlight, standing haunted and half real against the velvet sky. In the darkness, there is a strange, wry angle to every wall and roof, like the backdrop of some modernistic stage setting painted in black and

112

A meat market in Timbuctoo

silver by a madman. From the mud walls of the blunt and tumbling minarets, innumerable dead branches of trees, used for decoration, stand out at
right angles, and in the nighttime I half believe I see, in the ravens roost-
ing there, the black-faced ghosts of all the slaves that have been flogged to
death throughout the dark and bloody history of this savage place.

I stroll deeper into the city. Here and there a candle glows through some
open door, casting across the sandy path a pale, lugubrious light. A camel
sleeping in the lane suddenly rises noiselessly to his feet at my approach
—a shapeless, swelling apparition in the dark.

These lanes are not deserted after nightfall. The traffic of the day has
passed, but the traffic of the evening has just begun. Dark figures of women
drift up to me through the sand, and stand, and do not speak. They are
not prostitutes, but rather primitive daughters of a primitive black Eve,
hunting love and inviting into their arms the first person they can find.

Nevertheless I reach the courtyard before the Central Mosque. It is
utterly deserted. But here the night wind stirs, and brings from the far-off
edges of the city the faint, melancholy wailing of Arab pipes. I stop to
listen. From out of the air there also comes the distant throbbing of a drum;
but the wailing and the throbbing are so faint, so far away, they only lend
to the illusion that one is but half-awake, wandering in a labyrinth of dream
houses, among dream people, all buried in a starlit shroud of sand.

10

The Ghosts of Santa Sophia

✳ We spent a month in Venice. A month wasn't nearly long enough, but after that time we both began to feel the urge to fly again. Once more we unrolled our map of the world. Moye suggested Berlin. I voted for Malta. We compromised on Istanbul. A few hours later the Flying Carpet and its crew were in the air.

Our first stop was Vienna. Then to Budapest—to Belgrade—to Bucharest—through storms, across plains, over mountains—on to Istanbul and the Golden Horn.

As we approached, the sun was low in the west, beating against the vast land walls that stretch, with their hundred towers, straight across the peninsula on which stands Istanbul, once called Constantinople—before that Byzantium. Reflecting this fire rose a forest of minarets. The domes and the gardens, the castles and the seas, were suffused by the same violet haze that crowns Athens at the sunset hour. The Golden Horn mirrored the flaming clouds. The Bosporus, a deep blue ribbon, hewed its way between Asia and Europe, escaping from the Black Sea which stretched away to the north in deep, dark gloom. Gold walls and violet light, blue waters and sunset sky, all were softened and harmonized by the fast fading afternoon. And this concentration point of history and of splendor, this stage of endless epic dramas, this imperial city which next to Rome longest shaped the destiny of the world, lay, five thousand feet below, in the hollow of my hand.

115

Fifteenth-century Rumelihissar Castle still guards
the European shores of the Bosporus near Istanbul

Jason and his Argonauts first came this way, more than three thousand years before. Constantine and Justinian made it the center of civilization. Mohammed the Conqueror and Suleiman the Magnificent adorned it and glorified it. But not even they ever saw their capital revealed as it was revealed to me. They did not know, as I knew, how truly magical it was, how fabulously beautiful. They had not soared into space above their palaces, to survey their domains from the Black Sea to the Hellespont—the Dardanelles. This was within the power only of the jinn, and the characters out of storybooks who traveled miraculously across the skies aboard their flying carpets.

Long before we arrived at Istanbul I knew what most I wanted to see there—the Basilica of Santa Sophia. Pictures of this astonishing temple I had seen all my life; histories of it had filled me with an eagerness to enter its doors. Through those doors the ebb and flow of conquest, the emperors and the captains that ruled the earth, had passed for a thousand years before Michelangelo raised the dome of St. Peter's above the Eternal City.

There it was, a mile below, a monarch commanding two continents. Approached from the air the great Basilica seems to scorn all outward grace, relying on its enormous size and strength to capture one's eye. Instead of statues and lacelike stones, massive buttresses, solid and practical, ornament it heavy boxlike walls. Even the four minarets added by Moslem conquerors, rising above the granite mountain, are too incongruous to add much charm. In fact, from the outside, Santa Sophia is a disappointment. One might mistake it for a fort—until one sees the interior.

The first evening of our visit to Istanbul, a half-moon rose in the sky. Even though we had flown six hundred miles that day and well deserved a night of rest, I chose not to take it—not with this moonlight shining through the windows of the most ancient and most storied cathedral in the world. On such a night what might one not see within?

Alone, about nine o'clock, I went to the courtyard before the mosque and found it cool and calm at this late hour. The enormous mass of masonry, confused and meaningless in the dark, towered above. At the side door, now used for the entrance, a guard stopped me—it was late—the last prayers were being said—he would soon be extinguishing the lamps—I could not enter . . . unless I cared to contribute a little bakshish to him personally.

I contributed, took my shoes in my hand, plunged into the black emptiness, felt my way down a vaulted corridor, passed between two enormous marble columns, and there, moved to the depths by the incredible picture, I stood and stared. . . . "The terrestrial paradise, the second firmament, the throne of the glory of God. It rises to the heavens. It is the marvel of the earth," exclaimed a chronicler eight hundred years ago.

I knew just how he felt.

Had I entered this Temple of Divine Wisdom first by day, I am certain it would have been an adventure astonishing enough; but to have been drawn through the darkness into its appalling expanse of space, illuminated by the shafts of moonlight that streamed down through the forty windows of the most audacious dome in history, made me feel that I beheld a vision of a temple too aspiring, too vast, to be the handiwork of man.

Fourteen hundred years old—the first of the great Christian temples. Many others have since risen to compete with it, but as I stood within its walls I I felt this temple was still supreme among cathedrals, and would be always until the giants and angels who must have helped in building it came back to earth to build a greater one.

Once my eyes became used to the obscure light I began to move across the carpets, around the edge of the vault, past a row of marble columns—moving softly in order not to disturb the small group of Moslems bowed down toward Mecca. An imam led this late gathering of the faithful, and chanted forth his prayers to Allah, prayers repeated by the congregation as they knelt and stood and knelt and touched their foreheads to the floor in rhythmical, rustling unison.

The services were over, the last for the day. The worshipers, treading silently in their stockinged feet across the thick mats and carpets, flowed past my dark recess and out into the deep-shadowed corridor.

The priest alone remained, tiny and unreal in the presence of such soaring space, such huge dimensions, about him. And then he, too, without sound, without effort, in his long robes, seemed to float over the temple floor, and in slow and solitary dignity fade into the outer dark.

From out of this same dark, my friend the guard came in, extinguished the lamps, and disappeared, leaving only the beams of moonlight for illumination.

So utterly entranced had I been by the dim glory of my surroundings I had not given a thought to my own departure; and the realization that I was utterly alone within this haunted vastness strangely did not drive me out of it. Rather was I held, fascinated, by my nocturnal excursion into this moonlit and mysterious realm. There was no profanation here, no mock-heroic escapade, but reverence and wonder—reverence for the passion and the genius that built the temple, for the centuries that have consecrated it, for the millions of Christians and Moslems who have worshiped in it and approached nearer to

The great church of Santa Sophia, Istanbul

their God. I was possessed by an irresistible desire to rest peacefully in the dark shadow of this mother of all cathedrals, to enjoy the dream of fourteen hundred years of history, to possess utterly, for my very own, these carpeted floors, these columns torn from pagan temples, these mountainous marble walls, this soaring sensational canopy nearly two hundred feet above me, through which the moonlight streamed.

For three enchanted hours I roamed about my marvelous domain, touching, through the shadow veil, the pillars and the walls, the rostrum and the urns. I leaned back against a marble column and looked up at the incredible dome, a dome such as no man ever dared to build before, or has been able to build since. The master architect who designed it defied every structural law. Gravity was apparently dismissed. It should have fallen before it was half built, so ethereal it is, so flat, so fearless. And yet the innumerable earthquakes that have shaken the city to pieces have not so much as cracked this earth-scorning canopy.

How still the great mosque had become with the midnight hour; how peaceful its deep gloom! The weariness from six hours spent that day flying through the skies crept over me. My lodging was far away and the carpets in my secluded corner deep, and very soft. Perhaps if I rested throughout the night in this ghostly place I'd hear the chorus of angels that sometimes chant when no Mohammedan is near, or, like Jacob, see them mounting up one of the ladders of light that lead to Paradise.

I made a pillow of my leather flying coat and stretched on a carpet bed, still able to look out between the marble columns and up at the soaring canopy of dim stone sky. The moon continued to ride in the heavens, drifting around the circle of windows upon which the great dome spread its wings. That moon seemed determined to look through all the forty ancient panes; and as it wheeled, the angle of the shafts of light that fell upon the carpets at my feet wheeled too. I lay quite still, and watched the slow procession of these moonbeams, wondering if they were the ghosts of the emperors who once ruled Byzantium, the Christian kings who had worshiped here, the sultans of the Saracens . . . convening in this dark and overtowering vault from which all living human beings but myself had been driven out.

The first and proudest of these spectral shafts, if they were ghosts, must have been Justinian—Justinian, whose giant spirit conceived this glorious temple, who commanded his architects to build these walls, in order that Byzantium might behold the supreme manifestation of the worship of the Christian God, and remember the power and the glory of the imperial builder.

120

Who better had the right to lead the march of the ghosts than Justinian? It was his lordly gesture, in the year 532, that swept away acres of houses standing where he wished his great Basilica to rise. It was he who stopped all other works to marshal sixteen thousand builders under his authority, who scoured the empire for extravagant materials, who pillaged the colossal marble columns from the Temple of Diana at Ephesus, ransacked Baalbek for its riches, and levied from Athens, Delphi and Rome shiploads of treasures.

What matter if building costs soared into prodigious figures? Justinian was not the man to be dismayed. He merely seized the salaries of all the state officials, closed the schools and forced the army to fight without pay, thus providing forty thousand pounds of silver for the altar piece and half a million pearls for the sanctuary's curtain. Extortion, taxation, torture, robbery, played their part in the creation of this supreme monument to the Divine Wisdom of God.

Justinian's temple stood at last complete, faced inside with marble from a hundred lands, roofed (with the help of the dark and secret powers) by one miraculous, floating dome. This was the Emperor's triumphant hour. Surrounded by his glittering court, his generals and his ministers, accompanied by a thousand priests and a vast orchestra and choir, Justinian mounted to the silver altar and cried out for the multitudes to hear, "Oh, Solomon, I have surpassed thee!"

Yes—that foremost of the moonbeam ghosts—that was Justinian.

And the ghosts that followed—perhaps they were the other Byzantine kings; or perhaps Christian knights of the Crusades who had tarried here, bearing the cross and the sword with which to free the Holy Sepulcher.

And the final shaft but one, in the slow procession, was that Constantine XIII, the last Christian emperor of the Byzantines? Fate had forced him to watch his empire crumbling before the tidal wave of Saracens, until in 1453 the deluge came. Knowing his city was doomed and he about to die, he came into the imperial church to take the sacrament. He looked up at the huge mosaic figures upon the ceiling of the marvelous dome—Christ and the Virgin, the Saints and the Apostles. He knew they were soon to be flung from the thrones which they had graced nine hundred years. He kissed the great gold cross that hung suspended from the cupola. He knew that before the day was done a crescent would shine in its place.

And so it came to pass. Over the bodies of ten thousand Christian dead, Sultan Mohammed rode into the Basilica. The interior was packed with terrified citizens praying for deliverance, but deliverance did not come. Mo-

The glorious interior of Santa Sophia

hammed mounted to the silver altar, knelt toward Mecca, and gave thanks to Allah for the victory.

That brightest shaft of moonlight—the very last of all—that, surely, was Mohammed, for was this not the great Sultan's mosque as well as Justinian's church? Had he not transformed it? Had he not stripped it of every Christian symbol, appropriated its most valuable treasures, gilded over the mosaics of Christ, removed the altars and the crosses? Had he not spread verses from the Koran across these ceilings from which the saints had looked down? Had he not erected minarets from whose balconies the muezzins might call a Moslem Byzantium to prayer? He had found Santa Sophia the greatest church in Christendom. He had renamed it Aya Sophia, and turned it into the greatest mosque in all the Moslem world—and no man has been able to dislodge him from that day to this. How proud and slow his ghost marched past; proud of possession, proud of Islam, proud of Sultan Mohammed!

And on and on the shadow figures moved, pacing, with the wheeling moon, their path across the temple floor where they had known their mortal glory; until the moonlight waned, and one by one the specters faded back into their crumbling tombs. . . .

It was early dawn, and there was not a ghost in sight. The moon had entirely departed, and a pale gray light crept in through the windows of the dome. Cold, and a little apprehensive, I seized my flying coat and sought the door of the mosque. It was open, screened only by a heavy curtain of mats. The same guard of the evening before slept soundly on the floor of the stone porch outside, and I did not disturb him as I crept beneath the curtain and, shoes in hand, slipped past.

But I did not reach the street, for at that moment one of the muezzins was coming across the courtyard to ascend the minaret—and I stood still, seized by a fantastic idea. . . . The muezzin—the minaret of Aya Sophia—at dawn—the first call of the day . . . if only I could accompany him and hear him at close range summon Istanbul to prayer, my night's cup of adventure would be filled.

I spoke to him and indicated that I wanted to climb the minaret when he climbed. Never had I wanted anything so much. He looked at the guard. The guard slept soundly. He looked at the courtyard. Not a stir. He nodded ascent. Oh, Islam, Islam, how has your fanaticism faded!

Behind the muezzin, in the blackness, I felt my way up the spiraling stairs. We emerged on the high balcony with the sun just ready to spring out of

123

Asia, and all Istanbul, gray and misty, sleeping at our feet. Before us the dome of the mosque rose so close I felt that I could almost reach it with my hand. From the Marmora Sea the daybreak wind whispered past our minaret, blessing alike with its clear, cool touch the faithful and the infidel.

Allahu akbar—Allahu akbar. The muezzin leaned out to the east, out to the sun, and chanted in that weird, quavering whine always used, which sounds like mournful wolves a-howling. *Allahu akbar—God is great.*

Ashadu anna la ilaha illallah—I testify there is no god but God. There is no god but God.

The chanting priest now leaned to the north, toward the Golden Horn, the swirling, awakening Bosporus, the vague Black Sea—*I testify that Mohammed is the Prophet of God—Come to prayer—Come to prayer.*

He moved to face the west, the myriads of domes and minarets, the hundred towers of the great land walls, all tinted brightly with the first colors of the sunrise—*Hajju 'ala's—salaaaaaaaaat—Come to salvation—salvaaaaaaaashun.*

It was a futile call, an appeal in vain, apparently, for no one seemed to heed. The mosques are almost empty in Istanbul, the religious springs are dry. Mohammed's reign over Byzantium is tottering to a close. *Tout passe, tout casse, tout lasse.* Just how long until the crescent topples from Aya Sophia's dome, only a major prophet can foretell. But any minor prophet knows the time is not far off. Then bells will ring in the minarets, and back from exile will come the Christian saints to take their places on their thrones; and once more the doxology will fill the glorious Basilica as it did in the golden ages fourteen hundred years ago.

124

11

Galilean Days

✳ The armies of the First Crusade, fighting their way from Constantinople to Syria in the eleventh century, marched the eight hundred miles across what is now Asiatic Turkey in seven months. The Flying Carpet took just seven hours.

Moye and I left Istanbul behind one day at noon. We climbed and climbed above the minarets of Santa Sophia, waved good-by to the Golden Horn, and sailed up the castled shores of the Bosporus. Then we turned east, found the trail of the Crusaders and sped on toward the Holy Land. Our immediate objective was the Sea of Galilee.

The Sea of Galilee! In all the world has any lake a more romantic, a more poetic, history than this? Wherever Christianity has prevailed, this little sea is known and loved. Since the beginning of our era a halo of immortality has crowned its name. Its shores were the scene of Jesus' ministry; its waters bore Him many times; from its people came Peter and Andrew, James and John. Whenever He journeyed into the neighboring provinces it was to this haven He invariably returned. One can well imagine that when He hung upon the cross, slowly perishing from the torture and the thirst, His dying eyes saw the vision of the cool blue depths of Galilee.

And now, below us, the very lake appeared.

It is not a large basin, this so-called sea. From north to south it measures less than sixteen miles, and only seven miles across. But if it were larger, perhaps we should love it less. Mountains, treeless now and gray with stone, stand round about, broken only by the River Jordan, which flows in from the peaks of Lebanon and out to feed the insatiable Dead Sea.

We landed in a broad field beside the river, and remained for two weeks, held prisoner by the charm of this historic region. We climbed the mountains, tramped along the shore, and embarked on the lake in the tiny fishing boats.

The fishermen soon became our daily companions. I have never had companions I admired more, for, as is the case with fishermen everywhere, they had grown to be like the sea they continually contemplated—free, honest, natural, clean. It was not otherwise in Jesus' time. What greater tribute to a calling was ever made than this: that of the Twelve He chose for His disciples, seven were fishermen?

Among those following this profession, two Arab brothers, Akhmet and Ali, were my special friends. Like James and John they owned a boat together and, like those two disciples, observed the great tradition of their lake—the tradition of honesty, simplicity and fidelity. Ali was twenty; Akhmet twenty-one. The Galilean sun had burned into their dark skin a healthy ruddiness that found good company in their clear black eyes. They each wore a single white cotton costume made in the native style, and they were barefoot. They had no money—their sailboat was their only capital.

For several days, while Moye was occupied with the Flying Carpet, I accompanied these two brothers in their fishing boat when they set their nets or hauled in the catch collected the night before. Our oral communication was limited to the dozen English words they had picked up from occasional tourists, but in pantomime they were eloquent, so we got along.

Despite their lack of worldly goods, or perhaps because of it, they had the most untroubled, untarnished hearts I've ever met. They sang and sang all day, with shrill discordant voices—the way all Arabs sing. Akhmet, the elder brother, would chant out a line alone, and then the two of them would repeat the line in full-lunged duet. It was always of love they sang, for, like most young Arabs, they had incorrigibly romantic natures, responsive as the strings of a harp to any touch of sentiment.

> *Alhoub fi kalbi amanah, Kafia,*
> *Malakti kalbi bi ridayek*

was their favorite song, and Kafia the lady of their dreams.

126

Love in my heart is to be trusted, Kafia;
I can be trusted with your love.
Every shadow of my soul is yours, Kafia;
In your hands rests my destiny.

Tiberias, the once-royal city of Herod, was our harbor. From there, in the late afternoon, we'd sail close inshore up to the site of Capernaum, Jesus' adopted home, or across the estuary of the Jordan to Bethsaida where Peter and Andrew and Philip once lived. Today only a few stones and capitals strewn about among weeds mark the spots.

But before these ghost cities the fishermen cast with the same type of net, from the same type of boat, in the same free and hardy spirit, as two thousand years ago. At twilight Akhmet and Ali and I would fix one end of their net upon the shore, and then drag the weighted line, to which the mesh was attached, in a semicircle out into the sea and back to shore again. We slept near by to guard the line, and then, when it was dawn, we drew our catch to land, gathering the larger fish into baskets, and casting the very small away.

And upon me, always, was the consciousness that this shore by Bethsaida had seen things strange and wonderful. Here Jesus, standing in Simon Peter's boat, often taught the people gathered on the beach. Here, it is recorded, He said to Simon:

Launch out into the deep, and let down your nets for a draught. And Simon answering said unto him, Master, we have toiled all the night, and have taken nothing: nevertheless at thy word I will let down the net. And when they had this done, they inclosed a great multitude of fishes: and their net brake.

Such a miraculous draught of fishes from the Sea of Galilee has not, alas, been seen in many a day. The fish of late years have become few and small. There were several times when Akhmet and Ali and I toiled diligently before Bethsaida and, like Simon, took nothing. But, probably unlike Simon, we were not in the least made downhearted by a meager catch, for it meant there would be less marketing for the brothers to do and more time for us to sail, or explore the hills.

One such morning, after a particularly lean haul, we three stood on the pier at Tiberias looking about for new amusement to fill the day. I noticed the high gold mountain wall that rose up abruptly from the eastern shore of

127

Shepherds by the Sea of Galilee

the lake, seven miles away, and wondered what hidden ancient splendors might lie buried there. I had a sudden urge—the morning was so radiantly beautiful—I suggested to Ali and Akhmet that we sail across and spend the day on the other side, in "the country of the Gadarenes."

The two fishermen agreed, but on launching forth we found there was a dead calm. They took to the oars in a leisurely fashion, and I dived overboard and swam alongside. The water proved so cool and stimulating, I decided, after a mile or two of lazy paddling, that it might be amusing to swim all the way across.

From the center of the lake I could look around at the barren shores. Upon those shores, in the time of Christ, a dozen busy cities had stood, offering anchorage to large fleets of fishing boats built from the timber that grew in deep forests on the surrounding hills.

Of all this abundance, only Tiberias remains, now a squalid village. Except Capernaum and Bethsaida, even the locations of the other lakeside cities are lost. Gone are the fishing fleets. On the entire lake there are now less than twenty sails. I could scan the encircling mountains and not find one wooded spot to break their gauntness.

Among these mountains, the Mount of the immortal Sermon, above Capernaum, stood out most conspicuously. From Capernaum, Jesus and His disciples had climbed to this commanding altar and surveyed the entire sea spread below them, intensely blue amid the then green hills. Here was space for the crowds who flocked to hear Him speak in all His wisdom. . . . *Lay not up for yourselves treasures upon earth . . . for where your treasure is, there will your heart be also. . . . Take therefore no thought for the morrow: for the morrow shall take thought for the things of itself. . . .* No treasures upon earth, no thought for tomorrow—was that, after two thousand years, still the way to happiness? To look at my two Galilean companions, reared in the shadow of the Mount, one would think so.

All morning there had not been the faintest breeze. Not a single ripple disturbed the glazed surface of the lake. But Akhmet warned me that this quietude would not last; that on these hot August days the calm always gave way to a violent squall. . . . And just as Akhmet had prophesied, the wind, shortly after the noon hour, sprang up with astonishing suddenness; the whitecaps began to break about us—and the yellow mountain wall still lay a mile away.

The lake has been famous since Biblical times for these sharp summer storms. Utter cloudless calm all morning, and then, in the early afternoon—

swoop!—down comes a sudden vortex of wind, sucked into the basin by its subsea-level position; and in an instant the waters begin to foam.

It would have been the sensible thing for me to climb back into the boat and allow the fishermen to raise their sail and hasten to the shore. But having covered six of the seven miles, I naturally wanted to finish off the last remaining one, and so I stuck at it, through another half hour of wind and waves.

Reaching the foaming rocky beach at last, I lay down, half-drowned, beneath the great mountain wall, while Ali and Akhmet, having anchored our boat in deep water, swam ashore, dragging our sodden clothes behind them.

We had no hope of getting back to Tiberias before the wind abated, so we made ourselves at home in a sheltered corner of the cliff. Our little excursion had left us ravenously hungry, but as we had set out that morning unexpectedly, we had brought no food. However, for my two Galilean fishermen, that was not a serious matter. They just took their small casting nets from the boat, stood among the rocks along the shore, and fencing with the angry breakers, cast for fish.

The waves burst against them and over them, but they only laughed and braced themselves for the next assault. Their lithe and agile bodies, drenched with spray and sun, gleamed like polished copper as they swung their nets and wrestled with the sea.

Soon they had taken six fish—two for each of us—and proudly brought them back. Then while Akhmet built a fire from driftwood and dead reeds, Ali and I went to visit a small encampment of shepherds we had seen half a mile away. We returned with a basket of unleavened bread. By this time Akhmet had a grill of hot coals ready, and upon it laid the fish. Never in my life have I dined more royally.

Twilight was approaching before we thought of going home. But the wind still howled across the lake; and we did not dare start back until it blew less violently. However much the land of Galilee has changed since the time of the Apostles, the Sea of Galilee has remained the same—moody, tempestuous. Nineteen hundred years ago the first story of a Galilean storm, just such as this, was told. It has become one of the most familiar stories in the world:

When the even was come, Jesus saith unto his disciples, Let us pass over unto the other side. And . . . they took him even as he was in the ship. . . . And there arose a great storm of wind, and the waves beat into the ship, so that it was now full. And he was in the hinder part of the ship, asleep on a pillow: and they awake him, and say unto him, Master,

Ruins of the synagogue at Capernaum, on the Sea of Galilee, where Jesus preached and "gathered his first followers."

carest thou not that we perish? And he arose, and rebuked the wind, and said unto the sea, Peace, be still. And the wind ceased, and there was a great calm.

The stars were out before we were able to embark again aboard our fishing boat. Though the lake was no longer driven by the storm, it had not ceased to roll. Nor had the wind entirely subsided. Since it still blew fitfully against us, we had to use the oars, without the assistance of the sail. Akhmet sat at the rudder, and Ali and I each manned an oar, and stood as we rowed.

Alhoub fi kalbi amanah!

chanted Akhmet at the stern.

Alhoub fi kalbi amanah!

Ali sang after him, in rhythm with our oars.

Love in my heart is to be trusted . . . just an Arab love song, so popular locally that even I knew the words; yet now, sent ringing over the Galilean waves by these two simple fishermen, it seemed almost like the faint, imperfect echo of another, older love song—the divine love song once spoken to the music of these waters. For is not the refrain of that song, too, only the same simple message in a higher, more spiritual key—Love is to be trusted? These words, with their universal truth, rising in a great tide from the shores of this insignificant little lake, have swept like spring upon the spiritual deserts of the world, carrying the name of Galilee to the hearts of men.

During the second watch of the night the wind faded to a breeze, and then died away entirely. The Sea of Galilee slept, motionless, and on across it, guided by the outline of the hills, we rowed unto Tiberias.

12

The Holy Sepulcher

✱ From the moment the Flying Carpet left Istanbul behind and turned toward the Holy Land, the Crusaders had become our guides. And as the Holy Sepulcher had been their goal, so likewise it now became our own. The Crusaders had crossed the Taurus mountain range in southeast Anatolia with the greatest difficulty, and so did we. We tarried before Antioch, as they had tarried, and still in their tracks, flew on along the coast of Syria to Tyre, and Sidon, and Acre.

After our excursion to the Sea of Galilee, we continued south down the valley of the winding Jordan until we came to Jericho, a modern village built upon the ruins of the trumpet-tumbled walls. Here we turned to the west, rose four thousand feet out of the walled-in valley, sailed twenty miles over the wilderness of Judea, over the Mount of Olives—and Jerusalem burst upon us.

The soldiers of the First Crusade had attained this goal more than eight centuries before. Or rather, their remnant had, for out of every ten who marched forth from the cities of Christendom, only one arrived, and these, after three years on the way, were starving and exhausted.

Even so, the fanatical zeal that had driven them to the deliverance of the Holy Land still burned bright, and they did not falter at sight of the huge stone ramparts behind which an equally fanatical Moslem army watched and

The Damascus Gate, Jerusalem

waited. The soldiers of the Cross, gaunt and weary, but raised to a pitch of religious frenzy by their priests, hurled themselves against the walls, shouting their battle cry of *Deus vult!*—only to be hurled back with frightful losses.

Godfrey de Bouillon, greatest among their leaders, then decided on less zeal and more science. His engineers built a movable siege tower capable of overtopping the walls, and this was pushed forward. The Moslems flung fire and boulders against it, raised their rampart higher, and concentrated all their strength to meet the giant.

But the Crusaders grimly advanced. Only a foot remained between their tower and the wall. The tower's drawbridge was allowed to fall, and across it, led by the indomitable Godfrey, the Crusaders charged. *Deus vult!* God wills it! Seldom in history have soldiers been so fired by religious passion, seldom has any battle been so terrible. The Crusaders were fighting in the name of Christ. His sepulcher lay only a few hundred yards away. Nothing could withstand their frenzy. The Moslem ranks crumbled, the gates were opened from within, and the entire Christian army stormed exultantly into Jerusalem.

The soldiers went mad with joy. For this moment they had left their homes long months before. For this moment they had struggled three thousand miles through every obstacle. Their God and their dead comrades would be avenged, and the infidels who held Jerusalem swept from the sacred city they profaned.

The butchery was indescribable. Moslem families crowded for sanctuary into the Mosque of Omar—to be annihilated by the revengeful Christian sword. Not even the children were spared. The Via Dolorosa became a river of blood through which the conquerors waded to their goal. On a pavement of slaughtered bodies the Knights of the Cross knelt in pious prayer before the Holy Sepulcher.

And now from the Flying Carpet we could see below, amid the jumble of Jerusalem, the domes and towers of the church that marks this same historic spot—the spot where, so the holy legends say, Christ was crucified and buried, and on the third day rose from the dead.

In wide circles we sailed back and forth over the city. The present walls, though of later construction, rise on the ruins of the walls assaulted by the Crusaders. I could follow their entire circumference at a glance. This was the Jaffa Gate—this the Damascus Gate—this Herod's Gate. Where the wall turned the northeast corner, the Christian armies had maneuvered their

The Mount of Olives, seen from the tower of
the Church of the Holy Sepulcher

The Church of the Holy Sepulcher, Jerusalem

wooden tower. Looming above all other things, from the center of the great temple enclosure, rose the Mosque of Omar, which had served Godfrey's zealots for a slaughterhouse. Over thirty acres about the mosque spread the immense court, covering a sixth of the city—the same court that once supported the wonderful temple of Solomon. Eastward stood the Mount of Olives, crowned with churches; at its foot, Gethsemane. And over a ridge to the south the afternoon sun shone on Bethlehem.

It was already twilight when Stephens and I, on foot, penetrated the walls and entered the sacred city. Like all pilgrims to Jerusalem, the moment we had found a lodging and unburdened ourselves of our baggage we went straightway to the Church of the Holy Sepulcher. The route to the church led through the twisting, crowded lanes . . . past Jews and Arabs, priests and mullahs, Christians and infidels. Meeting every race and creed and costume in the world, we made our way down the narrow stair-stepped Street of David. Along this very street the Crusaders had hewed their way eight hundred years before.

The Church of the Holy Sepulcher is not the same as when Godfrey worshiped there—only the location. The present structure, restored behind a twelfth-century front, is not much more than a hundred years old.

Finding it, hidden away amid a labyrinth of lesser buildings, we entered a little door that penetrates the entirely unimposing Romanesque façade, walked through the cavernous gloom of an outer chapel into the main rotunda, and stood beside the hallowed Sepulcher.

Despite all previous warnings, I had hoped to find the church austere, simple, quiet—befitting the site it is supposed to honor. To make the pilgrimage and find miraculous peace and comforting at this shrine has been the life-long dream of so many millions of people. Thousands and thousands, during fifteen centuries, have made great sacrifices and endured great hardships, merely to come and kneel on this spot. To deliver it into the hands of those who would cherish it, two million Crusaders laid down their lives. If there is any sacredness in Christendom, surely it should be here.

But the astonishing, disillusioning reality! No Oriental festival was ever as blatant, as garish, as spurious, as the interior of this church at the present time. Decay and shocking disrepair are everywhere. Of the large sums given by the constant stream of visitors, no part ever manifests itself except in the form of gaudy tinsel ikons, soiled plaster saints, and dusty paper flowers. Rapacious "guides" dog one's heels. Moans and lamentations rise from the pitiful women who drag themselves on their knees to the Sepulcher and cover its marble slab with passionate kisses. Tourists are being photographed before the dilapidated altars. Wrangling priests of differing creeds glare at one another and grasp their holy candles like bludgeons, prepared to strike the enemy over his heretic head. These priests of rival Christian religions hate one another with an irreconcilable hatred. Actual fights among them are not infrequent, even at the Tomb itself.

At Easter, the high feast of all these brawling sects, the mobs of fanatics become hysterical and violent, their frenzies and antagonisms boiling over. Heads are broken, pitched battles occur, people have been beaten and trampled to death. At this season, lest too many of those who come for salvation should lose their lives, soldiers stand guard in the courtyard, trying to control the processions of turbulent pilgrims dancing and struggling around the Holy Sepulcher and shrieking "Christ is risen! Hallelujah!" If there were only a booth for red lemonade, a tin band, and fireworks at night through the dome, the Church of the Sepulcher at Jerusalem would be a complete sideshow of barbarism and buffooneries.

And this holy spot which has been the scene of such battle and bloodshed, such drama and sacrifice, for fifteen centuries, is without any proof whatsoever of authenticity. During the three hundred years following the death of Christ, Jerusalem was utterly destroyed, and completely rebuilt, several times. Not until 330, a lapse of time as long as that between the landing of the Pilgrims in America and the present day, was any thought given to the Sepulcher's location. Then Constantine ordered Calvary to be "found," and someone had a vision, and said, It is here! And that's all the proof we have.

These things I knew. Even so, respecting the overwhelming symbolism of the place, I came from far away to see it and entered reverently. I have recorded what I saw. And yet, despite the barbaric and unholy scenes, I left the Sepulcher as I had come—reverently, knowing that while one can doubt the authenticity of the church's claim, one cannot doubt the authenticity of the faith of the millions and millions of devout people who have worshiped there. Their adoration is extravagant, but in the simple hearts of those who pray, it is desperately sincere.

Those weary-looking women with distraught eyes, crawling on their knees oblivious of the bickering priests, were realizing the sweetest moment of their sorrow-filled lives. They pressed their lips to the dubious Sepulcher, and in their faces came a look that passed all understanding. They had brought their heartaches here; the touch of the Sepulcher opened the portals of their souls and healed the wretchedness. They *were* comforted. They *were* redeemed.

139

Bethlehem. In the center, the Church of the Nativity,
oldest Christian church in the world

The Garden of Gethsemane

Arab Information Center

The tinsel, the trash, the hocuspocus, was distasteful to me; but for each person like myself there are a thousand others whom these things console and spiritualize. Even if the Crucifixion took place a hundred miles away, even if the Resurrection had not occurred at all, the faith of the countless worshipers who have *believed* has made this place as sacred as if it were truly the scene of the Redemption. *Peace I leave with you, my peace I give unto you: not as the world giveth . . . Let not your heart be troubled, neither let it be afraid.* Peace—legions of the faithful have found it beside the Sepulcher. With all its falseness and its blatancy, this church is still the most blest of sanctuaries for half the people of an unhappy earth. In the face of such profound trust, such transcendent reality, who am I to scoff?

I burned a respectful candle where the mumbling pilgrims were burning theirs.

And when I had departed and reached the streets again, the night had descended, but the stars were shining in the sky.

13

After the Manner of Joab

✳ Our Flying Carpet safely housed, Moye Stephens and I stayed two months in Jerusalem. Every day and half the night we spent prowling through its ancient lanes, atop its walls, about its hills. Familiarity only made the city more interesting. We mixed with scholars, rabbis, priests, mullahs, eager to learn whatever we could about the inexhaustible subject of Jerusalem.

Of all the people we encountered, Dr. Jacob Spafford gave us the most enlightenment. For over sixty years, as a member of the American colony, he has lived and studied in Palestine, and has come to be recognized as the final authority on local history and archeology.

Doctor Spafford's stories of the Holy City were always vivid and dramatic; but one of them, a story of the original Jerusalem, the original city of David, captured our imagination so completely that it sent Moye and me off on the strangest adventure that had befallen us since our Flying Carpet left California.

This, briefly, was Doctor Spafford's tale:

Three thousand years ago Jerusalem was called the City of Jebusites, and was situated on top of a steep-sloped ridge [the Hill of Ophel] now well outside the present walls. The founders chose this spot because it stood just above the Fountain of the Virgins, the only constant spring in all the neighborhood. This spring flowed unprotected from a cavern at the base of the slope below the walls, and on into the Valley of Kidron. But the Jebusites, to assure their

143

water supply in time of siege, drove an inclining irregular shaft from the summit of the ridge, one hundred feet down through the solid rock, by which they could lower their buckets into the pool.

Thus they were able to defy even King David when, having subdued all Judea, he turned upon this last remaining unconquered fortress. As usual, the Jebusites felt themselves invulnerable. They mocked the besiegers and cried down to them that blind men and cripples could defend so secure a city [II Samuel 5:6].

But David was not easily discouraged. He doubled the intensity of his onslaught, and promised that he would make supreme captain of his host the first man who set foot within the stubborn citadel [I Chronicles 11:6].

And then one night during a lull in the fighting, Joab, one of David's officers, resting near the outlet to the Virgins' Spring, thought he heard the clink of copper buckets against the rocky cavity from which the water flowed. He waded into the grotto. The sound was unmistakable. Undoubtedly the Jebusites had a shaft leading from their fortress to an inner chamber of the spring!

This explained their endurance against the siege. But it also gave Joab a desperate idea. He undressed, left his arms and armor behind, and plunged into the pool. There *must* be an inward-leading channel—and there was. With barely enough space to breathe above the water level, he crawled along an utterly dark passage, and was rewarded for his daring by emerging into the vaulted pool where the Jebusite buckets were lowered.

He could see the outlines of this pool, for it was dimly lighted by oil lamps from above. He noted the bucket shaft, opening just above his head, and he saw that the shaft was not sheer but somewhat inclined. In fact, assisted by knobs and crevices, he was able to climb stealthily up the rock chimney to a point five times his own height. And there he found steps and a passage leading farther upward through the core of the hill.

With pounding pulse Joab slipped back into the pool, through the channel, and out again into the open night. Quickly he went to David's tent and revealed to the King what he had found, and asked for a small company to go with him in a daring attempt to reach the city by way of this newly discovered route.

At once David saw the possibilities of this plan. In an hour Joab and his few chosen followers were dragging their swords behind them through the water channel. The King, by prearrangement, crept up to the gates with his army.

144

As before, Joab climbed the shaft, and his men followed. They reached the rock staircase—the tunnel—more steps—another tunnel. On tiptoe, scarcely breathing, they crept up to the open entrance of the passage and emerged into the citadel.

Except for the guards on the walls all the Jebusites were sleeping soundly. Not even the watchdogs gave the alarm. Joab rushed upon the sentinels before they could cry out. The gates were flung open, and David's army poured in upon the helpless city. From that night to this, Jerusalem has been the capital of Israel.

But that is by no means the end of the story about this Virgins' Fount. Three hundred years after David's capture of the Jebusite city, Hezekiah ruled as king. The site of the city had still not been changed from the Hill of Ophel. During Hezekiah's reign the Assyrians invaded Judea, overcoming every obstacle put in their path. Jerusalem was their goal, and it seemed that nothing could stop them from attaining it. In this desperate moment the king thought of the Virgins' Spring, still flowing as it had flowed in the days of Joab. Why should this spring be allowed to supply his enemies as well as himself? Might it not be possible for him to tunnel under his citadel from Joab's grotto clear to the center of the city, and so divert the flow of water entirely into Jerusalem?

Hezekiah was a man of action. He ordered such a tunnel dug. Immediately a gang of miners assaulted the solid rock at the source of the flow, and, directing their tunnel through the base of Joab's vertical shaft, pushed ever deeper into the granite hill. Steadily the tunnel lengthened—high as a man and half that wide. But, fast as they worked, it was not fast enough. The Assyrians, fired by their victories, were sweeping on to Jerusalem with alarming swiftness.

Hezekiah was beside himself. He ordered a second gang of stonecutters to start at the point where the tunnel was to emerge into the cisterns within the city walls. They too dug into the rock at top speed, and pushed forward to meet the upstream excavation. Every man, woman and child was forced to contribute to this labor [II Chronicles 32:1-4].

For some unaccountable reason the two groups did not even attempt to dig straight toward each other. Each worked forward on a winding, uncertain course that turned and twisted in the most bewildering manner. The miners would suddenly abandon the forward thrust, and, retreating a few yards, strike off at another tangent. But by the grace of God, having cut a passage

145

over seventeen hundred feet long, they actually did meet, and with such precision that the levels of the two floors were no farther apart than the span of a man's hand. And at the spot where they met, an inscription in ancient Hebrew was chiseled into the wall. It read:

> The boring through is completed. And this is the story of the boring through: while yet they plied the drill, each toward his fellow, and while yet there were three cubits to be bored through, there was heard the voice of one calling unto another, for there was a crevice in the rock on the right hand. And on the day of the boring through the stone-cutters struck, each to meet his fellow, drill upon drill; and the water flowed from the source to the pool for a thousand and two hundred cubits, and a hundred cubits was the height of the rock above the heads of the stone-cutters.*

The moment the tunnel was completed, the old outlet of the spring was filled in with stones, and all evidence of it destroyed. And not one hour too soon—the Assyrians had reached Jerusalem. But as Hezekiah had planned, they found the neighborhood utterly devoid of water, and, driven off by thirst, retreated without striking a blow.

Two thousand years passed, and Jerusalem moved completely away from the Hill of Ophel on which the city of the Jebusites had stood. Ophel became a barren mound, neglected and forgotten. But a hundred cubits below, the water from the hidden Virgins' Fount flowed on through the centuries of accumulated silt that almost choked the tunnel, emerging into the Pool of Siloam, which became, in its turn, the only constant spring for miles around.

Not until modern times was the Fount of the Virgins reopened and Hezekiah's tunnel rediscovered. As a small boy, fifty years ago, Doctor Spafford was one of the first to crawl through. Only a child could have done this, so filled was the gallery with silt, and so near the ceiling was the water. A schoolmate of his, on a similar adventure, found the famous inscription.

In 1907 a society of English archeologists cleared out the entire passage, and restored the Fount to general use. Once again the water flowed freely through the rock as in Hezekiah's time, and what is more, the vertical shaft near the

---

*This inscription was removed intact and is now in the Imperial Museum in Istanbul. The ancient measurement of the tunnel is given as twelve hundred "cubits." It also measures seventeen hundred feet. From these figures the hitherto unknown length of the cubit was fixed for the first time—seventeen inches.

146

upper end, through which Joab had climbed to capture the city of the Jebusites three thousand years ago, was found intact.

Moye and I listened, deeply interested, to this story, one afternoon at tea—and from his glance, I knew that the plan which had occurred to me had also occurred to him.

That night we left Jesrusalem by the Zion Gate and, following a rocky path, stumbled down into the steep wadi of the Kidron, with the vast walls of the Temple enclosure rearing above. We meant to explore for ourselves the scene of Doctor Spafford's fascinating chapter from Jerusalem's ancient history.

A lantern lighted us on our way to the Pool of Siloam. At this midnight hour the pool, so busy with water carriers by day, was entirely deserted. Descending fifty feet of stone steps we reached the stream, and by the light of our lantern looked closely at the large fissure from which the water flowed. It seemed much like the source of a hundred other rock springs we had seen, there being not the slightest indication of the dramatic tunnel within. But we knew its secret, and were determined to penetrate as far as might be possible.

Hiding our clothes and wearing only canvas shoes, we plunged through waist-high water into the inky cavity. This was the spot at which the second gang of miners had begun to excavate.

By the light of our single lantern, we could see quite clearly the chisel marks on the walls, marks there since 700 b.c., but fresh and clear as the day they were cut. Underfoot, the silt, twelve inches deep, made a soft cushion on which to tread. The splash of water as we forced our way forward echoed down the black and hollow gallery, as if the ghosts of Hezekiah and his hard-pressed miners were crying out against this visitation, fearful that we were the Assyrians learning at last the vital secret of the city.

At first there was ample room for our heads and shoulders, for the tunnel near its exit was ten feet high. But shortly the roof descended and the walls closed in, so that Moye, who was well over six feet tall and proportionately broad, had to bend his head and walk sidewise.

The passage wound and writhed. Why was it not cut straight? Why this molelike burrowing? At six hundred cubits we came to the intersection where the two gangs had met. Here the level of the floor rose about seven inches; and the dimensions of the tunnel and its workmanship changed abruptly. The two groups must have had entirely different tools and differ-

147

The Pool of Siloam

ent specifications. But that they ever met at all, with each group blindly chiseling its own aimless course through the solid rock, will always remain one of the marvels of ancient engineering. That they did meet, the ancient inscription proved. We thrust our lantern into the gash in the rock wall where Hezekiah's tablet had rested—the tablet that had remained in darkness, unread by human eyes, for twenty-seven hundred years.

Another six hundred cubits of waist-deep water, of grotesque shadows and eerie echoes, of bumped heads and skinned shoulders, and a vaulted pool suddenly opened up at the left. This we knew must be the entrance to Joab's shaft, for by pushing on a few yards farther, we emerged into the grotto of the Virgins' Fount and saw the stars again.

This was the place where Joab had first entered the cavern. We followed his course back to the vaulted pool, and turned our lantern full upon it.

For some reason the 1907 excavators had blocked access into the shaft from the main tunnel by a masonry wall, six feet high, but with an opening of several inches left between the top of the wall and the rock roof above. Moye, with his large stature, could not hope to pass this barrier; but, being of a more slender build, I was able, by smearing my body with wet mud, to squeeze over the partition and drop in a heap into the three feet of silt and water on the other side. Reaching back through the gap I seized the lantern from Moye and, ignoring his protestations, left him in the dripping darkness, seated none too comfortably on the very floor of the tunnel, with the waist-deep stream of the Virgins' Fount flowing calmly past his ears.

"No loitering, now," he growled across the wall, knowing I meant to climb Joab's shaft if I could. "This is not my idea of a place to spend the night."

"Oh, stop grumbling!" I exclaimed. "I may find a couple of Jewish princesses up there, imprisoned in an underground dungeon. If I don't come back you'll know I have."

"If you don't come back, and damned soon, I'm going home!"

But with no light and no clothes, this did not seem likely.

Standing in the shallow water, I looked about me. This was the very pool into which the Jebusite women had lowered their buckets in the time of David. I listened, almost expectantly, for the clink of the descending copper. Complete silence. I raised the lantern overhead. There was the shaft, four feet square, just above me. If Joab could climb that shaft with his company of men, I could climb it too! Taking the handle of the lantern in my teeth I laboriously began to raise myself, an inch at a time, up the rock, taking advantage of every knob and digging my toes into every

149

crevice—the same knobs and crevices to which Joab had clung a thousand years B.C. In a few moments the top of the vertical shaft was reached—it wasn't more than thirty feet in height—and there began the steps, hewed out of the same rock, leading farther upward. I crept on, crouching to avoid the low rock ceiling. But I did not crouch low enough. My head struck a hard and heavy object. Startled, I turned my lantern upon the ceiling. There, almost rusted away, hung an iron ring, eight inches in diameter and three thousand years old, from which undoubtedly the Jebusites had hung their lanterns to illuminate this passage to the well. It may have been the glimmer from a lantern hanging on this very ring that had first guided Joab up the shaft to the capture of a city.

The capture of a city! I wondered what lay ahead of me. . . . What would I find deeper in this ancient and almost forgotten gallery? Might not some turning lead secretly to the tomb of Solomon—to the legendary treasure stored beneath the Mosque of Omar—to the True Sepulcher itself? With increasing tenseness I moved forward, hand and lantern extended, antenna-like, before me.

But at this moment a faint, faint, far-off cry, coming from the other side of the spirit world, from across the land of the dead, floated out of the darkness below. In sudden alarm, I started backward, slipped on the treacherous wet rock, and fell with a crash on the hard steps. And as I fell, the lantern struck against the wall and instantly went out.

The cry was only Moye's voice, calling out in impatience from the bottom of the pit. But in this tomblike place the twisting of the sound, over the masonry barrier and upward through the tortuous channels, distorted it into the most inhuman cry I've ever heard.

Realizing this though I soon did, I still sat huddled against the clammy and invisible rock wall for several seconds in complete panic. Then at the top of my lungs I called back down the black shaft, "Moye! Moye!" The sound of my own voice shouting through this evil place only exaggerated my alarm . . . until from far away came an answer—that same ghostly cry. The words echoed and rolled and faded as they ascended. But I could distinguish them. I was not abandoned. There was another living human being in this Stygian labyrinth.

I forgot all about the Jebusites, all about Solomon's treasure. My only thought now was to get out. With caution increased ten times over, on hands and knees, I felt my way downward—down to the rock steps—down the sloping tunnel—more steps—more tunnel—groping blindly, feeling

150

ahead for security before I moved. And then after what seemed miles I reached a place where there were no more steps—only a drop—and I knew that this was the brink of the thirty-foot pit.

There was no hope, without light, of ever finding my way down the pit by way of crevices that had helped me up. They were too scattered, too hard to locate. Nor was there any hope of immediate help from Moye, who because of his height and girth could never climb through the opening over the masonry barrier. I could wait until he had found his way, without light and without clothes, at two o'clock in the morning, back to our hotel, and waked the porter and hired an assistant small enough to squeeze through the opening to rescue me with a lantern. But even if Moye were able to find someone unsuperstitious enough to enter the tunnel at night, they could not return before I had endured hours of waiting.

Yet there was only one other alternative—to jump.

I decided to jump.

This would be unpleasant enough, though not, I knew, really dangerous. It was almost certain that the three-foot cushion of mud and water below would break my fall; but for some moments I still hesitated on the brink, summoning up sufficient courage to launch into the blind chasm. There was no point in waiting . . . I must get down . . . I lowered myself over the rim, kicked away from the rough wall—and dropped.

It probably didn't take me long to fall twenty-five feet, but that blank instant in which I could neither feel nor see was one of the longest moments I have ever lived.

The jolt, when I banged into the shallow pool, sent me sprawling across the mud floor. And there I sat, too stunned and faint and knocked about to move.

"Well, Brother Joab," came Moye's voice over the barrier through the murk, "did you find your Jewish princesses?"

"No," I answered, sick and shaking.

We later found out that the Joab shaft no longer has an upper exit, for the entire surface of the Hill of Ophel, where it formerly emerged, is buried deep under twenty-five centuries of accumulated debris. Solomon's treasures may indeed be somewhere in that shaft, and the mummies of all the mighty Hebrew kings . . . or perhaps those lovely Jewish princesses, languishing in a dungeon and waiting to be rescued, far below the citadel of the Jebusites. I still do not know—but Doctor Spafford says it's most unlikely.

14

The Enchanted City

✳ Once upon a time in the far-off ancient days there was a great king living in Arabia, who by means of a magic talisman had been able to gain dominion over the jinn. With the assistance of these jinn he built for himself a capital that became one of the wonders of the Arab world. It was a city grander and more beautiful even than Thebes—a magic and mysterious city such as one encounters only in myth and fairy tale. He called his city Petra.

Now in no sense was Petra like other cities. It was located in the wildest mountains in the middle of a barren wilderness in the land of Edom, south of the Dead Sea. Unless one knew the country well, one might not have found it, for the main entrance was just a crack in the mountain wall. This crack led into a deep, sunless canyon, and the canyon into the city.

But once one had reached Petra itself, no sight could have been more wonderful. All about were vast palaces and tombs, beautiful and noble beyond belief, carved with hammer and chisel out of the solid rock.

But the king of Petra did not spend all his time building tombs and temples. Besides being the lord over the jinn, he was also the most dreaded robber in Arabia. Sallying forth from the hidden canyon in the rock, his robber bands would drive the passing caravans into the impregnable fortress. And no revengeful army could pursue them; so narrow was the single canyon corridor that four soldiers could block it against four thousand. The city became a vast fortified storehouse where gold and pearls and silk were piled in fabulous array.

Gorged with wealth and power, the arrogance of the people of Petra knew no bounds. They conquered all the neighboring nations, and driving their prisoners of war up to the great altar built on top the High Place over-looking the city, they slaughtered thousands of these living victims as sacrifices to their gods. To Petra its rulers dragged captive artists and sculptors from Athens. Grander and grander grew their temples, conceived in gigantic scale and executed with miraculous perfection by Greek genius . . . all in the solid sandstone cliffs.

Proud as they were in life, the Petrans became prouder still in death. The construction of their tombs became their great concern. Each noble set himself to carve from the glowing rock a tomb more stupendous and more magnificent than his neighbor's. To hew burial chambers in the solid rock as wide and deep and tall as a palace of King Solomon's was the task of the jinn . . . but only the sensitive hands of the Greeks could carve the graceful colonnades and cornices and statues across the façades, all in one superlatively beautiful piece.

To what length might not this bold and beauty-loving race, with their slaves, the giants, have gone to rival the glory of the gods, had not their king, the source of their power, at last brought about their destruction through his own vanity and pride!

He saw the tombs of his nobles rising higher and more regal every day. More and more envious he became of their display, and more and more resentful, until, in a passionate and violent mood, he commanded his enslaved jinn and his artists to carve for him a temple-tomb such as the world had never seen, nor would ever see again—a temple that must overshadow the efforts of the nobles as the moon outshines the stars. And it must be so beautiful in form and color and ornament that whoever looked on it, no matter in what age to come, would fall in love with it, and remember it until the end of his days.

So the king commanded, and he was obeyed. From out of the living rock the temple-tomb appeared, in one miraculous piece, colossal, and yet delicate, perfect, classic in its beauty, a poem in burning stone, a vision of the glowing sunset reproduced by the hand of a Phidias out of the rose-red rock.

The king looked upon this perfect thing—and loved it no less than other men. Then, fearful lest a rival try to build a fairer monument than this,

154

he made a sacrifice to the gods of the architect who had conceived it, and decreed that no more rock tombs should be built.

All the people of the subject nations flocked to Petra to see this master-piece. It became the city's crowning glory. But it soon proved to be a fatal passion for the king. The nobles, envious of their ruler's overtowering monument—a monument so completely obscuring their own—plotted against him, and murdered him.

What madness was in that act! With the king, the power of the Petrans over the jinn departed. He alone had known the secret charm that held them in thrall.

When the last heartbeat of their master had ceased, the jinn found themselves free. With one accord, these terrible spirits burst the bonds that had bound them to their hated overlords, and with a single magic word enchanted the whole of the glorious rock city they had helped to build.

This was centuries ago. But Petra is enchanted still, unchanged, in all this time—its tombs, its monuments, the proud and lovely burial palace of the vainglorious king—all, all standing as on the day when the revengeful giants cast their magic spell. The sunset glow that bathed the city at that moment was captured and enchanted too. It still shines in undiminished glory on the temple walls. And, as the king commanded, to this hour whosoever looks on the unearthly beauty of his temple falls in love with it, and remembers it to the end of his days.

This is a true story.* I know—because I've seen Petra with my own eyes. I've stood before the enchanted temple, face to face. . . .

Stephens and I flew to Petra in our Flying Carpet. And what a beautiful and romantic journey it was! From Jerusalem, we had sailed on south toward Egypt—over the oldest trail of travel in the history of the world. We had seen the wonders of Egypt from the air—and marveled. But when we heard of Petra we said farewell to the Pharaohs to seek a rarer prize.

Petra! The Flying Carpet was given its sailing orders. We rose above the housetops of Cairo, soared out over the gardens of the Nile, circled the Sphinx and zoomed the Pyramids.

---

* Those who wish a less fanciful version of the rise and decline of this extraordinary city may find numerous literal records concerning it written by archeologists and historians. But to me, as to anyone who has actually stood in the midst of its strange silence, any literal account of the place is more difficult to believe than the tales of enchantment which the neighboring tribesmen tell as truth. In the face of Petra's riddles, reason becomes unreasonable, but magic grows commonplace.

And then the Carpet, flashing gold and scarlet in the burning sun, headed for Arabia.

Cairo was soon out of sight. Once more the wastes of sand stretched to all sides. The Suez Canal, dotted with tiny ships, appeared below—and disappeared behind; and desert without end, scarified and gutted by the sun, rolled on.

For three hours we flew straight east, across the base of the Sinai Peninsula, on through the land of Edom. Petra was too well hidden among a maze of rocky canyons for the Carpet's crew to find it from the air, but we located the oasis of Maan which we knew to be nearby, and spiraled down to earth.

Two Bedouins, who said they had no fear of Petra's jinn, offered themselves as guides to the enchanted city. At dawn next morning Moye and I stood before the hidden entrance of the secret canyon corridor. Here the guides were left behind. I wanted no conducted tour through this magic realm.

Amid the wild and tumbled country on all sides, we could have passed by the canyon and never noticed it. Only the Stream of Moses, the same stream the prophet brought forth with his miraculous rod, betrayed the entrance, for the rivulet suddenly turned from the open valley and struck straight into the mountain wall.

We followed the stream and found ourselves at the bottom of a tremendous split in the rock, overhung on either side by black precipices three hundred feet high that shut out the sky and the sun. These evil cliffs seemed only to be waiting for a human being to enter there, in order to close in on the ribbon of space that separated them and grind to bits their helpless victim.

Uneasy and hesitant, we moved deeper and deeper into this appalling gorge. We could stretch forth our arms and touch both walls. At times the daylight almost disappeared. This was not a corridor for the passage of mortal men, but for the efreets and the demons who shunned the sunshine and moved, with the bats, always in the gloom. This was the enchanted entrance to the enchanted city. No wind stirred; no flower bloomed . . . a world petrified and deserted centuries ago.

But I knew it had not always been like this. The canyon floor was still paved with well-worn blocks of quarried stone; the walls were lined with altar niches where statues of the gods had stood. Along this corridor the wealth of Arabia had ebbed and flowed; the caravans, laden with silk and

156

The narrow rock defile leading to Petra

pearls, had passed, musical and slow, in never-ending streams; the retinue of a king, returning from Jerusalem, had filled the living canyon with the clatter of its cavalcade; and the charioteers, driving forth their thundering vehicles, had cracked their whips, and shouted, for all the seething throngs to hear—Make way!

For over a mile we crept along the tortuous abyss. Gloomier and gloomier it grew, more overhanging, darker and more sinister.

And then we turned a corner in the canyon, and, suddenly, out of the gloom, a glorious burning pool of carved rose light sprang from the cliff of a transverse gorge running at right angles, and smote down upon our two tiny figures in the canyon like a blow from the mace of the Sun God.

We could only stand and stare, believing we beheld a vision, a miracle of immaterial light and loveliness, appearing at the end of this sunless chasm. The vision took shape, and became reality . . . a cameo temple carved from the coral-red rock, lifting its radiant and exquisite face high up the towering cliff. For the first few moments we made no effort to understand the heavenly apparition. We only let ourselves be flooded by the sunrise glory that fell in splendor from its walls.

Surely, I thought, this great jewel must be the temple-tomb raised by the genius of Greek art, with the power of the jinn, at the order of the king of ancient Petra . . . "a temple-tomb that was to overshadow the monuments of the nobles as the moon outshines the stars, a temple such as the world had never seen nor would ever see again." So the king had commanded, and the artists and the jinns had obeyed . . . thus had the legend run . . . and from out of the living rose-red rock the temple-tomb appeared in one miraculous piece, colossal, and yet flawless, a poem in burning stone, a magic moment of the glowing sunset reproduced by the hand of a Phidias . . . "and whosoever shall look upon it, no matter in what age to come, shall fall in love with it, and remember it to the end of his days."

I looked upon it, and in that moment, as the king would have desired, felt all the powerful, magical attraction of its sheer beauty.

Moye much less so. Moye was the artisan, not the dreamer. He noted that the façade was one hundred and fifty feet high, and a hundred feet across; that the great rock chamber within was forty feet square and forty high; that the temple was supported by graceful Corinthian columns; that cornice and architrave, capital and cupola were adorned with the most exquisite and elaborate carving—garlands and flowers, angels and goddesses, standing forth in delicate relief; and all, all, in the solid rock.

158

The rose-red city of Petra

But I did not analyze these things. To me this was a true work of enchantment. How else could one explain the way the sunshine turned the temple walls to sculptured flame? What else but the magic of the jinns could have painted so glowing, so vibrant, a coral color into the sandstone precipice? I accepted it utterly, unquestioningly, as one accepts a rainbow arched across the castled clouds, or moonlight on the sea.

Reluctantly, we left the royal temple-tomb behind, and moved on.

The transverse gorge in which the temple stood now led us into Petra proper. But whereas the first canyon had been almost a tunnel in the rock, this second one was two hundred feet across, opening wide to the sunshine and the sky, and lined with temples, temples, in endless procession, all cut, like the royal tomb, from the solid rock. Here too the sandstone dazzled one with its brilliant and varying hues. In the interiors, the stone carvers had taken full advantage of this painted rock, and produced effects in natural color on wall and altar and ceiling that the greatest artist in the world would have been proud to achieve. Obviously these were the tombs of the nobles. No wonder the king had feared their marvelous display and needed all his riches and authority to surpass them.

But Petra is not all gorges and tomb-flanked canyons. The valley soon opened into an enormous amphitheater two miles across, walled in by towering and fantastic precipices utterly barren, utterly untraversable. In this amphitheater, before the time of the enchantment, had lived the people who had spent their lives robbing caravans, hoarding riches and building stupendous rock mausoleums.

In the midst of all this majesty and this magnificence, Moye and I spent several days, crawling about the tomb-studded cliffs, and climbing to the holy High Places where stood the great rock altars down which blood in great streams, pouring from slaughtered prisoners of war, had flowed in sacrifice.

There was not one corner of Petra which we did not explore. But all the time the coral miracle of the king's tomb had been foremost in my thoughts. This beckoned to me continually across all the other wonders of the enchanted city. Each day I had wandered back for a secret tryst with the radiant temple, and now that a full moon was shining down on the sandstone wonderland, I slipped away, for the first time at night, from the cave where we had pitched our camp, and walked alone up the gallery of noble tombs that led to the great jewel.

How pale and beautiful these tombs appeared in the soft, silver night

160

and yet how sinister! Created to shelter Death, they seemed like phantom dwellings for the evil spirits of the nether world—shadow spirits which even now moved and peered at me as I strode past.

But I pushed on through the enchanted vale, between the high rock-monster walls, skirting the black lakes of darkness that alternated with moonlight along the way. I tried to whistle a bit, to drive the ghosts out of my path and announce to the ambushed demons that I was not afraid.

Whistling, but fainthearted, I went to keep my moonlit rendezvous.

How changed I found my temple—yet not less beautiful. If its burning beauty of the day had disappeared, a softer, gentler glow had come into its face. I had believed nothing could be lovelier than its coral color inflamed by the sun. I now saw that there *was* something lovelier—its coral color subdued by the moon. Had a perfume come from the place, or swelling radiant music, with such magic and mystery already suffusing the temple, I would not have thought it strange.

Better to behold this overwhelming vision of beauty, I backed against the cliff wall opposite. I could picture to myself the day when the king of Petra, with envy of his nobles burning in his soul, rode to this spot where the narrow entrance chasm opened into the sunlit gorge, and pointing to the glowing rose cliff opposite, commanded his Greek sculptor to carve there the royal temple-tomb, beautiful and proud beyond all other mausoleums in the world. I saw the Greek sculptor bow in obedience and summon the enslaved jinn. Terrible and roaring in their chains these giants attacked the solid rock with drill and mallet. Thousands upon thousands of cubic feet of red sandstone were chiseled from the face; and the stream of jinn carrying away the huge rock fragments on their backs were never-ending. Beneath the furious bombardment, the cliff took shape—the columns and the capitals appeared, the statues grew in beauty on the walls.

The rough façade stood ready for the Greek sculptor's final touch, and from his hands it re-emerged, smooth and delicate. The interior chambers were hewed clean, the great entrance door framed in fragile decoration and the sun invited to drench the finished temple with fire.

And then the sculptor bade the king look upon his tomb. I could imagine the king returning, borne on his litter of gold, and stopping, speechless, before the miraculous mausoleum—"so beautiful in form and color that whosoever looked upon it should fall in love with it and remember it to the end of his days" . . . and every one who stood before it fell in love with it —the king, who most loved beauty, most of all.

161

But did the king's mummy ever rest within that great black vault opening wide its framed portals behind the shining colonnade? . . . Did not the jinn at the very moment of his death enchant the city? Indeed, they must have, else this pink and silver dream beckoning to me in the moonlight would have been in ruins, and desolate, a thousand years ago.

Grateful, I looked up at the temple's sublime face with humility and worship. I had not worshiped anything in such a long, long time. It was as if I had been saving all my homage for this vision of beauty, for this enchanted hour. . . . "Eternal, silent, beautiful, alone . . . eternal, silent, beautiful, alone"—a line from the poem this temple had inspired in a poet's heart, but I meant it to be from my own heart, a tribute and a dedication. . . .

The months have passed since that memorable night. I have encountered other things and other faces I have loved. But until the end of my days, I shall remember, as one of the great loves of my life, the enchanted coral temple, alone and beautiful, in the moonlight.

PART TWO

THE GLORIOUS ADVENTURE

15

The Call of the Wanderer

"Come, my friends,
'Tis not too late to seek a newer world.
Push off, and sitting well in order smite
The sounding furrows; for my purpose holds
To sail beyond the sunset . . . till I die . . .
To strive, to seek, to find, and not to yield."

✳ "To strive—to seek—to find—and not to yield" caught my
fancy as I sat before the fire with a volume of Tennyson's poems opened to
"Ulysses." What a fine refreshing purpose—"sail beyond the sunset till
I die!" This clear call to leave behind the outworn, too familiar life and
seek a newer world found a responsive chord in my own restlessness. I
thought to myself: Of all the great figures in history, did not this royal
vagabond who spent his days in finding the extraordinary, in meeting new
experience, in knowing every thrill and beauty and danger the world could
offer—did he not have the fullest, the richest, the most enviable life of any
man who ever lived? When the fates had spun his thread of destiny to
a close, how unregretfully he must have faced the end! How proudly he
could have said:

"*I die content.* All times I have enjoy'd
Greatly, have suffer'd greatly, both with those
That loved me, and alone; on shore, and when
Thro' scudding drifts the rainy Hyades
Vext the dim sea; I am become a name;
For always roaming with a hungry heart
Much have I seen and known; cities of men
And manners, climates, councils, governments,
Myself not least, but honour'd of them all."

And more. He had ruled his island kingdom of Ithaca in his youth; for ten years he had battled on the ringing plains of windy Troy; he had sailed the oceans with his ships, tasted of the lotus fruit, struggled with the cannibal Cyclops, dwelt with Aeolus, the king of the winds, heard the singing of the Sirens. He had braved the monstrous Scylla to escape the whirlpools of Charybdis; he had even descended into hell, before the intervention of the gods brought him back home to his faithful wife—and Ithaca.

As I thought of all this stirring drama, my own life, imprisoned by apartment walls, surrounded by self-satisfied people, caught in the ruts of convention and responsibility, seemed drab. In my own way I too had been a wanderer. I had tasted the drug of romantic travel, and I could not rest from it. I had seen the sun rise over the Alps from the summit of the Matterhorn; I had tramped the Pyrenees, and basked in the warmth of Andalusia; I had watched the moon sail across the sky as I sat enthroned on a fortress gun at the supreme summit of Gibraltar. From the high passes of the Himalayas I had seen the roof of the world lifting up the heavens with pillars of gleaming ice. The tropics I had known, and the northern blizzards; and I had learned to love the poetry and the majesty of the ocean from the fo'castles of a dozen ships. I had "enjoy'd greatly, suffer'd greatly, both with those that loved me, and alone; on shore, and when . . . the rainy Hyades vext the dim sea."

And now this slippered ease before the hearth—how barren and profitless it seemed! How dull it was "to pause, to make an end, to rust unburnished!" I rose from my deep chair and moved restlessly to the window. The ships and the gulls were sailing down the Hudson and out to sea; and I envied every sailor who would wave farewell to the skyline of New York, and turn his salt-stung face to some strange enchanted land beyond the far horizon. Suddenly I became bored and impatient with everything I had and was:

bored with people, bored with knowledge. I realized I didn't want knowledge. I only wanted my senses to be passionately alive, and my imagination fearlessly far-reaching. And, instead, I felt I was sinking into a slough of banality. Adventure! Adventure! *That* was the escape; *that* was the remedy. I knew there was no turning back once one had broken from the nest of colorless security, and spread one's own young wings, and visited the tall strange treetops across the valley that had always been beckoning.

I had once spread my wings—and now that I had returned to my nest again, I was dissatisfied. I had security, and I did not want it; I had comfort, and I did not enjoy it. I wanted only to sail beyond the sunset. I wanted to follow Ulysses' example and fill life once more to overflowing. Ulysses' example—and then the idea flashed through my brain: Ulysses' very *trail,* his *battlefields,* his *dramatic wanderings*—why not follow these too?

My sudden enthusiasm for this glorious idea swept away all practical obstacles. No matter if no one knew exactly where the Sirens were—I'd find them; or if scholars disagreed about the Cyclops' cave—it must be *somewhere.* I'd go to Ulysses' own island of Ithaca and embark for the walls of Troy; I'd visit Aeolus and his cages of the winds; I'd brave the enchantments of the dreaded Circe; I'd swim from Scylla to Charybdis and taste the lotus in the lotus land.

As I stood looking out on the teeming Hudson, the whole smoldering idea caught fire: I must climb Mount Olympus to call on the gods; Delphi, to consult the oracle; and Parnassus, to invoke Apollo; Athens—and the Hellespont—and the classic isles of Greece. Homer would be my guide; the *Odyssey* my book. What matter if Greece was a barren waste—it would not be for me; or Troy a grass-grown mound of earth—*I* could see its lofty gates and its towers gleaming in the sun. Wherever Ulysses went, there I would go; across whatever seas he sailed, there would I follow. Why wait to embark? Below my window lies the port; the vessel puffs her sail; there gloom the dark broad seas. Come—come—my friends,

> " 'Tis *not* too late to seek a newer world.
> Push off, and sitting well in order smite
> The sounding furrows; for my purpose holds
> To sail beyond the sunset ... till I die ...
> To strive, to seek, to find, and not to yield."

16

Throne of God

✳ Crash! The lightning in a rage split the writhing firmament from Thessaly to the Cyclades in one blazing, blinding glare. Streaks of fire burst into the inky darkness, inflaming the abyss about me and lashing at the clouds that hurtled past. The far-darting thunder, peal upon peal, roamed the Aegean Sea, plunged across the Vale of Tempe, and echoing back from the walls of Ossa, shook the granite rocks I sat on.

The wrath of Jupiter had burst on me. Hidden by the seething darkness he charged across the sky, for I had violated the sanctuary of the immortals; in his wrath he flung the lightning at my head, for I had challenged his omnipotence; with his thunderbolts he sought to hurl me bodily back to earth, for I had dared to climb the utmost pinnacle of Mount Olympus and seat myself on the very Throne of God.

Midnight was a strange hour to be on top of Olympus. It was bad enough insolently dislodging Jupiter by day from his own castle, but to cling tenaciously to it all night as well was nothing short of sacrilege. Small wonder he assaulted me so savagely. But how could I retreat! I was trapped ten thousand feet high, atop a towering rock chimney up the precipitous walls of which I had laboriously climbed that afternoon, clinging fearfully to the little crevices that allowed one to ascend only an inch at a time. It would have been suicidal, now that night had come, and the rain, and the clouds, and the lightning, to try to climb down. No, by all the gods, I would not, could not, move.

It was consoling, however, to know that if I were annihilated by outraged Jupiter, I would not suffer alone, for Roderic Crane, my American companion, and little Lazarus, a heroic half-grown shepherd boy who alone of all our retinue dared climb the final peak with us, stood defiantly by my side.

By desperate effort I was able to find amid all this darkness some small gleam of consolation. My position corresponded to that of a journalist whose house was wrecked over his head by an earthquake—discomforting, yes, but magnificent copy. Roused by "the surge and thunder of the *Odyssey,*" I had embarked resolutely on Ulysses' trail in hope of finding some of the glorious adventure he had found so plentifully three thousand years ago. And here, at the very outset, was a reception to Greece, romantic and tempestuous beyond my most extravagant hopes. I felt that if this midnight battle with the gods was a sample of the adventure in store for me, Ulysses' shade would soon be looking on from Hades with envious eyes.

Even before leaving faraway New York, Roderic and I had chosen the pinnacle of Olympus for our first great goal. The ascent of this immortal altar was to be a pilgrimage in quest of atmosphere and stage setting, and of proper adjustment to the spirit of our expedition. We had been born and bred in a nominally Christian civilization where any heathen belief in the efficacy of the ancient Greek divinities was looked on as a bit out of style. But if we were going to revive the classic days of Homer and relive the life of Ulysses, I felt it imperative (despite Roderic's skepticism) to try to resurrect this fine old fashion in religious faiths; I felt we should get acquainted with Zeus* and Athena, with Hermes and Neptune, who had been to blame for all the good and all the harm that came to our hero. So we hastened eastward to find and climb this deity-crowned Olympus, "where the dwelling of the gods standeth fast forever."

Our approach was from Salonika. On a hilltop behind this ancient city, we had looked southward and first seen the most celebrated mountain in the world. My pulse increased at the very sight of it—Olympus—the far-off, unapproachable capital of classic Greek mythology, and Greek art and culture and life itself. To honor the gods of Olympus, the sublime temples of Greece rose in marble majesty; in the image of Olympian gods the hands

---

* No attempt has been made to be consistently Greek or consistently Latin in the terminology of the classic gods. Sometimes I speak of "Zeus," sometimes of "Jupiter." Generally I have tried to choose the more familiar term.

of Phidias and Praxiteles gave posterity such sculpture that each poor fragment is enthroned by modern art, and guarded as a priceless possession. In the shadow of Olympus, Homer sang the greatest poetry ever sung before or since, and in the name of Mount Olympus the most happy and sin-free religion the world has ever known bloomed for centuries.

And yet I had always felt that Olympus, like the other beautiful legends of ancient Greece, was only a myth, a vague representation of divinity and immortality, which no longer really existed in this iconoclastic age.

The view from Salonika disillusioned me, for now a massive, purple, peak-ridged mountain loomed in the distance, a ten-thousand-foot mountain touched with snow and diademed in clouds; and that mountain, as firm, as real, as tangible as the earth, was Olympus, the golden throne of Zeus.

I was delighted to find it so beautiful. We saw it first at twilight, when obscurity had invaded the slopes, and the shadows were deepening in the gorges. But far above, its pinnacle still shone into the night, soaring toward the heavens, slowly—like a prayer.

For a long while Rod and I sat quietly, watching the picture fade. Then, without any warning, my companion asked me if I thought he would be alluring to Venus if we ever *did* get to the top.

"Yes, Rod," I replied a bit acidly, starting homeward as a gesture of remonstrance against his lack of reverence for poetic moments. "With your mustache and line of Negro stories I'm sure you'll prove irresistible. Just the same, I want you to promise me you won't start any scandal with a goddess right at the beginning of our trip. Things are going to be complicated enough as it is."

Next day, scorning to waste another hour on crass material matters like equipment and provisions and directions, we hurried off to visit the gods, and at Larissa in Thessaly, on the opposite side of the mountain from Salonika, made ready for the grand assault.

The mayor, acting under official orders, much to our disgust attached a young army of gendarmerie to our train "to protect you from the bandits," whereas, next to the gods there was nothing in the vicinity we wanted to meet quite so much as the notorious Olympus bandits who have terrorized the district for generations. The idea of being romantically held up for ransom so captivated our fancy we had seriously considered advertising in the local paper for some gallant robber band that would oblige us.

And now the mayor had spoiled it all. We stormed against such a military burden. But all our protestations were in vain. So in ceremonial grandeur we moved Olympusward.

The second night found us sleeping on the ground at a shepherd's camp not far below the summit. Never shall I forget those Arcadian hours. We moved back two thousand years and lived again in classic pastoral Greece. The shepherds with their sunburned curls, in their coats of skin and felt, carrying their crooks, and playing their melancholy pipes amid their tinkling flocks might have stepped straight out of mythological literature. To make the setting truly a poem, the full moon rose over the pine-clad summits that walled us in, and glowed upon our campfire, revealing the stilled herds upon the hillside and casting fantastic shadows among the rocks that might have been Pan and the Centaurs joined in their nightly dance.

It was on this night that Lazarus, the shepherd boy, annexed himself from out of nowhere to our retinue. We glanced up from our campfire to find him standing just inside the circle of the light, with an expression of wonder and curiosity on his firelit face—foreigners—and such strange ones! He was leaning on his crook looking so shy, and yet so fearless—so wistful, and yet so self-sufficient. At close range he proved an extraordinary little satyr. He had never owned a hat other than his mat of sun-bleached hair; he had never had a home other than the hillside. He was as uncivilized as any of the half-wild goats he shepherded—and as hardy. Whatever initial distrust the child had of us was changed to idolatrous worship when we expressed amazement and admiration on seeing him rake out several glowing embers from the fire and carry them in his bare callused hands to another spot. Our compliments so touched his affection-starved heart that he was our very shadow until our climb was over and we had left him behind still in a state of high excitement over the greatest adventure that had ever befallen him.

Next morning in the sharp mountain air we moved in gay procession on up the canyon—nine soldiers, fifteen shepherds, four mules, six dogs, two Americans—and Lazarus.

So far, the procession had proved much more interesting than the mountain. From Salonika, Olympus had appeared pinnacled and defiant. Now, at close range, all we had found was a rather barren hillside—and here we were almost at the top—or so it seemed.

Never were appearances so deceiving. Our young shepherd-guide, realizing we had a shock in store, had rushed on ahead to the crest, calling back for us to hurry, hurry. When we gained the rim, there stood Lazarus, his piquant face a wreath of breathless excitement, his crook outstretched over a sudden canyon that dropped dizzily away, on the other side of which soared a fluted, stalagmite tower of naked sparkling rock. The great spire burst on us so dramatically—a smooth, swelling mountainside, and then, presto!—this amazing picture. We had been ascending only the shell of a vast and irregular amphitheater from out of the middle of which, a thousand feet below us, this arrogant tower sprang, to rise a thousand feet above.

No one needed to tell us that the spire was the throne of Jupiter. Several of the neighboring peaks, while almost as high, appeared to be easily scalable, but the summit of this one seemed as far beyond reach as heaven itself. The ancient Greeks felt they were safe in placing their gods on such an intimidating pinnacle-top, because it was past belief that any mortal man could climb its shaggy walls and shatter their theology. So right they were in believing the summit unconquerable that, though Olympus has been for three thousand years the most famous mountain in the world, the oldest in song and story, the heaven of a great and beautiful religion, it remained the last accessible mountain to be climbed.

Our crater crest was only a box seat for all this drama. That was not enough. We must have the stage itself. Our army captain insisted the peak was "impossible"—only three times in three thousand years had it been surmounted by mortals* We must have ropes, we must have guides, we must have permission from the army, we must have—we never heard what came next, because before he was well started on his "can't be's" and "must have's" Lazarus and Roderic and I were far down the jagged spur that connected our crest to the base of the tower, hell-bent for the Homeric heaven.

We completed the descent into the intervening chasm and reached the great chimney. Scampering up it like one of the goats he tended, Lazarus beckoned us on. Painfully we followed him an inch at a time, clinging to this crack, feeling for the next crevice, not daring to look down at the clouds that were gathering below. Several times the shale gave way beneath us, and our hearts almost stopped as we looked into the gulch and saw how far an avalanche would take us.

Nothing made Lazarus stop. He moved relentlessly on, calling back encouragingly, returning to redirect our missteps, supplying such an abundance of moral support that he actually got us up the last grim battlement and led us with a shout over the top.

Roderic looked eagerly about for Venus; I for Jupiter. Not one single god or goddess was to be found. This did not mean, however, that they had meekly abandoned the throne room to the three infidels. We later learned

* The tower may have been climbed by people unknown to our guides. The surrounding peaks, offering no special difficulties, are frequently visited every summer.

that their disappearance was just a strategic move which would allow them to punish us all the more effectively.

Jupiter had seen us crawling like flies up to his inviolate sanctuary, and, realizing that we were determined to seize the summit, had flown away to marshal his armies of defense. In consequence, when we did attain his empty throne a phalanx of black clouds with glowering faces was already sailing ominously past, entirely obscuring the long-anticipated panorama.

There was no time now for Roderic to lament Venus' lack of hospitality. The clouds were rapidly rising nearer and nearer from out of the chasm. Scarcely had we gained the summit when Lazarus began to implore us to escape from the chimney-top while the atmosphere was still clear enough to make descent possible. We could see the situation as plainly as Lazarus, but before we fled we were determined to leave behind a carved record of our conquest. On top a great flat boulder right at the point of the needle, the Swiss climber Boissonnas, who in 1913 was the first mortal to scale this highest tower of Olympus, had built a three-foot rock cairn as a monument to his significant achievement. On the same boulder were the engraved names of the two other parties who followed. And here too, fog or no fog, our names, as the fourth party, must be emblazoned as a sort of visiting card for Jupiter when he returned.

Hurriedly we scraped away at the rock with our knives—closer crept the clouds. Lazarus became frantic at our indifference to the trap enclosing us. But we saw only the magnificent CRANE and HALLIBURTON we were carving eternally into Jupiter's throne. The final E and N were completed. We pocketed our knives and harkened at last to Lazarus' wails of distress—too late. One sweep of the wind, and the fog, with startling suddenness, from all directions at once, had thrown its impenetrable blanket over us. We drew back from the brink, in alarm.

"Oh, it will soon pass by," I said encouragingly to Rod. "It's still two hours before darkness. Things will clear up in time."

"I hope so," he replied, shivering a bit from the damp clinging mist. "We really can't spend the night up here—we haven't our nightshirts."

But things didn't clear up. The fog only grew thicker and wetter. Twilight was approaching, and in the secret mind of each of us apprehension was growing. We had left our coats behind with the soldiers, and already in the sharp wind that was driving the fog across our ten-thousand-foot perch, we were beginning to be uncomfortably cold. There was nothing we could do in the way of exercise to keep warm, for the needle's point was literally a point with abysses always just a few feet away that prevented our enjoying any resuscitating calisthenics that demanded more floor space than deep breathing.

To keep up our spirits, Roderic resorted desperately to his banter. Under the circumstances it proved inefficacious, for Lazarus couldn't understand one word of English, and I was too occupied with anxiety to listen. Realizing his audience was reduced to one, he gave up, joined the gloom group, and waited for the most unwelcome night that ever enfolded Mount Olympus.

There was no hope of escape now till morning. We must protect ourselves as best we could in anticipation of a long and painful exposure. Some sort of shield against the biting wind would help a little, so the three of us, creeping cautiously through the fog on hands and knees, collected all the loose rocks we could find in the few square feet that measured our cage and piled them into a low wall abutting the boulder on top of which the Boissonnas cairn was built.

The cairn itself would have tempted us as a convenient quarry for building material, had the destruction of this historic monument not been the height of dishonor and the depth of sacrilege. Little in size and crude though it is, it marks one of the symbolic episodes in the history of the world—the first ascent of the mountain of the immortals, and the first overthrow of the king of all the gods from this last refuge which, defending itself for three thousand years, had defied, by its precipitous walls and surrounding chasms, the assaults of every unbeliever.

No, there were enough other rocks. And when these were in place, we raised over them Lazarus' shepherd's crook (which he had clung to all the way up), decorated at the top by my red bandanna handkerchief, our flag of conquest.

Night came all too soon—black, grim, threatening. Roderic and I had Lazarus to worry about now. We reasoned that his resistance to the exposure, which we simply must endure till morning, was not so strong as ours. We reasoned wrongly, for the young shepherd very shortly made it clear that his only apprehension was for *our* safety. And when I recalled his method of transporting live coals, and his mop of sunburned hair, and his wind-tanned face, I came to the conclusion that if any one of us survived the night it would probably be boy-Lazarus.

It was eight o'clock now. The sun would rise about five. Nine hours of this! We may as well relax to the situation, keep our circulation going and try to enjoy what we couldn't avoid. The summer was well advanced, so that the temperature would hardly drop to freezing. If the weather got no worse it would be merely a matter of enduring a cold, disagreeable nine hours—not of endangering life or limb.

The weather did get worse—much, much worse. Jupiter was only imprisoning us with the fog. And now that we were helplessly pinned to the needle point, he prepared to charge furiously with every element at his command and sweep these usurpers over the brink.

At nine o'clock, with one frightful crash of lightning the outraged god sounded the charge, leaped into his chariot and, lashing his mighty horses, drove thundering upon us. His first hurled bolt missed its mark, ripped past us and struck the wall across the canyon, shattering a portion of it and sending the fragments dashing down the precipice. On rolled the Olympian cavalry of clouds to blanket the mountain anew in a fresh barrage of mist. The battalion of winds charged against our bastion, overhurling our flagstaff and slashing our brave bandanna into shreds. Apollo's archery followed close behind. A hundred million raindrop arrows he shot into our faces and drove through our flapping clothes. Back and forth, over us, under us, the great chariots rumbled.

We grew wetter, colder, more miserable. To leave our little shelter and try to stand against the onslaught would be cruel punishment; to remain, with the icy water pouring in gullies over us, was just as cruel. The dilemma was abruptly solved by an especially furious assault of the wind, which, accompanied by a cloudburst, flung itself with a roar against our battlement and toppled it precipitately onto our heads.

I gave myself up for dead. I hoped I was dead—anything to escape the unendurable plagues of cold and rain. I lay stiff and aching under my granite grave, until I heard Lazarus, somewhere in the melee of arms and legs and stones, shout some terrible blasphemy at the elements. Here was the old fighting spirit! Rod and I joined in the chorus and supplemented Lazarus' profane-sounding vituperations with a fine string of our own.

This castigation of the gods only increased their indignation. It rained harder than ever. I do not believe Jupiter would have let us live through one more hour of this exposure had I not thought of a perfectly obvious method of gaining relief from his wrath—sacrifices! How *stupid* of us not to have thought of this even before beginning the ascent. No wonder he misunderstood our intentions. A ram offered up that morning at our hillside camp would undoubtedly have assured us bright skies and a clear picture of the classic world from Olympus' top. While we had carelessly forgotten to bring along up the precipice any fat rams or wreath-hung bullocks, it might not yet be too late for some modest offering of propitiation.

Quickly I made an inventory of all our sacrificial properties, and in the torrential darkness commandeered whatever was disclosed. I should have liked to sacrifice Roderic's mustache, but it was undetachable. With this great prize eliminated, the collection was not very impressive. It consisted of one pocketful of sour, weatherbeaten goat's cheese (from Lazarus), and a small bottle of *mastika,* a highly alcoholic Greek liquor which tastes so much like stale paregoric that even though it had been given to me by the shepherds for just such emergencies as this I would rather have frozen to death than drunk it. This *mastika* would be a splendid gift to Jupiter—since I couldn't swallow the awful poison anyway.

We were sorely handicapped by not knowing much about classic sacrificial ritual. Burning the offering on pyres was one way, but with our cheese dissolved to a soupy consistency, and with our matches floating around in our pockets, and nothing but dripping granite for fuel, we gave up *that* plan.

There was only one thing left to do—drop the irresistible gifts solemnly into the abyss.

Overboard went the cheese, and as the *mastika* was poured after it, I suggested to Jupiter that he take note of our homage sufficiently to call off this damned shower bath.

And would you believe it?—not fifteen minutes afterward, the rain desisted; the Thunderer's chariot rumbled away over Thessaly; the cloud cavalry drew aside its evil veil, and there, hanging radiantly in the southern sky, the moon that we had seen at the shepherds' spring the night before smiled again.

Even so, though the rain had lasted hardly more than an hour, we still had six or seven hours more to endure our sodden clothes. It wasn't nearly so bad, though, now that we could see one another, and know that we were free of any further persecution from the gods. Rod began to renew his interest in Venus, and to regret that after all we had gone through, his grooming probably wouldn't be as chic as he'd like to have it if she happened to return home in the morning to look him over.

A thousand more years passed, and then in the eastern heavens, far out over the Aegean, a gray light grew. Land and ocean began to unfold. Before Aurora's radiance, Diana waned, and drooped, and sank to sleep, and left her rival in undisputed possession of the Grecian world.

177

In the startling glory of the sunrise, Roderic and Lazarus and I almost forgot our frozen limbs, and failed to notice one another's weary faces. It was just as well, for I'm sure our appearances and expressions must have been not far removed from those of three half-drowned alley cats. Even these poor creatures would have forgotten their misery when the chariot of the Sun drawn by his glowing horses not rose but exploded from the sea, scattering golden fire against the defiant walls of Mount Olympus.

As the sun climbed upward into the storm-cleared sky we found ourselves pinnacled in a range of peaks—all, all Olympus. From the foot of this throne of God all classic Greece rolled away, to Pelion and Ossa, to the plains of Thessaly, and the Vale of Tempe, to Mount Parnassus capped with snow, and the eternal isles of the Aegean. The valley toward the north opened toward Macedonia and Thrace. This valley was once the home of the Centaurs, and the happy land where Orpheus enchanted all nature with his music. Toward the west we saw the pass of Pitra through which the Persian barbarians under Xerxes, having crossed the Hellespont on a bridge of boats, invaded Greece to fight the battle of Thermopylae. To the south was Thermopylae itself, and far, far across the eastern ocean—but no farther than the gods could see—the walls of Troy!

What exultation danced within me! The afternoon before, Greece had been only an ocean of clouds, and veiled Olympus just one more mountain. Now, in all its splendor, I could see what I had come to see—the Greece of myth and legend, of heroic deeds and godlike men, of Achilles and Ulysses, of Zeus and Athena, the immortal Greece of Homer's epic poetry, all beheld from the sacrosanct summit of Mount Olympus—"Olympus, where the dwelling of the gods standeth fast forever."

The sun was well up now, and as we looked out on it, drinking in its life-giving glow, an eagle came flying toward us from over the abyss. Nearer and nearer he drew until we could mark his beak and claws. Then just as the great bird on outstretched wings sailed above our heads, he glanced down at us, gave one vigorous scream and flew on. I confided in Roderic that I believed the eagle was Zeus in feathery form returning to investigate his invaded habitation. I wanted so much to call him back and further explain our position. I wanted to express my appreciation for his gracious reception of our sacrifice. But my wish was only vanity—he was gone.

Roderic was painfully bored with my childish idea about the eagle, and said my mind must be a bit touched from the ordeal of the night before. He assured me the eagle was only a grouchy bird, and my god-infested Olympus only a high and barren hill. He even claimed that the rain had already all but stopped before I made the sacrifices. It was apparent Roderic had become very cynical since Venus had failed to appear. In fact, he admitted that so far as *he* was concerned the Greek gods were a complete flop.

Yet even if he were right and rid of all illusions, and even if I were only inspired by crazy dreams to crazier action, was I not the richer of the two for having indulged myself in the poetic notions of that fine old Greek god faith? Its fancy, its grace, its lyrical appeal, that had their haunts in shaded dale, or piny mountain, in the sea and the running brooks; these things the rationalists cannot know or love. They have their faith of reason, but their hearts still have no language. Their civilization cast down the gods of Greece, and ever since, in cultural darkness, on hands and knees it seeks the shattered torch of Beauty and Humanity that from the lighthouse of Olympus illumined once the Western world.

17

We Charge Parnassus

⁜ Back at Larissa with our laurel offering, we took a motorcar next morning for Parnassus, and watched this sacred mountain grow in grandeur as we sped across the plains of Thessaly—on to Delphi which lay on the mountain's southern slopes.

The celebrated shrine is situated eighteen hundred feet above the Gulf of Corinth, on the side of a wild, spectacular gorge that in itself fills one with awe, and reverence for the gods. Our motor ground up the steep slopes of the rocky canyon and deposited us at the hotel. At once we hurried out to the holy precinct, knowing, of course, that the oracle had been dumb for twenty centuries, and that the shrine was only a field of prostrate ruins; yet still believing that in a place of such dramatic associations, there must be adventure awaiting two faithful pilgrims like ourselves who came bearing fresh laurel wreaths from Tempe. Anyway, we had determined that such a small obstacle as lack of a prophet was not going to interfere with our purpose. Having put so much store by this visit, we were going to consult *an* oracle if not *the* oracle.

Reaching the sanctuary, we inquired where the vapor crevice was. Legend has it that goats browsing on these Delphian slopes of Mount Parnassus were thrown into convulsions when they approached a certain deep cleft in the side of the mountain, from which a peculiar intoxicating gas arose. The

The ruins of Delphi, Mt. Parnassus in the distance

goatherd on inhaling it was affected in the same manner as the goats. The local inhabitants imputed the convulsive ravings, to which he gave utterance under the power of the exhalation, to Apollo's divine inspiration—and a temple was straightway raised on the spot. I felt that if the vapor could hypnotize goats and goatherds it could do as much for Roderic, so we decided to seek the crevice, over which he agreed, grumblingly, to sit and breathe deeply of the Apollonian chlorine.

To our complete disappointment we learned there was no longer any crevice, nor any mystic vapor. How annoying! We must find a substitute. The hotel bar offered possibilities, but it was a problem to know which alcoholic aroma would have just the proper degree of intoxication on Oracle Roderic. Scotch whisky might stimulate beyond the point of receptivity; champagne might incline the prophet to rash and overoptimistic promises; certainly the dreadful native Greek *mastika* would never inspire anybody to foretell anything but death and disaster. I'd never want my fortune told with *that*. And then we opened a beer bottle. Instantly I knew we had found the correct asphyxiator. Rod's eyes took on a glazed, faraway expression. He began to laugh softly. I jerked the potent bottle away from him, since it would never do to go into the mesmeric trance in the hotel bar. People might misunderstand.

Residing in our hotel at the time was an arresting young English poet who was so highly amused at our oracular efforts that we decided to give him a leading role in the ceremony. In ancient times there was always a consecrated priest who interpreted the oracle's mumblings, and Mr. William Watson Wright could play the priest's part to perfection, as he had the most gorgeous pink beard that ever adorned a pallid white face. Roderic was more than agreeable for this assistance since he was foreseeing some difficulty, even with the divine inspiration, in putting his prophecies into the customary iambic verse upon which I insisted.

Our priest was well informed on Delphic ritual. It would not be possible, he said, for the oracle to become the purveyor of divine auguries without first seeking absolution from all earthly contamination in the sacred Castalian fountain which gushed out of the rocks near by from beneath a great hewn-stone altar. The water was like ice, and Roderic demurred from immersion in such an arctic bath. So we compromised on a sprinkling baptism. I managed to get enough water down his back, however, to cleanse away a good part of his iniquities. He squirmed and quarreled, but when I reminded him how countless his sins were, he accepted the purification more gracefully.

183

The Castalian Spring at Delphi

I was thoroughly enjoying my role of purifier when the priest announced that all Delphic pilgrims, as well as prophets, had to purge themselves in this same magic spring before consulting the oracle. Roderic joyfully agreed with him and revenged himself by giving me as thorough a drenching in holy water as I had given him. We then decided the priest was not going to escape, and although he strenuously insisted that Delphic dignitaries were already sacred and needed no further cleansing, we determined to make an exception of him. And so, breaking all precedent, we gave the immaculate Mr. William Watson Wright the most violent purification ever applied in the long history of the Castalian spring.

Thus prepared to receive Apollo's divinations we sought the Rock of the Sibyl, where, although there were no noxious vapors, there was at least a crevice. The laurel we had been saving for this very moment was now brought forward, and, while it refused to bend into a crown for the prophet's head, I managed to balance a nice sprig fetchingly over one ear. Everything was set now for the administration of the beer-bottle afflatus.

The priest drew out the cork and rested the gas tank on the rock beneath Rod's nose. Once more he breathed the celestial ether; once more he seemed to be transported to another, fairer land. Priest William now told me to put my question.

"Will my Odyssey be a success?" I asked reverently. "Shall I get safely to Troy, and then hold fast to Ulysses' trail? Will the gods blow me home for Christmas, or will Neptune persecute me and keep me ten years from Penelope?"

The interpreter turned to the laureled oracle and repeated my question. The prophet took several more deep inhalations from the malty depths and began to mutter the reply. The priest clutched his pink beard tensely, and, putting his ear close to the entranced clairvoyant, slowly translated, extemporaneously, the holy gibberish:

"The — shade — of — dead — Ulysses — on — your — undertaking — smiles.
  You'll — meet — with — many — labors — set — against — you — by — great — Zeus.
But — through — your — comrade's — brav'ry — you'll — escape — from — all — the — guiles
  Of — Circe — and — the Sirens — if —— Rod Crane's — advice — you'll — use."

185

This oracle business wasn't so bad after all. I decided to ask another question that was troubling me:

"Shall I ever be recognized as a writer?"

Once more the prophet breathed deeply from the supernal flask:

"You — must — conquer — Mount — Parnassus — if — to — fame — you — would — aspire,
And — from — its — highest — summit, — as — the — sun — bursts — from — the — sea.
Invoke — the — god — Apollo — for — his — literary — fire.
But — even — then — the prophet, — if — you — want — *his* — frank — opinion,
Believes — that — wholesale — groceries — are — truly — your — dominion."

"Tell the oracle his opinion is not required," I retorted. "Also tell him that he's not yet answered my question, and that if he will give me a favorable reply I'll pay his hotel bill." (In ancient times a bribe was known to have influenced the divine responses more than once.) Our hotel expenditures would cover two days or more. The offer had instant effect:

"If — these, — my — words — of — wisdom, — onto — paper — you — will — write,
A — hundred — thousand — people — in — your — story — will — delight."

Ah, worthy oracle! Wise Apollo! This inspired medium had now best be disenchanted quickly lest he also ask for his railroad fare and change his mind about my literary future. The holy incense was removed; the prophet's vision came back to Delphi; the priest let go his flaming beard. We called the ceremony to a close and adjourned to the hotel.

As we walked back, the oracle's first sincere response to my inquiry relating to my literary career, kept ringing in my ears: "You must conquer Mount Parnassus, if to fame you would aspire, and invoke the god Apollo for his literary fire, as the sun bursts from the sea." Roderic and I with Olympus only three days behind us had had enough mountain scaling for a while, but with the oracle offering this one and only hope of fulfilling my aspirations, I must charge Parnassus—and at once. So in an hour we were off up the eighty-two-hundred-foot slope of this great symbolic mountain that has been sacred from time immemorial to Apollo and the muses.

All day long, from eleven in the morning till sundown we pressed upward as fast as our guide and pack horse could walk, through cool, murmuring pine woods, across little flat plateaus, past the famous Korykian Grotto where the most notorious Bacchic festivals of antiquity were celebrated, reaching the higher slopes covered with huge tumbled blocks of jagged stones around and over which we had to pick our way with the utmost care.

The sun was low in the west before we arrived at the ruined chalet in a little valley some thousand feet below the summit. Here we spent the night. How luxurious a fire and shelter seemed in comparison with the ordeal on top Olympus! At four in the morning we moved on up the last great dome in ample time to reach the top before sunrise, and dropped onto the summit boulder to recover our labored breath.

Every moment now the light grew brighter, and disclosed more distant miles. Olympus, and Ossa, and Pelion, to the north, thrust their summits through the mist. To the south, the Gulf of Corinth opened at our feet, and the Peloponnesus spread beyond.

Any further inspection of the landscape was cut short by the sun's imminent arrival. It was just on the point of rising out of Skyros, one of the far Aegean isles. Hurriedly I made ready to pray to Apollo, in keeping with the oracle's bidding, "as the sun bursts from the sea." Here it came . . . a great glow diademed the rocky island . . . brighter . . . clearer . . . with a shower of light it broke through the horizon.

"O great Apollo, god of poetry, thou who walkest over the mountains and the waves, leaving thy robe on the ocean foam, thou god of harmony, thou inspiration to music and to art, hear my prayer. Grant unto me but one of thy thousand sunbeam shafts with which thou kindlest the creative fires. Guide me and encourage me with thy light. Let me be touched by thy grace, that I may see clearly, and follow only, in the songs I wish to sing, that which is true, and beautiful, and enduring——"

"—and, dear Apollo—" Roderic, praying vigorously alongside, interrupted my invocation by speaking right out loud—"please bless Mama and Papa, and make me a good little boy, forever and ever, Amen!"

187

18

Acropolitis

※   The bluest waves I've ever seen sped past as our coastal steamer from Delphi crossed the sunlit Gulf of Aegina. The island of Salamis rose abruptly on our left. We rounded a small promontory and steered straight for the mainland that now loomed ahead. Roderic, leaning over the rail beside me, suddenly gripped my arm, and raising his hand with a dramatic gesture, pointed to——

I saw it! A surge of rapture swept through me. There before us, painted against a violet veil of mountains a league or two from the sea, lifting high into the air its temple-crowned rock-altar, spread beneath its halo of immortality, gleamed the most radiant, the most delicate, the most sacred shrine we were to find in all our pilgrimage—*Athens!*

A single beam of sunlight, pouring through the flocks of clouds that roamed across the Attic plain, fell like a searchlight on the Acropolis. Enthroned on its crest, the far-famed Parthenon, haggard but still majestic in its columned splendor, sprang forth from the shadows, the crown of glory set on the brow of this queen of classic capitals.

That evening as Roderic and I dined in the shadow of the Acropolis, rising black and sheer against the stars, I thought: How beautiful it would be, on such a lovely night as this, to climb up to the battlements of that high pin-

Royal Greek Embassy Press & Information Service

The Acropolis of Athens

nacle and look out on the mountains and the sea! I knew the waning moon would rise, perhaps two hours later, the same moon that, full, had shone so brightly several nights before on Mount Olympus. I had also learned in advance that the Acropolis was open to the public for three nights each lunar month when the moon was at its zenith. But by three days we had missed this period of dispensation. That afternoon, the Acropolis gate, as usual, had been made fast at sunset, and two thousand years ago the Acropolis walls had been made proof against just such invaders as myself.

"Remember the Persians," whispered Temptation. "They found a secret stairway. Perhaps it's still there."

"But it's so dark—you'll break your neck scrambling up those rocks," admonished Discretion.

"Then take matches, fool!" was the sharp retort.

I took matches, my own and all of Roderic's, since he was too busy getting us settled at the hotel to want to accompany me on any marauding expedition our first night in Athens, and on second thought, while the maître d'hôtel wasn't looking, seized the pink candle from our table. As I bade my companion good-by, it was agreed that if I did not return before dawn he would mount to the Acropolis next morning as soon as the gates were open, and join me in order that we might see the Parthenon together by sunlight. Then I moved forward to the grand assault, sparkling inside that such a noble and novel adventure was still left on earth. My complete ignorance of the citadel's vulnerable points, of the distribution of night watchmen, of any helpful information whatsoever, made the expedition all the more alluringly hazardous. I would have an opportunity of finding out all these things for myself.

It was obvious, even as I climbed the encircling highroad to the Acropolis gates, that the eastern and southern walls were eliminated. They towered straight up above me, sheer and naked. Perhaps the western end, containing the formal entrance, would be less hostile to my plans.

As anticipated, I found the bronze grill doors immovably locked, and there was no climbing over them, for they were only indentations in a great marble surface. I whistled enticingly for the night watchman, prepared to force the entrance with drachmas. Only Echo heard my notes. I could look through the grill, straight up the broad marble steps that led beneath the Doric colonnade of the beautiful Propylaea, the monumental gateway which rose above me, pale and mysterious in the starlight "like a brilliant jewel on the front of Athens' coronet." This glimpse into the forbidden

192

The Propylaea, gateway to the Acropolis of Athens

sanctuary only fired anew my eagerness to reach the Parthenon. I wanted to bend asunder the cursed bronze bars and beat them into submission. But only trinitrotoluene could have done that.

Casting about impatiently for new routes, I observed a rocky terrace to the right, and, crawling up this with the aid of my walking cane, I saw that it continued in the form of a ledge, at a not unscalable angle, on up the foundation of the charming little temple of the Wingless Victory. In my enthusiasm over the finding of this steep but adequate rock ladder, I clambered along it with such careless haste that a shelf of loose gravel was dislodged. Rattling noisily down the slope it crashed onto the tin roof of a modern cottage, the home of an Acropolis warden, which, because of the darkness, I had not even noticed. Instantly a half-dozen huge watchdogs came bounding out of nowhere and in a savage chorus announced to all Attica that I was trying to steal the Parthenon. The warden rushed after them, jabbering and storming and gesticulating. While it was all unintelligible to me, I supposed he meant "Come down."

Smarting from the humiliation, I turned to the left side of the entrance pylon, to see what the northern slopes had to offer. In a moment I realized this was the weak link of the fortification. The rocks were creviced and caverned, and unguarded by any Acropolean hellhounds. Before I had gone a hundred yards, I came by chance, in a small hollowed-out cave used for a chapel, upon the famous Klepsydra Spring from which, though it is now isolated outside the walls, the Acropolis garrisons in classic times drew their water.

I continued my scramble, in and out, over and under the topographical confusion, and presently found myself before the mouth of a grotto. Grateful for my pink candle, I lighted the poor little thing, and plunged into the abysmal blackness of the interior. Here, surely, I would find the secret stairway. But each fissure of the grotto ended in a blank wall. I was only in the ancient shrine of Pan—a shrine dedicated to the pastoral god in tribute to the assistance he lent the Athenians in the battle of Marathon. The dark and twisted cavern rocks cast such a weird reflection, the light of the flickering candle was so ghostly, I thought once or twice I saw the grinning old goat-foot seated in the shadows, ready to make my blood run cold with some mischievous snort. But of secret steps there was none.

Back in the open once more, I found a faint path, and followed it hopefully. It led straight up to a deep artificial breach in the cliff face which obviously had once been a sort of postern gate to the Acropolis. The en-

Into this throng of worshipers I too must go; into the temple. Bending low, moving forward noiselessly, clinging to the shadows of block and battlement, watching for the figures of night watchmen, I crept toward the Parthenon. The massive steps were attained. A moving, half-veiled shadow, I climbed them one by one, and, unchallenged, reached the refuge of the marble forest.

What loveliness rose all about me! Broadside against any colonnade the moonlight streamed, leaving a swath of silver, then of shadow, then of silver, then of shadow, down the lofty aisles. On across the gleaming flagstones I slipped on tiptoe. The cella wall toward the sea inside the portico was shattered, leaving receding stumps of marble that climbed like a gigantic stairway to the cornices. On hands and knees I pulled myself up these huge blocks until I reached the crowning stone, and could stand and look back upon the enchanted picture.

Never have I faced a scene that stirred my very soul so deeply as this picture of the brooding, broken Parthenon spread below me in the moonlight. The sight of its haggard marble, its butchered glory, made me faint and weak within. A lump of bitterness filled my throat, and a rage swept over me against the Venetian vandals who had wantonly gutted this sublime Palace of Art.

With all its prostration, the Parthenon is still the most overpowering ruin on earth—overpowering not from magnitude or richness, but because of its serene and classic perfection of form. Its terrible beauty is intellectual, not sensual. It was reared to glorify Athena, the Goddess of *Wisdom*. It was the ideal of intelligence supreme expressed in marble. From cold stone, the artistic giants who built the Parthenon embodied the spirit of the "Greek Fire" that has civilized the world. In Pentelic marble they wrought this immortal monument to the Greek passion for Knowledge, for Culture and for Freedom. In this moonlit temple spreading in silver shades below me, I beheld "the supreme effort of genius in the pursuit of beauty," the triumph of the ideal by which men once were able to become like gods.

But beware—what was that hollow sound? A night guard with a lantern emerged from nowhere and glided along the portico. No harm would come to me were my presence detected. I should only be expelled! . . . so I stopped breathing till he got away. Then cautiously I crept down the stair-stepped wall-end and looked about for new delights.

One need not look far in the Acropolis, since every time-worn block has beauty and every inch of it has memories. The spirits of "half the immor-

The Erectheum, showing the Porch of the Maidens

talities of earth" haunt this hallowed scene. Here Pericles stood, there Phidias trod; here Socrates taught philosophy to young Plato, there Alexander the Great piled his captured shields. I scarcely knew which way to turn. In the dilemma my eye caught sight, a hundred yards away, of the exquisite little "Porch of the Maidens," one of the most delicate and beautiful creations of a supremely artistic age. The portico roof is supported not by columns but by six figures of marble maidens—and oh, what lovely, gentle, lifelike maids they are, standing there so easily, so reposed, with slightly bended knee, and carrying the simple architrave on their graceful heads as if it were the most agreeable duty in the world! The diaphanous draperies ripple in soft and supple folds from their young breasts. Their marble hair waves tenderly about their mobile faces. The moon, still in search for beauty, had climbed to just that fortunate corner of the sky where her beams could fall luxuriously on these enchanted maidens, nor yet reveal the black recess behind, so that they floated, pale and pearl and phantomlike, against a curtain of dark velvet. The beauty-seeking moon seemed to know that here, at last, she had found beauty, and to linger with this long-sought prize, pouring out upon their faces all her radiant benediction.

In a deep-shadowed corner of the portico I found a smooth, broad step, and stopped to worship a moment at the feet of the ghostly maidens. How sweet it was to relax amid such loveliness! In the intensity of the day I had not thought to rest, but now a dreamy lassitude came over me, and I half forgot the world. The breeze from Mount Hymettus, blowing like a soft caress, whispered songs of bees and pine trees' murmurings. All the earth, outside my shadow, was gowned in silver mystery. Touched by its hypnotic spell I drifted with the moonlight into half-haunted dreams, and thought I heard a marble maiden speak:

"There's a stranger lying on the steps, Persephone."

I listened—it was the corner figure.

"A strange hour for visitors; I wonder what he's doing here?"

"It must be to sleep. He hasn't moved for half an hour."

"But I'm *not* asleep," I blurted out, moving around the corner to where I could come closer—and immediately hated myself for fear I might have disenchanted them.

"Well, what then *are* you doing?"—how relieved I felt!

"I mean no harm; I slipped up the steps on the north side to pay homage to your moonlit loveliness."

"Oh, I see," said the corner figure. "But I didn't know that route was open."

"It most certainly isn't," I answered with a laugh. "It's blocked by a tin wall. I had to crawl over it like a lizard."

"Please don't say *lizard*," she exclaimed. "They've been creeping over us for two thousand summers, and we detest the name."

"*Two thousand summers!*" I gasped. "And I thought you were not a day over eighteen."

"Oh, but we're immortal."

"Have you names?" I asked hesitatingly.

"Why, certainly. I'm Philomela."

"And I'm Persephone," said her neighbor.

"And you?" I asked, looking at the third figure.

"Oh, she's dead," said Philomela sadly. "Flora used to stand there, until Lord Elgin carried her away long ago. Somebody put back a substitute— but she's only terra cotta. Electra is on the other corner. Cyrene stands behind her, and Thalia's behind me. Have you a name?"

"Yes." I told her what it was. "Not very classic, is it? I live in America."

"America—? I never heard of it. Is it as far away as Thrace?"

I gasped again. "No-o. Hardly as far as that."

"Why have you come to Athens?"

"Well, you see, I'm retraveling Homer's *Odyssey*. I climbed Mount Olympus recently to propitiate the gods, and then came here on my way to Troy."

"You climbed Mount *Olympus!*" exclaimed Philomela. "What desecration! Father Zeus should have hit you with a thunderbolt."

"He tried to," I exclaimed, "only I dodged. But enough about me. What brought *you* to Athens?"

"Why, we were hewn out of Mount Pentelicus and set up here during the Golden Age, as part of the temple to mark the spot where Athena strove with Poseidon for the possession of the city."

"Who won?" I asked simply.

"*Who won!*" exclaimed Philomela. "What *stupidity!* Athena won of course and became the patron goddess of Athens. The whole Acropolis is dedicated to her."

"Were you here when the Persians came?" I asked, trying to change the subject.

"Oh, no. We just missed that, fortunately. We've heard all about it, though. That must have been a dreadful time. Only a few hundred helpless people who couldn't go with Themistocles and his fighters to Salamis barricaded themselves here. Xerxes and his entire army attacked the Acropolis, but you see how strong it is. The poor little garrison might have held fast till the Greeks came back from the sea fight, if some traitor hadn't shown the Persians the secret entrance. The garrison was surprised and easily overcome, and every standing stone on the Acropolis was leveled to the ground.

"We missed all that, as I say. Still, we have had enough tragedy since. It's been nothing but heartbreaks and violence all our lives. We were sculptured during the great war with Sparta—under the most trying circumstances. We've been hurled to earth more than once. You see we've lost our arms and noses; it's only a miracle we stand here at all. The Romans left *us* intact even though they did carry away hundreds of our neighbors. Several times during the Byzantine period we were all but dragged to Constantinople to enrich some Christian church. Why, our temple *was* a church for a thousand years.

"Bad as that was, it wasn't half so bad as the Turks. They made harem quarters out of us, and stuck a minaret up beside us. And then—the Venetians—" I thought I saw Philomela's eyes fill with tears—"they were fighting to dislodge the Turks from the Acropolis. One of their dreadful shells fell into the Parthenon and exploded the powder magazine stored here. I'll never forget that terrible moment if I live another two thousand years. There was a burst of fire; the Parthenon roof was blown into the air—I saw it all—and almost half the columns were hurled down. The explosion nearly rocked us over, too. It was agony for a long time after that—all the sculpture on the Acropolis was hacked and stolen by everybody. Lord Elgin tore Flora from us, and allowed our architrave to collapse. Soon after, the Turks pounded us with cannon for a whole month, fighting with the Greeks in their War of Independence. That was the time our faces suffered so. Now, we're well cared for—now that it's almost too late and we are disfigured and separated."

"Oh, my Philomela, you are still the loveliest, and still the most admired little monument in all Greek architecture," I said consolingly. "Remember, even the moon, who has seen the beauty of every land, seemed to stop in her course tonight to honor and to brighten you. Think of me, immortal maiden, who must grow old and perish, while you may drink the sunshine of two thousand summers more, and come to life on every moon-mad night like this. If I could only stay and talk to you—I've never known an ancient Greek before—how happy I would be! But you see the night has passed— the moon is trembling in the west—dawn will be here so soon—I must hide back in the shadows before the watchman comes. Here's a little blue flower

I found beside the Klepsydra Spring as I was looking for the secret gate. Make it immortal like you, Philomela, so I may never be forgotten. Good-by, Persephone—good-by, Electra. I'll see Flora someday soon, and I shall tell her you miss her, and need her, and love her, eternally—good-by."

Sadly I crept away—back to my dark recess. I had waited a moment too long, so enslaved was I by the charm of the marble maidens. When I moved, the dawning light had disclosed my presence to the guards. I heard footsteps coming toward me; someone touched my shoulder. I squeezed my eyes together lest I behold some ogreish night watchman. But there was no escape. I screwed up my courage—and looked!

Everywhere was brilliant morning sunshine—and there, smiling quizzically down at me—stood *Roderic!*

19

On the Trail of Ulysses

✳ The mountains of the mainland of Greece rose behind us; the mountains of an isle of Greece before, and all about us the blue Aegean sparkled in the brilliant summer sun. Roderic and I looked out on this panorama of land and sea from beneath the awnings of a small, leisurely-moving steamer that we had boarded at Piraeus shortly after my heroic return from Marathon. Having crept northward along the coasts of Attica and Euboea, the little ship had now turned straight to the east and bravely headed for the rocky isle of Skyros right in the middle of the Aegean. From time to time we looked ahead inquisitively at the approaching island for we were soon to disembark on its storied shores and make it our residence for a week.

A perfect picture of ennui, Roderic sprawled in his deck chair trying to look bored, and succeeding very well. I sat beside him, busily engaged with my pen and notebook.

"Writing a love letter to one of your Marble Maidens?" he asked with a tinge of ridicule.

"I'm writing books," I replied loftily. "I've just begun Chapter Nineteen. Want to hear it?"

"No-o-o!"

So I began to read:

"'The year 1194 B.C. found ominous war clouds gathering over Greece.

Paris, a Trojan Prince, had violated the home of Menelaus, King of Sparta, and carried off his beautiful wife, Helen, to Troy. It has been cynically intimated that Helen may have put Paris up to it. But Sparta didn't appreciate these circumstances, and with righteous indignation rushed to arms to bring back by force the errant lady. Bound by sacred treaty, Sparta's allies under the supreme command of Agamemnon, Menelaus' brother, came to her assistance, and at Aulis, forty miles north of Marathon, the hosts began to gather.' "

"That certainly is an original story," Roderic remarked sarcastically.

"Don't criticize so soon. That's only the historic background. Before I get too deep in this book I think I should explain to my readers—the oracle promised me a hundred thousand, you know—how Ulysses came to leave home, and where he went first on his travels—since we are going everywhere he went."

"I think so, too. And how well you explain it! You don't even mention him."

"Oh, give me a chance. In the next paragraph I add that he was one of these allies. Listen to this:

" 'In his remote little island kingdom of Ithaca, Ulysses was loath to take part in a conflict so utterly unrelated to his own affairs. He had been married to Penelope, the most faithful of wives, not so long before, and a baby son, Telemachus, had made him the happiest and most contented king of all the Greek states. The very last thing on earth he wanted just now was to leave his happy home and go roistering off with an army to slaughter the citizens of an almost unknown city just because one of its princes had stolen somebody's wife who was probably no good anyway.

" 'The moment Ulysses realized, however, that it was impossible to escape his oath of allegiance he assembled his company of twelve hundred Ithacans, and his fleet of twelve ships. Having rounded Cape Malea—' that's the southernmost tip of the Greek peninsula, Rod—'he delivered his military contingent to Agamemnon at Aulis. There he threw his amazing vitality and enthusiasm into the Greek cause, and, with his crafty counsel, became the brains of the Greek army.'

"That brings him round to this side of Greece," I added, laying down my notebook, "and into our present territory. Aulis is just behind us on the other side of Euboea."

"If we're following Ulysses' trail, why didn't we start out from Ithaca, and come to Aulis?"

204

"Because we're going to Ithaca in the end—if we aren't seduced by the lotus fruit, and you don't make a fool of yourself over some Siren. We didn't go to Aulis because there's no way to get from Aulis to Skyros."

"I don't understand *yet* why it's so necessary for us to take all this time out from our trip to Troy for a visit to Skyros—that is, as far as our Odyssey is concerned. You did say something about Achilles being in hiding there, and about Ulysses going after him to bring him back to fight with the Greek army. I asked you if Achilles was a conscientious objector, and you gave a sigh of despair and bought me some chewing gum. That was probably just because you don't know yourself what it was all about."

"Then listen to this—and learn," I said, picking up my notebook again and turning to another page of Chapter Nineteen.

" 'In the Aegean, some seventy miles northeast of Athens, lies a rocky little island called Skyros. Though sadly neglected by nature it has its claims to immortality no less than the other long-celebrated isles of Greece. Delos is famed because it gave birth to Apollo and Diana; Cythera, because Venus was born from its waters; Lesbos, because in her palace there "burning Sappho loved and sung." The renown of these islands rests solely on their ancient glory, but Skyros can boast not only of an abundance of classic associations, but of possessing a modern halo as well. Its ancient fame is due to the fact that Achilles, the most heroic of the Homeric Greeks, made it the home of his late boyhood, and that it took no less a person than Ulysses to win him away. Skyros' modern distinction comes from its having sheltered, since April 1915, the grave of one of the finest and brightest spirits that the twentieth century has produced.' I'm not going to mention *him,* though, till I get to the next chapter.

" 'Achilles,' I continued reading, " 'at the time of his residence in Skyros was a comparatively unknown youth. He had been sent to the king's court there in the disguise of a girl, by Thetis, his mother, who, warned by the oracle of fatal consequences if he went with the Greeks to Troy, hoped to protect her son by thus removing him from the scene of danger. King Lycomedes, never dreaming that the tall handsome "maid" was not a girl, established him as lady-in-waiting upon Deidamia, his daughter.

" 'We do not know how soon Achilles revealed himself to Deidamia, but it was inevitable that they should fall in love—his disguise notwithstanding. The princess and her "lady" became inseparable, and no one objected; they occupied the same apartment, and no one suspected.' "

Roderic would have interrupted me here with some facetious comment about such goings-on, had I not rushed ahead into the next paragraph.

" 'Meanwhile, the Greek armies had gathered at Aulis and were ready to set sail, when a soothsayer confided to Agamemnon the fact that Troy would never fall without the aid of a young man by the name of Achilles. Wishing to leave nothing undone that might help the expedition to succeed, the Greek commander asked Ulysses to seek out this Achilles person and bring him to their ranks.

" 'By some unknown divination, Ulysses learned that the object of his quest was in hiding at the king's court at Skyros, and set out to find him.

" 'Disguised as a peddler, he gained access to Lycomedes' palace, and spread before all the court maidens an assortment of female finery, in the midst of which he had craftily placed a glittering shield and a sword of bronze. Achilles instinctively pounced upon these beautiful weapons, and thus betrayed himself to the artful Ulysses. Once detected there was no great difficulty in persuading him to join his countrymen in the great war. Together the two young men that were destined to become the most celebrated characters in Homeric literature left Skyros for Aulis. As for Achilles, the fateful prophecy of the oracle in due time came to pass.' "

"Did Deidamia shoot herself when her lover skipped off?" Rod asked with his usual irreverence.

But I never got to answer his question, for at this point a blast from the ship's whistle announced that we were drawing near the mountain-bound little harbor and must prepare to disembark.

Aboard the tender which came to meet us was a very agreeable young Greek. On hearing Rod and me speaking American he introduced himself to us in our own language. He knew the States well, having run a fruit store in Omaha. And when he learned that this city likewise claimed Roderic for its own, he looked upon my companion as a blood brother, urging this fellow Nebraskan to accept his hospitality—such as it was—during our visit.

While I did not hail from Omaha, and was therefore not of the sacred fraternity, he agreed that I might come along too.

What was his name?

"Achilles."

We fully expected him to add that his wife's name was Deidamia, and that she was the daughter of Lycomedes, the mayor, but on inquiring we found he didn't have a wife.

He *did* have one of the most picturesque homes on the island, in the little city likewise called Skyros, built upon the site of King Lycomedes' capital.

206

Gleamingly white, the snug house was stuck precariously upon the side of the citadel hill, and buried under grapevines.

When the afternoon of our first day's residence here had cooled, and the shadows were lengthening, Roderic, our host and I strolled along the beach beneath the towering cliffs, where the original Achilles, draped modestly in his hateful garb, had walked beside his Deidamia. Then as the same deep violet hue that suffuses Athens at sunset began to spread over land and sea, Achilles from Omaha guided us up a steep winding path that climbed to the decaying citadel crowning the hilltop—the same hilltop in all probability where the palace of King Lycomedes had stood. It took small imagination to picture the crafty Ulysses himself, bent low under his pack of peddler's wares, climbing our very path.

The sun had gone down before we reached the top, but what a soft calm glow it had left behind! The classic Achilles, looking out on this same purple picture, must have stood where we stood, and with his Deidamia close beside him watched the island-flecked Aegean fade on just such gentle summer evenings as this evening. Here Ulysses spread his baubles before the maidens of the court; here Achilles seized the sword and went to his destiny; here Deidamia clung tearfully to him, the last night of their union; here the princess sat, when he had sailed away, and, looking across the sea toward Troy, besought the gods to protect her lover and bring him soon and safely back to her empty arms.

As we rested in the hilltop-darkness, vigorous native music began to drift up to us from the big café on the square below—a wedding, we were told. There was a wild syncopation to it, a shrill barbaric lilt, that set one's blood to tingling. Achilles, having dined us, led the way down to the animated scene of action and turned us loose among the revelers.

They were dancing the *sirtos,* a national Greek dance, the origin of which is lost in the past. Deidamia may have danced it with Achilles; Ulysses with Penelope; Helen with Paris (probably better than with Menelaus); Roderic and I danced it with the buxom black-eyed maids of Skyros whose children unto the tenth generation will dance it at every wedding festival such as this.

Being the only strangers present we were given a hearty welcome. *Mastika,* such as we had propitiated the angry Zeus with on Olympus, was poured in a continual stream into our glasses. Not to drink the distasteful fluid would seriously have offended our bridegroom host; to drink it was to run the risk of becoming as uproarious as the other guests. We drank.

The music grew wilder, the long line of dancers more reckless. Roderic and I broke into the jiggling circle, joining hands with these modern bacchanals. We jiggled on the right foot, jiggled on the left foot, stepped and dipped and stepped and dipped; jiggled on the right foot, jiggled on the left foot, stepped and dipped and stepped and dipped. There was intoxication in the piercing pipes—hour after hour—men and women—boys and girls—not one ever left the dancing ranks except to seize another drink of *mastika*. The wooden floor resounded to the rhythmical stamp of our feet; there were shouts and hot laughter; the leader of the swaying line, holding by his left hand the bride, who in turn led the others, pranced and leaped and twirled and postured, until his legs could endure no more. The moment he dropped from line another took his place, eager to excel his predecessor's prowess.

Toward morning Rod and I had learned the leader's antics as well as anyone—and drunk as much *mastika*. The musicians, inexhaustible, were playing more violently than ever, and swaying on their benches, half delirious from their own music. In a new outburst of enthusiasm one tottering old graybeard with a wild yell plunged into the circle alone and cut the most amazing capers.

Away went the last leash on Rod's inhibitions. A most dignified youth generally, he now became fired with a sweeping impulse to lead the line. Snatching off Achilles' flaming red "cholera sash" he wound it about his own waist, and, encouraged by the cheers of the multitude, showed Skyros how *really* to lead the *sirtos*. He added a clog to the jiggle; he clicked his heels in the air; he kicked the candles out of the chandelier; he was superb. And all about, led on by the clogging, abandoned Roderic, the line jiggled on the right foot, jiggled on the left foot, stepped and dipped and stepped and dipped till the sun came up, and the music died, the last drop of *mastika* had been drunk.

O Ulysses, if some Greek boy married some Greek girl the night you arrived at Skyros, what a perfectly *swell* time you must have had!

20

I Swim the Hellespont

We all have our dreams. Otherwise what a dark and stagnant world this would be. Most of us dream of getting rich; many of us of getting married; and some of us of getting unmarried. I've met people whose great dream it was to visit Jerusalem, or Carcassonne, or to look on the seven hills of Rome. I'll confess to a sentimental lifelong dream of my own—not of riches, or weddings, or Jerusalem, however—something far less reasonable than that. I've dreamed of swimming the most dramatic river in the world—the Hellespont. Lord Byron once wrote that he would rather have swum the Hellespont than written all his poetry. So would I!

Sometimes, once in a long, long while, sentimental dreams come true. Mine did, and it was as colorful and satisfying as all my flights of fancy had imagined it would be. To me the Hellespont was not just a narrow strait of cold blue water, discharging the Black Sea and the Sea of Marmora into the Aegean. Far more than that: it was a tremendous symbol—a symbol of audacity, of challenge; of epic poetry, and heroic adventure.

The nature of the Hellespont's first records seem to have set an example for all the historic events that have clustered about it. Its very naming is a dramatic story. The name of "Hellespont" ("Dardanelles" on the modern maps) goes back to legendary ages, receiving its title from "Helle," the King of Thessaly's daughter who fell into the channel from the winged ram with the golden fleece, on whose back she was fleeing from her enemies.

Through this same Hellespont, Jason, in his immortal ship, the *Argo,* sailed in quest of this same fleece. For ten years, from 1194 to 1184 B.C., the fleets of the Greeks were beached at its entrance, while their armies, led by Agamemnon, Achilles and Ulysses, thundered at the lofty walls of Troy. It was across this stream that Leander nightly swam to keep his clandestine trysts with Hero. In the very wake of Leander, in one of the most spectacular military exploits in history, King Xerxes of Persia, the mightiest ruler of his time, crossed from Asia to Europe with a colossal army for the invasion of Greece. Here in the following century Alexander the Great ferried his Macedonians from Europe to Asia to begin his conquest of the world. Back once more in the fourteenth century rolled the tide of invasion from east to west: this time the Turkish conquests that were to turn the Hellespont from that day to this into Saracenic property. Through this strait the piratical Turkish cruisers moved for generations, making all the eastern Mediterranean a Turkish lake. Since 1600 Russia has fought periodic wars for the possession of this storied channel. And now the shores of this same Hellespont are dotted with the wrecks of sunken Allied battle fleets and strewn with the graves of a hundred thousand French and English soldiers, whose blood was squandered in rivers in the desperate attempt in 1915 to plant the Allied flags over the rocks where Hero joined her drowned romantic lover in dim antiquity. Indeed, one's spirits surge to read the amazing record of this fateful stream and realize how repeatedly it has shaped the destiny of the world.

This, then, is the Hellespont, and the scene where my dream came true.

Nature was most capricious when she created this eccentric corner of the earth. She drives the enormous volume of the Black Sea past Istanbul through a narrow channel called the Bosporus—and then again by more reluctant, prolonged, tortuous degrees, through a winding canal-like gash in the mountains, forty miles long, and from one to five miles broad. Down this insufficient Hellespont, with Europe on her right side and Asia on her left, the Black Sea, unleashed at last, rushes at top speed, foaming with indignation at her long imprisonment. For ten thousand years she has poured herself into the greater ocean, season in and season out. Tides she scorns. South—south—south, her waters always swirl so that one may well call the strait a river since but for its briny nature it qualifies in every respect to this term.

Few watercourses can boast of having seen the rise and fall of as many stately cities on its banks as can the Hellespont. Of these the two most familiar to us (though they have long since crumbled into dust) are Sestos and Abydos: the former on the European side of the narrowest part of the Hellespont; the latter almost opposite on the Asian, some three miles away. And why are these two cities, from among the scores of their contemporaries, alone favored with immortality? Is it because of their great military conquests, or their celebrated soldiers, or their marble temples? No, none of these. They are immortal because a youth—an undistinguished, undescribed youth of Abydos, named Leander—tragically loved an equally undistinguished maid of Sestos named Hero: and legends of love refuse to die.

One loved fiercely in legendary Greece. Hero, priestess of a temple though she was, and consequently sentenced to a loveless life, was no less human than her lay-sisters. She craved love as they, and when on the occasion of the popular Sestos Temple festival, her eyes caught the concentrated glance of a graceful and sturdy youth, she did not run away. The moment he guardedly spoke to Hero, her vows, her veil, quite properly, lost their power. She learned that his name was Leander and that he had sailed across the straits in his boat from his home in Abydos to attend the festival. They must not be seen together, since she was a priestess, prohibited by the gods from the society of man—*by day*. But that night, might he come in the moonlight, to the temple garden? Find me the girl of ancient Greece, or modern Greece, or any other land, who would have said no.

And so they met in secret, high on the Sestos cliffs, and looked out over the glittering ripples of the Hellespont that swirled ceaselessly past. And the next night again, and the next. All went well until one of the temple orderlies saw the lovers together and betrayed them to his superiors.

In a rage, the head priest seized the unfortunate girl. He dragged her down the cliff path to the very edge of the Hellespont, and then up to the top of a tower where the wretched maiden was left in solitary imprisonment, safe from the approach of any more sacrilegious lovers.

From his homeward-bound boat Leander, in the moonlight, had witnessed the figures entering the tower-prison that rose above the wave-lapped rocks, and in his heart he rejoiced. They were casting her into his very arms—for he was the strongest swimmer in Abydos.

Impatiently from his Asiatic shore he watched the sun go down beyond the cliffs of Sestos, across the swirling Hellespont. While they were only three miles away, it was necessary to take horse and servant and ride upstream along the Abydos side until he reached a point well above Sestos. Sestos lay sharply upstream, and the tideless current, squeezing through the narrowing channel, raced past at such a rate that no swimmer, save a god, could have swum against it. From above, though it would require four miles or more of furious swimming to reach Hero's tower and not be carried past, he might hope to succeed.

Strange and desperate things are done in the name of love. Shortly after nightfall, Leander, ready to face any obstacle for one caress of his mistress, plunged into the Hellespont. He had hoped Hero would guide him by means of a light from her tower window—nor was he disappointed. A spark from her small oil lamp cast a faint path across the water. Thus directed, he steered his course to Sestos, and drew himself up on the rocks beneath the tower. Hero was half expecting him to come, and watching. Tearing the cover of her couch into strips, she made a rope by which on the hidden off-shore he could pull himself up to her apartment. And then, what an eager reunion!

Partir, c'est toujours mourir un peu. Yet part they must, while darkness hid them.

The journey back, though difficult and cold and unrewarded, was not so long as the first crossing, for the Abydos point extended deep into the stream and assisted the swimmer to reach the Asian shore.

Did I not say that love drives us to desperate ends? Again the next night, undiscouraged, unsubdued by the sinister river's power, Leander swam his way back to Hero's arms—and many nights that followed.

But high on Olympus the fates were spinning to an end the immortal lovers' thread of destiny. They saw the storms and the winds that were churning the Hellespont as winter seized the land; they saw the madness for Hero that burned increasingly in Leander's heart, driving him recklessly into the face of any danger. Indeed, whom the gods would destroy, they first make mad.

And it *was* madness for the youth to defy the furies on such a night as this, and attempt as usual to swim across to his mistress' tower. Heaven and earth warned him back. But Hero's eyes beckoned, and to them he surrendered. Plunging through the surf, he met the oncoming rollers. He looked anxiously for the little lighthouse. Nowhere was it to be seen, for the storm had obliterated the faithful lamp.

The usual hour of Leander's arrival had come and long since gone; and dawn, shrill and ominous and glowering, found Hero still at her heart-

212

breaking vigil. And then she saw that Leander had come at last. There on the seething rocks below her window, the strong white body of her lover lay, tossed at her feet by some pitying water god. A flame swept through Hero's heart. In despair she cried out Leander's name, and plunged from her window into the swirling waters.

And so today because a man died for a maid, and a maid for a man, Sestos and Abydos are not forgotten as were their great contemporaries. Time annihilates all things but romance. In every land, in every generation it is romance that the human heart perpetuates. I do not doubt that in some distant time, when our modern world is dust, the story of Hero and Leander will stir mankind far more than all the futile foolishness of our own unheroic age.

Three thousand years later, Lord Byron was so gripped by the sapphire beauty of the Hellespont, and by the drama of its storied shores, that he ceased his restless wanderings and for an entire year rested in a charming little house at the very edge of the water near the site of Abydos. Like every true romanticist, Byron was deeply moved by the story of Leander, and decided, being a swimming enthusiast, to try to swim the Hellespont himself.

Early in April 1818, accompanied by a friend, he undertook the crossing from Sestos to Abydos. Finding the water of an icy chillness, the two swimmers postponed their venture until the following month. It was the third of May when the attempt was made again, and although, as Byron wrote in one of his notebooks, "the water was still extremely cold from the melting of the mountain snows, we swam from Sestos to Abydos." This was slightly incorrect, because, as the poet added, he began the swim high above Sestos to make sure of gaining the sand point at Abydos. "The whole distance," he continues, "from the place where we started to our landing on the other side including the length we were carried by the current was computed roughly by our companions at upward of four English miles, though the actual breadth is less than two. The rapidity of the current is such that no boat can row directly across. Its rate of flow may be estimated by the fact that the whole distance was accomplished in one hour and ten minutes. The English consul at Dardanelles could not remember the straits ever having been swum before, and tried to dissuade me from the attempt. The only thing that surprised me was that, as doubt had been entertained of the truth of Leander's story, no traveler had heretofore endeavored to ascertain its practicality."

The poet, on landing safely at Abydos, in one of his typically facetious moods, celebrated his swim in the following familiar verses:

"If in the month of dark December,
  Leander, who was nightly wont
(What maid will not the tale remember?)
  To cross thy stream, broad Hellespont!

"If, when the wintry tempest roar'd
  He sped to Hero, nothing loth,
And thus of old thy current pour'd,
  Fair Venus! How I pity both!

"For *me,* degenerate modern wretch,
  Though in the genial month of May,
My dripping limbs I faintly stretch,
  And think I've done a feat to-day.

"But since he cross'd the rapid tide,
  According to the doubtful story,
To woo,—and—Lord knows what beside,
  And swam for Love, as I for Glory;

" 'Twere hard to say who fared the best:
  Sad mortals! Thus the gods still plague you;
He lost his labor, I my jest;
  For he was drowned and I've the ague."

It was not many years after this that Byron followed Leander to Hades.
However, the house in which the poet lived at Abydos on the edge of the
Hellespont continues to stand intact to the present day, for Roderic and I
occupied it.

In the actual wake of Ulysses at last, we had left Skyros behind, and, like
Ulysses, returned to the mainland of Greece—he (proudly escorting Achilles)
to reunite with his fleet, we to find a ship that would take us to Troy at the
entrance to the Hellespont.

We found such a ship, but not being on the warpath for the recovery of
anybody's wife, as was Ulysses, and having all the time we wanted to indulge
in side excursions, we did not disembark at once on the long sandy shore of
the Trojan plain where the eleven hundred and eighty-six Greek ships were

214

drawn for ten long years. Instead, we passed by for the moment, a stone's throw from it, and twenty miles on upstream to Abydos, to investigate the Hellespont swim.

We found any "investigation" unnecessary. The sites of Sestos and Abydos were conspicuously, unmistakably, there. At the former place the acropolis ruins establish its exact location. The Mound of Xerxes, up the slopes of which Abydos climbed, and the sand peninsula, which is a spur of the mound, establish Abydos with equal certainty. The only way to "investigate" my ability to swim the intervening distance was to dive in and swim. As previous endurance tests I had swum the Nile and the Mississippi, but either of these was mere paddling compared with the Hellespont.

The first problem was to reach Sestos, the starting point, in a boat big enough to buck the savage current, and yet small enough to escort and safeguard me on my return journey. The Turkish officials (suspecting we were British spies) made this exasperatingly difficult. In order to move at all against the relentless flow of the water and constant south wind it was necessary to push off at 4:00 A.M., at which time the elements were comparatively calm. Each morning for a week the police delayed our departure till almost noon, by which time all the oars and sails we could muster were utterly futile to combat the onslaught of the current.

Each day with renewed determination we tried to beat and tack our way upstream with every device in our power. Back and forth, back and forth, sailing endless miles in the blistering sun, trying to gain a yard. Then by sunset, utterly exhausted, we would look back toward the Asiatic shore to find we were still just off the Byron house, *exactly* where we'd been that noon.

On the eighth day, in desperation, we managed to sail straight across to the European shore, and, though we were almost as far from Sestos as ever, we were at least free of the obnoxious and suspicious Asiatic officials.

That night we spent in one of the Gallipoli battlefield graveyards, with thousands of wooden markers of thousands of British soldiers spreading grimly across the hillsides. We slept on the ground, using a grave for a pillow. Next morning long before daybreak, when the wind was stilled, Roderic and the two boatmen and I each took an oar, and heading our sailboat straight upstream, bent to the task. One moment's relaxation, and we would lose ground. For five hours we fought our way toward Sestos—and attained it. But this was not enough. Being by no means a swimmer of Leander's caliber I thought it wise to take the precaution Byron had taken, and continue on upstream some two miles more above Sestos in order to give myself more time to get across before the current swept me past Abydos point.

Finding a semisheltered cove, we anchored our craft and waded ashore for a rest. From the top of the bluff we could see Abydos—dimly visible through the summer haze—about five miles away. Up to this moment we had been much too busy to think about a meal. Now with our first object attained we turned ravenously to our provision basket. It was absolutely empty. During the night the two Turkish boatmen had consumed every vestige of our food. Not so much as a crumb of bread was left. No, not quite so bad as that—a small can of Norwegian sardines they had been unable to open. It was this or nothing. Roderic, realizing I had to make the swim, magnanimously insisted I consume the entire available supply of fuel—so I did.

Then at two o'clock I removed my clothing, and, my heart pounding with excitement, stood at the water's edge, praying to the water gods to deliver me safely on the other side. The summer sunshine blazed from a cloudless sky on the sinister, sapphire stream that lapped invitingly at my feet. With nerves keyed up to the highest pitch, I yet held back in fear lest I fail. Despite the fact that Xerxes had scourged the Hellespont with chains in punishment for having destroyed his bridge of boats, I knew its beautiful, villainous waters had not been humbled. Here was my Siren Dream, beckoning to me. This was the Great Hour. I recalled a similar moment, in Japan, when on a zero January morning I faced the iceberg of Fujiyama at the timber line, ready to plunge up the glassy slopes to the blizzard-swept summit. Again, and stronger, came the spiritual exultation, the sudden strange pulse of power that makes cold chills of courage race through one's blood. My body whispered: "You cannot possibly swim five miles in such a current," but Inspiration shouted: "This is the *Hellespont*—what matter if it's fifty!"

I plunged.

The Asiatic shore across the channel rose hazily. I struck out straight for it, with Roderic and the boat hovering close beside.

Before I had gone half a mile, whatever "form" I may have begun with soon vanished, and I thought only of covering the greatest possible distance with the least possible exertion: backstroke, side stroke, dog paddle, idle floating, any old thing to keep going. A big Greek steamer bore upon us, rushing furiously downstream. It was our place to get out of the way. The officers on the bridge, not seeing me in the water, made frantic gestures. To protect me, our sailboat stood its ground in the very path of the oncoming

216

ship, and the steamer had to take a violent veer to one side to keep from colliding with our craft. As she passed by, not forty feet away, the officers hurled upon our heads every unprintable name in their broad vocabulary— but it was all Greek to us.

By half past two I looked back toward Europe to find, to my alarm, that I was already abeam the Sestos bluffs. It made me realize how relentlessly I was being swept downstream. And Xerxes' Throne, the conspicuous last-chance goal above Abydos, where the Persian king sat to watch his army cross the Hellespont on a bridge of boats over the very channel I was swim-ming, seemed to have moved laterally miles up the coast, though not to-ward me.

Before three o'clock I was in midstream. The wind had constantly in-creased, and was now churning the water with whitecaps. Every few min-utes I was half drowned when the resentful waves broke unexpectedly over my head. It seemed to me I swallowed half the Black Sea. Nausea seized me so painfully that several times I was ready to give up. But the increasing cold was the worst thing of all. The water flows so rapidly that even the surface has no opportunity to be warmed by the sun. After the first hour I began to grow uncomfortably numb.

However, the Throne of Xerxes was not far off now. All along, this had been a guide point. And yet, as I drew near to it, I realized the ricocheting current was sweeping me parallel to the shore about ten times as fast as I was approaching it. The trees and rocks began to gallop past. From midstream I had calculated that I would land half a mile above the tip of Abydos point, but the mile soon became a quarter, a sixth, a tenth. After two hours in the water, within three hundred feet of shore I was being swept past the "last chance" of solid ground, just as, and where Leander had been swept twenty-five hundred years ago . . . and should I fail to reach the beach by ever so little, the current would drag me across the Hellespont, back to the European shore whence I had started.

Never have I felt such utter despair: a five-mile swim—my Hellespont—to miss achievement by one hundred yards! Never have I struggled so desper-ately. My eyes became blurred, seeing only the land not far from me. I ceased to know where I was, or what I was doing, here in this cold, tormenting, boundless ocean. Mechanically I thrashed the water with my weary arms and legs.

Then—bump!—my *knees* struck bottom. I was swimming hysterically in

217

less than three feet of water, for the shore sloped so gradually that, even at three hundred feet out, the water was not waist-deep. With not one second to lose, I stood upright, and staggered ashore, with Rod, who had jumped into the surf, right beside me, and flopped on the last foot of ground at the point.

And so the Hellespont, that treacherous and briny river, was swum once more. Though I am but one of several to have battled successfully with its evil current, I have a distinction no one else can claim. Leander swam to look into a lady's eyes; Lord Byron, that he might write another poem; but I can boast of being the only person, dead or alive, who ever swam the Hellespont on a can of sardines!

21

The Windy Walls of Troy

If you had to choose the most romantic corner in the world, what corner would you choose? I know mine. It is a corner that has fired imagination for three thousand years. It is a corner packed with stirring drama, touched by pathos and deluged with poetry. Such bitter tragedy it has known; such vivid personalities. It is the corner that Homer has immortalized in the first great masterpiece of European literature. It is Troy.

How many a night, as a very small boy, I was rocked to sleep on my father's lap to the romantic tales of this romantic city! Hector and Paris, Ajax and Achilles and the crafty Ulysses were my intimate childhood companions. A hundred times and more I heard the story of the wooden horse, until, if my father failed to recite every smallest word in the telling, I would know it and solemnly correct him. And a hundred times my eyes filled with tears when we came to the place where, in the final sack of the city, Achilles' son, Pyrrhus, slew the good King Priam on his very altar, and where the little son of Hector was torn from his mother's arms to be hurled from the walls. Oh, how I loved Hector, and how I hated the arrogant Achilles! No Trojan could have lamented more bitterly than I the sight of Achilles' chariot dragging the body of my favorite up and down beneath the walls, before the eyes of his wife and mother and father. I never forgave Achilles this. It only increased my pro-Trojan sympathies, and made me suffer the more that my heroic, unconquerable Troy should fall before the miserable treachery of a wooden horse.

How vividly my five-year-old eyes saw it all from the high battlements of my father's lap! How many beastly Greeks (before I went to sleep) I pursued in wild flight across the Trojan plain, back to their ships at the edge of the Hellespont! I never grew tired of Troy and its bloody drama. *These* stories had guts. Peter Rabbit! Uncle Remus! Bah! They were for idiot children.

The years passed, but not my ardor for Troy. Many of my childhood friends became strangers, but not Hector, nor King Priam, nor the ever-interesting Ulysses. I go to sleep once more with Greeks and Trojans battling in my brain, not curled up on my father's lap, but stretched beneath the stars on top the walls of Troy itself, against which the Greeks flung their armies for ten long years in the most celebrated siege in history. For twice ten years I had sought to attain these very walls. I had arrived at last.

And I had come the same way Ulysses had come—from the sea. The Hellespont business with its struggle and its surrender, its exhaustion and its exultation, lay several days away. I was still suffering from the cold, but I was inexpressibly happy. From the end of the sand pit where I lay for a few moments, none too conscious, Roderic had dragged me back to the boat and, in a determined effort to revive benumbed circulation, beat me till I howled for mercy. Lord Byron remarked in his Hellespont poem that the Hellespont gods were a very plaguing lot, for they had given him the ague and drowned Leander. I didn't know exactly what the "ague" was before my own adventure with the Hellespont gods. I certainly learned.

That night, back at the Byron House, I shivered and shook and swallowed brandy in the very same room and for the very same cause His Lordship had shivered and shaken and swallowed brandy a hundred years before. Between the shakes and shivers Rod and I discussed transportation to Troy. Byron made the forty-mile round-trip journey on horseback from "our" house. The fatigue that resulted he offers as one of the reasons why he failed in his first attempt at the Hellespont swim, undertaken immediately following the ride. After we looked at the dilapidated horses, and the wooden saddles still in service, we didn't wonder. They only made us resolve more firmly to cover the twenty miles by water as any good disciple of Ulysses should.

So a second time (having just passed close by the first time), we drew near the curving strand of the Asiatic side of the entrance to the Hellespont, where in 1194 B.C. eleven hundred and eighty-six Greek ships had been beached on the arrival from Aulis. Here the Trojans, having hastened from the gates of their city three miles inland, were drawn up awaiting the first onset of the enemy.

The oracle had prophesied that victory should be the lot of that side from which the first victim of the war should fall. Knowing this, Protesilaus, a Greek, drove his ship forward in order that of the thousand vessels, it should be the foremost prow impressed upon the sand, and leaped to the beach into the midst of the shouting Trojans to perish instantly at the hand of none other than Hector himself.

Eight hundred years after, 334 B.C., Alexander the Great, in his conquest of Asia and of the world, pushed his own ship ahead exactly as Protesilaus had done, so that he himself might be able to leap ashore where the Greek ships had been drawn, and be the first of all his army to tread on Asian soil.

There were no shouting Trojans to obstruct Roderic's and my disembarking, nor any Macedonian armies to applaud. Only a few curious sea gulls screamed at us as we lowered the sail of our *caïque* in preparing to land.

Our boat having departed, we made a reconnaissance of our position. The bluff of Rhoeteum, topped by the tomb of Ajax, rose at our left; the promontary of Sigeum, topped by the tombs of Achilles and his friend Patroclus, at our right. These rocky landmarks have not changed a foot since the ships of the Greeks first sighted them. But the two miles of marshland, river delta and beach, between, may have receded or advanced several hundred yards during the three thousand years that have passed. It could not have been far from our point of disembarkation, however, that the Greeks established and occupied their fortified shore-camp.

Sighting the village of Kum Kale a short distance down the beach, we struck out toward it, crossing en route the almost dry bed of the Scamander River where it empties into the sea. At the village we found a road which we were told led to "Hissarlik" (the modern Turkish term for the site of Troy). One mile, two miles, three miles, we followed this trail across the plain where the Trojans had pursued the Greeks, and the Greeks in turn the Trojans. How many a heroic warrior had fallen in our path! And the gods, even Zeus himself, had moved on this honored ground to assist the army they favored. The midsummer sun beat down upon us; the stones in the road were sharp and painful. But none of these things did we heed. We noticed only the abrupt flat-topped hillock that now arose before us— all that was left of the lofty walls of Troy.

It was a thrilling moment. The same picture had opened up before the eyes of King Xerxes four hundred and eighty years before Christ. In that year the great Persian, leading his vast army toward the Hellespont, "reached the Scamander River and went up to the citadel of Priam, desiring to see it." One hundred and forty-six years later, Alexander, having survived his dramatic leap into the brine, crossed the plain as Xerxes had done before him, and encountered the ruins of Troy. He was only twenty-two at the time of his visit and, being an incorrigible romanticist, was imbued with as much hero worship as any other young man at this romantic time of life. He claimed descent from Achilles, his great example as a man and inspiration as a warrior. In imitation of this heroic ancestor's pursuit of Hector three times around the walls of Troy, the young Alexander, before entering the sacred city, removed his heavy armor and ran three times, in the tracks of Achilles, around the walls. Having honored his hero in this way, he carried a garland of flowers over to the shore of the Aegean and placed it reverently on the tomb of the great Achilles.

The Romans believed Troy to be the cradle of their race, for was not Aeneas, who planted the first seed of their empire in Italy, a Trojan hero who had escaped death at the hands of the Greeks when the city fell? In consequence, a long series of Roman emperors came to the Troad and with beating hearts made a sacred pilgrimage across the same bloodstained ground. Julius Caesar came here in 48 B.C. and thought seriously of making Troy the capital of the Roman Empire. Augustus, Hadrian, Marcus Aurelius and a dozen more great Romans landed on the Troad shores and came to Troy along the same route Rod and I were following in quest of the most dramatic corner of the world.

The mound took shape as we drew near—a serried, creviced mound some eighty-five feet high and a third of a mile high in circumference. Eagerly we reached its base. There I suddenly stopped and began to take off my shirt.

"Dick!" my companion exclaimed. "Put your clothes on. You know how easily you sunburn."

"Just taking off my armor, Rod. Here, hold the shining greaves," I said, handing him my pants.

"*Now* what are you going to do?" He was always fearful of my foolish enthusiasms.

"I'm going to do an Alexander the Great, stoopid. Get out the alarm clock and see how long it takes me. And when I've passed by the third time, drop your red bandanna so I'll know. It would be so unclassical if I got mixed up and ran around four times, wouldn't it?"

222

"Shall I climb to the tower and pretend I'm Helen?" he asked with a touch of sarcasm.

"Oh, yes," I agreed. "With your mustache you look *just* like her."

The rocks he threw at me fell short, for I had departed on my "circum-cursation."

There is a wagon road around three sides of the mound. The fourth side is over a rough spur upon the extremity of which Troy was built. Running was easy enough along the road; only the hillock was difficult to cross, for there was no path, and I had to pick my way among trenches and brambles.

Roderic refused to take my homage to Achilles seriously. As I passed beneath his "tower" the first time, he threw more rocks and ribaldries at me. I ignored his irreverence and trotted on.

At the second turn he dropped his red bandanna from the mound top, but I wouldn't be fooled. I *knew* he was just trying to deceive me. The third circuit ended in a burst of glory and perspiration. The entire run of a mile had taken scarcely ten minutes. I hope, however, that neither Achilles nor Alexander was as hot and thirsty when they finished as I.

"Now I suppose you'll want to walk the three miles back to Kum Kale and scatter daisies on Achilles' tomb just because Alexander did," was the greeting I got from Rod.

"What a noble idea!" I really thought so. "And you can put a garland on Patroclus' tomb. Achilles and Patroclus; Alexander and Hephaestion; Roderic and Richard. Let me have my shining greaves, Rod. We can be over there in less than an hour."

"I'll not stir one foot!" he exclaimed. "The bats in your belfry multiply like rabbits. You haven't even seen Troy—you've just run around it, and you want to go dashing off to sentimentalize over somebody's tomb, who, I'll bet, isn't buried there anyway. It's two o'clock and I'm going to have lunch if I have to eat it off your prostrate form. You never *would* take time to eat or sleep if it weren't for me."

"Oh, all right." When Rod did get stubborn he was a regular tyrant. "Let's have a look at the beans."

After lunch we climbed together to the highest point of the mound to look about. A tossing sea of trenches and broken walls and ruins spread before us, without order or significance—the abandoned excavations of Schliemann and Dörpfeld, the two celebrated German archeologists who first uncovered Troy a generation ago. Few of the trenches penetrate the outer slopes, so that from the plain the mound appears almost as undisturbed as the day these "scientists of the spade" first saw it. Only when the rim has been gained, and the "crater" spreads before one does the vastness and completeness of the excavation become evident.

Few achievements in archeological records have been as full of interest as the unearthing and rediscovery of Troy. Until 1870 "Hissarlik," covered with grass and underbrush, was to all appearances just another flat-topped hillock rising out of the broad, rather barren plain that encloses it on three sides. But in 1870, Dr. Heinrich Schliemann, a man of consuming enthusiasm, assaulted the mound with the firm belief that it was the site of Troy and if explored would reveal more than rock and earth.

His hope was amply realized, for by digging to the bottom of the hill he uncovered the remains of *nine* successive cities built one on top of the other, the bottommost dating from 3000 B.C.; the topmost being of elaborate Roman construction and lost to view about A.D. 500. Dr. Schliemann naturally believed the Homeric Troy was one of the lowest layers of ruins, not realizing that five prehistoric settlements had preceded it. It was only after his death in 1890 that his successor, Dr. Wilhelm Dörpfeld, discovered that the sixth layer from the bottom and third from the top was the long-lost Troy. It had escaped previous detection because the Roman builders in leveling the Homeric ruin for their own citadel had scraped off the higher masonry in the center and dumped it on top of the lower at the edges. Schliemann, digging in the middle of the hill, thus missed the object of his quest. It was only when Dörpfeld encountered the outer rim that the true situation came to light. That Schliemann after twenty years of unfailing faith and unwearying toil should have died just before the great discovery, was a tragedy indeed.

It has been more than fifty years since the excavations were first begun, and some thirty since they were abandoned. In consequence, grass and debris have once more begun to claim their own. Even so, since several of the trenches are fifty feet deep and a number of the uncovered walls thirty feet high, it will take another lapse of centuries before the ruins of the nine Troys are once more buried from view.

Of the sixth city very little remains, for even before Homeric Troy was razed by the Romans, local conquerors had made a stone quarry of its walls to fortify new cities in the surrounding country. In fact, only one Homeric wall of imposing dimension stands, and one great tower facing the Hellespont. But this tower fortunately is part of the Scaean Gate which played such a heavy role in the *Iliad*. All the other conspicuous ruins are Roman.

224

Eagerly, Roderic and I, on distinguishing this landmark, made our way to the top of the Scaean Tower. The wind, sweeping always southward down the Hellespont, blew steadily against us. "Windy Troy!" How often Homer mentions the wind! I well understand why this tower was the chief observation post of the city. All about us spread the treeless, uninhabited Trojan plain with the sparkling blue Hellespont clearly visible three miles away. The islands of Imbros and Tenedos loomed out of the ocean to the west, and far to the south, half lost in summer haze, Mount Ida, the station from which Zeus watched the great conflict, dominated the scene. The Scamander and Simois Rivers, so frequently mentioned by Homer, still drain the Trojan plain, but in summer they are only dry beds and so were invisible from our tower. Farther along on the narrow spur, the end of which is crowned by the ruins, one sees a Turkish farming village built of mud and purloined blocks of hallowed Trojan marble. From this village an occasional farm hand comes to greet strangers and ask for baksheesh. Otherwise, not a human being is to be seen.

Enthroned on the very stones where Helen had pointed out to Priam all the Greek leaders assembled in the plain, and for ten years had watched her Greek kinsmen and her adopted Trojans slaughter one another in her name, I sat all afternoon with Homer's wind burning my face and whipping the grubby pages of my schoolboy *Iliad*, carefully brought from America in anticipation of this magic moment. There I vividly relived the drama that I had first taken part in on my father's lap.

With my imagination aroused by the history all about me, I read and read and read, at fever heat. The *Iliad* ceased to be words on paper. It lived and it throbbed. I tried to shake off all modernity and be a Trojan.

The thrilling pages turn and turn. Paris, bearing the easily persuaded, immortally beautiful Helen, lands on the Hellespont shore and brings her into the city through the Scaean Gate. From my tower the Trojans descry the thousand ships of the pursuing Greeks, creeping over the horizon far out in the Aegean, and marshal on the shore to oppose them. Protesilaus perishes, but the Trojans retire to the city. For nine years they are besieged. Then when Troy is wearying of the struggle, Achilles, the bulwark of the Greeks, withdraws from the fight because of his quarrel with Agamemnon, and Hector, taking the offensive, kills Patroclus, Achilles' greatest friend.

Maddened with grief and rage over the loss of one so dear to him, Achilles, with a grim thirst for revenge, re-enters the ranks and after a furious quest for Hector meets him below my Scaean Tower. Before the murderous eyes

225

of the flashing Greek even the bravest of the Trojans quails. He turns to escape. Once, twice, thrice, around the walls of Troy, the doomed Hector flies. Hecuba and Priam, his royal parents, and Paris and Helen watch with anguished eyes from this tower top.

On the opposite side of the city Hector tries to gain the Dardanian Gate. Achilles interposes. There is a desperate fight to the death which we cannot see. I pray to Zeus, as I prayed at five years of age, to give Hector courage, to go to his aid, not to let him perish miserably at the hand of Achilles. But the pages in my hand cry out that Hector is sinking—is dead—with the bronze spear of Achilles in his throat. Another page—there is a wild shout of triumph from the plain. Achilles, lashing his chariot steeds, dashes past beneath the Scaean Tower, dragging by the heels the stripped and bloody body of my beloved Trojan. Priam, at the agonizing sight, tries to rush out that he may die with his son. Hecuba goes almost mad with grief. Andromache, Hector's wife, tries to throw herself from the walls. Helen, the cool, the imperturbable, must witness this further havoc she has wrought to a city. And the war, and the pages, move on.

Achilles' reign of terror is short-lived. A truce is declared, and Paris, coming upon Achilles unarmed, treacherously shoots him with a poisoned arrow in his one vulnerable spot—his heel.

Hector gone, Achilles gone, Ulysses now becomes the dominating figure in the war. His leadership, I know, is destined soon to end the struggle, for the pages of my story are turning fast, and few remain. Few remain, yet what a bloody tale they tell!

They tell that the Greeks, apparently, have raised the siege and gone away, leaving behind the fateful Wooden Horse.

With songs and procession the Trojans roll the strange statue back across the plain, and demolish a section of wall that blocked its triumphant entrance—and night comes—and Troy is drunk with revelry.

It is too dark to read. I toss my book aside. The sun has gone down behind the island of Imbros in the shadow of which the Greek fleet is hiding. I know it is hiding there. I have known it for twenty years. I know that the Wooden Horse is a clever stratagem of Ulysses; that Ulysses himself is hidden inside along with a score more of daring Greeks. I do not need my book to tell me of all the fury that is to be let loose before the night is gone. I stand upon my Scaean Tower, and breathlessly wait for the storm to break.

Behind me the Trojans, completely occupied with feasting, are not aware that Ulysses and his followers are stealthily emerging from the horse. Before

226

me through the starlight the Greek army, returned from Imbros, is stealing across the plain and up to the gates of the doomed city. Quietly, cautiously, they are massing in deep ranks below the Scaean Tower. There is a stifled cry in the darkness below. Ulysses has run his sword through the Trojan sentry. Groaning slowly, the gates open. The Greeks rush in. There are shouts everywhere, and slaughter. The city is helpless; no one is spared. In the midst of the carnage, King Priam hurls a feeble spear at Pyrrhus, Achilles' son, and invites his own destruction.

Helen, more beautiful than ever, awaits the end serenely. Menelaus seeks her out, determined to satisfy his ten years' hate and his honor as an out-raged husband and king. But when he finds her, she is still so fair, still so much the woman he has loved, that he flings away his sword (somewhat to Helen's disgust) and kneels in homage at her feet—while outside all the streets run with blood, and the red fires mount to the heavens, and Troy becomes a smoking shell of ruins.

Ruins, yes—immortal ruins. Not for three thousand years has a day passed but some Greek, or Roman, or Byzantine, or modern Occidental has dreamed of Troy, or read of Troy, or gone to Troy. Its fame is imperish-able; its romance is inexhaustible. To our own faraway new world its great name has echoed, and I, for one, am proud to have answered its calling, to have lain atop the crumbling battlements in the twilight with the wind whimpering fretfully through the grass-grown ruins, and with the ghosts of Priam and Hecuba, Helen and Andromache drifting beside me, as each night they mount to the Scaean Tower to watch, with hollow anguished eyes, the ghostly horses of the ghostly Achilles dragging Hector's shadowy body before the silent, sleeping, sorrow-laden mound that once was Troy.

22

Lotus Land

✳ Ulysses was almost the last chieftain to leave the Trojan
shores with his remaining command of men. His successful stratagem with
the Wooden Horse had increased his already great prestige so enormously
that even Agamemnon came to consider him the wisest and ablest of all the
Greek captains, and requested his services in the difficult task of demobiliz-
ing the spoil-laden army.

Increasingly restless from this delay, Ulysses and his twelve ships at last
set sail for Ithaca. To reach this island it was necessary to voyage six hundred
miles, traverse the entire length of the Aegean, double the southernmost point
of Greece where Cape Malea looks out on the southern sea, and then, turning north, sail far up the west coast of Greece.

Each ship had held a hundred men ten years before when they came to
the wars of Troy. Scarcely half as many were returning, for the Ithacans had
always been in the thickest of the fight, and the Trojan arms had wrought
destruction in their ranks. This remnant of six hundred was further diminished by fighting on the Thracian coast where Ulysses landed his men to sack
the city of Ciconians who had been allies of Troy during the war.

Leaving behind seventy more men, dead or captured, he set out again, and,
favored by wind and wave, scudded past Lemnos, past the familiar shores of
Skyros (what tragedies had come to pass since Ulysses had first set foot ten

years before on that little isle!), past Delos, past Milo. The war-worn soldiers paid small heed to these romantic islands. They were too eager for Ithaca.

The southern course was ended, Cape Malea was rounded, and all was going well. The helmsmen joyfully turned the prows of the twelve ships to the north into their own Ionian waters.

But alas! The offerings to propitiate the gods for a safe and quick return were evidently not sufficient, for none other than Ulysees himself was destined to ever reach Ithaca.

Scarcely had the last ship passed the cape when heavy currents began to resist them, and the north wind, sweeping down the Ionian Sea, blew so fiercely that they were driven helplessly before it, far out into the boundless Mediterranean. Seven days, eight days, nine days, they were sped southwestward, cursing the perverse winds and this further delay in their homecoming.

On the tenth day, in utter ignorance of their location, they sighted a great verdant island with palm trees reaching out from the shore. To the weary Greeks this meant fresh water, a cool refuge from the sun and an escape from the tossing sea.

As they drew closer, a deep curve in the shore and a glittering white beach indicated a safe haven. Impatiently, they turned their ships toward it. With one final stroke of the oars, the twelve ships were driven high upon the sands of the harbor—the harbor of modern Houmt Souk, the little metropolis of the island of Djerba which now belongs to the French colony of Tunis and is located just off the African coast not far from the line that divides Tunis from Italian Tripoli.

To investigate what manner of people lived here, Ulysses sent out three of his men. Straightway they found a road, leading, beneath a great aisle of waving palm trees, from the beach to a village. Never had they seen such a luxuriant land. The flowers, the ferns, the soft, moist, musical wind would have been acceptable to any traveler, but to the Greeks who had endured the past ten painful years in a barren military camp, this lush tropical garden seemed like the Elysian Fields. I know, because I, too, went there straight from Troy.

Ulysses' men came at length to the settlement half hidden beneath hibiscus trees with their flaming blossoms and palms heavy with dates. They met the residents there, and found that they were a mild-eyed, melancholy, hospitable people who lived on a honey-sweet fruit. The Greeks were cordially received and fed this flowery food, which they learned was called the lotus.

230

"Now whosoever of them did eat of it had no more wish to bring tidings, nor to come back, but there he chose to abide with the lotus-eating men, ever feeding on the lotus, and forgetful of his homeward way." To all of Ulysses' men who tasted of this enchanted fruit,

> "Most weary seem'd the sea, weary the oar,
> Weary the wandering fields of barren foam.
> Then some one said, 'We will return no more.'
> Hateful is the dark-blue sky,
> Vaulted o'er the dark-blue sea.
>
> Death is the end of life; ah, why
> Should life all labor be?
> Surely, surely, slumber is more sweet than toil, the shore
> Than labor in the deep mid-ocean, wind and wave and oar;
> O, rest ye, brother mariners, we will not wander more."

Still on top of the Scaean Tower, Roderic woke up the morning after the fall of Troy, with a yawn. "Tennyson was right, Dick:—'Surely, surely, slumber is more sweet that toil.'"

"*I* should say it is, thou sluggard. *I* was up at sunrise to find if anything was left of the Trojans. Nothing is. They're all dead and the Greeks are all gone. There's not one in sight even on the beach. I've been out to see if they left anything for our breakfast. Behold! One watermelon, one armful of bread, one pocketful of cheese. And what's more, I've engaged two horses with lovely wooden saddles to take us back to Abydos. I know having to get up and eat cheese is an awful hardship, but you'll recuperate when we get to Africa."

We walked the last few of the twenty miles to the Byron House (I suspect Byron, who likewise rode back from Troy, did too, if he had a saddle like ours) and that night on a steamer were once more in pursuit of Ulysses. No ship plied from the Hellespont to Djerba; so we had to return to Athens to look for further transportation.

As ill luck fell on Ulysses on leaving Troy, likewise did ill luck fall on me. Awaiting Roderic at Athens were cablegrams calling him home—after I'd spent weeks training him to put up with my disposition! His loss was a heavy one for me. From the first he had been the steadying, responsible element of our expedition, always good-humored, especially under trying circumstances, always generous, always right. I felt safe to plunge into any caprice no matter how indiscreet, if I knew the cool-headed Roderic was there to see that I didn't get hurt. And so long as I traveled under his watchful eye (as at the Hellespont swim) I never did.

After his departure I wandered about Athens at loose ends, trying to find a boat to Djerba, and not caring much whether I found one or not. At Piraeus I interviewed innumerable sailboat captains, trying to persuade them to take me to the lotus land. No one would venture the nine hundred miles across the Mediterranean in a small sailing vessel, even though I offered the boat's weight in drachmas. The best thing I could find was a Greek freighter bound for the city of Tunis, from which port I could probably re-embark for Djerba. It would take two passengers. I was one.

The other was a prince, not by royal inheritance, but by attributes of mind and heart. A professional German-Swiss ski master, he spent his winters in the Alps, and his summers wandering about the world with a knapsack slung on one shoulder and a violin on the other. He was twenty-six, a graduate of the University of London where he had been an active Fabian, a brilliant linguist, and a gifted musician. Yet with all this he had deliberately chosen the rugged life and, except for his summer excursions, never left his mountains.

He told me of the exhilarating Alpine winters and of the miles he swiftly traveled on his skis. I told him of my Hellespont adventure and the Odyssey I was attempting to relive. We had several things in common. We both revered Rupert Brooke. We had both swum in Lake Geneva in the shadow of the Castle of Chillon. We had both climbed the Matterhorn to watch the dawn break over the Alps. Here was an interesting substitute for the sorely missed Roderic, and he agreed that if I would go with him to Carthage, just outside of Tunis, he would go with me to the lotus land.

We woke up the first morning out, to find to my inexpressible delight that our lumbering freighter was just off Cape Malea, with the island of Cythera close ahead. Over this very spot the twelve ships of Ulysses had sailed. Just as their helmsmen had done, our helmsmen turned us sharply to the west. We cleared the cape, with a strong northeast wind, such as drove the Ithacans to Africa, blowing the smoke from our stack ahead of us. In my mind's eye I could see the Greek crews struggling to hold against the elements, and their despair when they saw Cythera disappearing to the north.

In three days we passed Malta where both Ulysses and I were to come at a later date, and finally entered the harbor of Tunis.

I was not at all unwilling to visit Carthage, despite the fact that my labors at Lawrenceville with Virgil's *Aeneid* had not especially endeared me to

Dido's capital. After the death of Hector, Aeneas had been the greatest defense of my pet Trojans, and for that service I was glad that he had escaped here to Carthage after the sack of Troy, although as a man he had always bored me to death with his monotonous, incessant virtue.

The two-hundred-mile voyage along the Tunisian coast to Djerba was made painfully in a small sailing vessel. Leon and I could have covered the distance by motor in one tenth of the time, had I not been determined to approach the enchanted island from the sea, as Ulysses had approached it. True, our craft was crowded with pigs and cows, which at times got very obstreperous. To restore order, Leon would unsling his violin and put them to sleep with *"Du bist wie eine Blume,"* and *"Stille Nacht, heilige Nacht,"* which he sang divinely. When we weren't clinging to the gunwales for dear life to keep from being pitched overboard, he taught me to yodel and smoke hashish. The latter proved so delightful, I didn't care whether we *ever* got to Djerba.

But we did. I knew it was lotus land from afar: the dense fringe of palms silhouetted against the clouds and the indigo sky, the white ribbon of beach, the clear green water into whose transparent depths one could look and see the sandy ocean floor, and the rainbow sails of the fishing boats—blue, rose, orange, violet, bobbing in scores over the sponge fields at the entrance to the harbor. All this told me that here was the place whose flowers and fruits had seduced the Greeks so completely that they forgot the world and wanted only to dream away the rest of their lives in this enchanted garden.

After seeing Djerba I really didn't blame them. Leon and I went there planning to stay only two days ourselves; we stayed twenty, and even then left with the same reluctance Ulysses' men had shown three thousand years ago.

As our little boat docked at the pier, I looked scrutinizingly at the crowds that watched us land, to see if they were "mild-eyed and melancholy," and if they languidly bore the branches of the lotus tree. Not one of them did. Instead, a number of brisk French customs officials in white uniforms came to meet us, and, behind them, half a hundred chattering Arabs who were about as unmelancholy a lot as a flock of blackbirds. There were color and motion and life in every direction. Ulysses wouldn't know the place today.

The road, however, to the city of Houmt Souk has probably changed very little. There are still the same tall palm-tree lanes, the same hedges of flaming hibiscus, the same fragrant breeze that never lost its tang of salt, and the same countless millions of lavender crocuses that showered the fields like lavender rain, and hid the earth on every hill and dale with a blanket of bright lavender.

Ulysses certainly didn't have two French-speaking porters to carry his baggage and escort him to a neat little hotel, as we did, where Madame asked if we would have red wine or white.

That very day was the date of the big monthly fair. The tiny arcade shops were packed with visitors from the hinterland—tall, arrogant Arabs wrapped in unbleached woolen garments, and gliding along in their bright yellow slippers.

In the great square before the mosque, the perishable products of the island were piled in blazing array: baskets of enormous gold pomegranates, tons upon tons of fresh-gathered olives awaiting the auction block and oil press, great branches of rich red dates, little hillocks of bright oranges, huge oily lemons competing with the splash of tangerines for brightest hue.

The piles of octopuses and other piscatorial foods of like strangeness we found on sale reminded us of the brilliant-colored fleets of fishing boats we had seen scouring the sea just outside the Houmt Souk harbor. This looked as if it might be a jolly adventure—to spend the day in diving for sponges or octopus or whatever it was they went out to get. Our hotel proprietress only said the word and a dozen sailboat owners were at our door ready to accept paying passengers for the day. The price was adjusted by the harbor commissioner, and since the construction of each boat was exactly the same, and the sailing skill of each captain alike unknown to us, the only point left on which to pick our boat was the appeal of its colored sail.

Leon and I carefully looked over the field. All blue sails we eliminated. They were too nearly the color of the sky. The green ones were not bright enough; the salmon proved a bit dingy on close inspection. Leon at last decided on a brilliant red, while to me the yellow seemed the most alluring. But no, Leon stubbornly clung to red.

"Oh, don't be so selfish," I said to him with some impatience. "The yellow is the much more lively and inspired color. Don't you remember how the yellow sails flashed brightest when we first saw them from across the Bay of Gabes? I *insist* on yellow."

"Don't be so selfish yourself," he retorted. "Red is the great primary color. It's the color of wine and rubies and love and warm lips and blood—and this is the only sail in the fleet with that color. It's unique; it's distinctive; it shows a soaring imagination."

Neither of us would budge an inch. Then I thought of a magnificent compromise.

"Leon! I have it! Let's take an orange sail. That's red and it's yellow too. It has all the red love and red lemonade and red flannel underwear, et cetera, you demand, and also my yellow sunshine and optimism and gold. That would satisfy everybody."

"Dick, you're a genius."

So we picked out an orange sail that was sponge-gathering on this day and, once more the best of friends, scudded in a ten-foot boat over the white-floored harbor.

About three miles out, the skipper rolled up his sail and cast overboard a metal cylinder with a glass pane in the submerged end. Being watertight, the cylinder sank only about a foot and floated there. It was big enough to receive one's head in the open end. Thus freed from the ripplings and light reflections on the surface of the water, the sponges growing forty feet below on the sandy floor were visible. At this extreme depth the sponges were safe, for the diver who accompanied each boat was never skillful enough to work so far under water, nor was it possible to handle forks of such a clumsy length. In fact, the forks were rarely made more than twenty feet long.

At first, though it was easy to see the innumerable fish moving about (and not difficult to drive the sponge fork into the unsuspecting creatures), I was quite unable to detect the gray-green sponge from the rest of the scattered marine life on the bottom. But little by little Leon and I came to recognize them. Sometimes they were a foot across and when logged with water presented a serious weight problem.

Our diver was a lad of about eighteen. With a clip over his nose, he would swim to the floor and either tear the sponge loose himself and drag it to the surface, or else, if the water was shallow enough, direct the long fork, held onto from the boat, into the poor sponge's heart.

Leon and I soon had enough of spearing them. We wanted to dive for them, and when Abdulla, the boatman, discerned a fat prize in about twenty-five feet of water, we took off our clothes, put clips on our noses and went after it. I'd never descended into water of more than swimming-pool depth in my life, and didn't know the most elemental rules of "deep" diving. The boy seemed to be as much at home in the cold, green depths as the sponges. If he could be, I could be.

Oh, how wrong I was! Before I'd driven myself down fifteen feet, the pressure on my lungs and heart became so painful, I came scrambling back to the surface half-suffocated and gasping for air. Leon had experienced the same thing. Evidently we couldn't make our living gathering sponges at *this* depth. But we *would* have a sponge even if we had to capture it in the bath-tub.

Abdulla was loath to retreat to more shallow fields; the reward there

235

wasn't worth the trouble. We settled that by offering him twice the value of a day's yield in deep water. Being very willing to humor us at this price, he raised the famous orange sail, and away we sped half the distance to the harbor, not stopping till we reached ten-foot water.

Here we tried it again, and with better luck. The sponges thus close to shore were miserable, anemic little ones, so in order to help out we brought up handfuls of starfish, oysters and sea shells.

We found it great sport, after we became somewhat accustomed to the pressure, snooping over the ocean floor in these tropical sunshiny waters, meeting the fish face-to-face, and getting acquainted with a beautiful new emerald world we had never known. After the first day of practice I was able, by breathing deeply several times before submerging, to ravish a sponge at twenty feet, while Leon took naps on the ocean floor and decided to give up being a wandering minstrel and become a mermaid.

For the next two weeks Leon and I wandered aimlessly about the island, ever charmed by its flaming colors, and its relics of ancient civilization. From dimmest antiquity it has been a flowering oasis along the desert coast of Tunis, and every succeeding conqueror that has flourished in the Mediterranean has occupied, developed and greatly prized Ulysses' lotus land.

Twenty miles across, it afforded ample opportunity for excursions. We swayed on camelback to the far points of the island, looking for deserted beaches on which to swim, watching the olives pressed to oil in crude stone mills a thousand years old, gathering oranges with the hospitable farmers, living on native bread, melons and gigantic pomegranates, idling along the paths under the clouds and the blue African sky, or across the fields which seemed to glow a brighter hue each day with the tidal wave of lavender crocus.

Leon never parted from his violin; he played it in squalid villages where he always collected more children than Hamelin's Pied Piper. He played it on the starlit beach if we stopped there to pass the night. Best of all, he played it when we called on the rural French-conducted schools. Here he completely hypnotized the awed little Arabs with his sunburned smile and his simple German melodies that kept them still as mice. Visitors may come to Djerba, and visitors may go away, but the laughing brown children of this enchanted island will never forget the bronzed, bare-legged man from the far-off world who never grew tired of making sweet dreamy sounds come from his magic bow and box.

And so the slumberous summer days drifted languidly along in this land where it is always afternoon. Whether it was Monday or Friday, June or

236

September, we did not know or care. We had tasted of the lotus, and like Ulysses' men wished to roam no more. Just what Djerban fruit it was that bewitched the Greeks, we do not know. Some say the jujube, once, though no longer, found on Djerba; some say it was the red dates for which the island is famous, and which the Greeks, accustomed to a harsh diet of meat and cereals, found irresistible. I think that it was no one of those things, but all; that the "lotus" was just the general seductiveness of the island. Certainly the effect was the same on the Ithacans and on us.

Only by making ourselves a sacred promise that we would return to Djerba the moment our present expedition was completed, could we set a date for our departure—and that was not to be until the moon, which had enchanted my Marble Maidens two lunar months before, and which was now waxing rapidly, should reach its fullness.

Jealously we watched it grow, until our last night came. Tomorrow we would turn away and, in Ulysses' tracks once more, follow him to the Cyclops' cave.

When the evening was well advanced, Leon took his violin, and we strolled out into the luminous white-walled city to find a quiet refuge and to play a sad farewell to lotus land.

We passed the mosque. The door was flung wide open, and the courtyard was deserted. Ghostly white in the blue moonlight, the minaret rose above the trees, above the walls, above all the earth, into the blue African night and the stars. Braving the wrath of Allah, we entered the courtyard. No one challenged us; so we climbed the ancient circular stair through the impenetrable ink to the muezzin's topmost balcony.

There was the shining Mediterranean over which Ulysses had come and over which he had departed. Inland the spectral olive trees, wave upon wave, dotted the lavender land, and all about us clustered the white, still, starlit city. Leon removed his violin from its battle-scarred case and ran his bow affectionately across the strings.

"What shall I play for you, Dick?"

Any music would have been so painfully beautiful in this high, calm minaret, it did not much matter.

"Do you know the overture from Mendelssohn's *Midsummer Night's Dream?* That's what this evening is, Leon."

He knew it well. Clear and fine, this titillating, dancing, elfish music floated from our tower, so shy at first the people in the streets below did not know whence it came, or if it came at all. Little by little, the violinist took courage, leaned more firmly on his bow, and with increasing resonance poured out the *Dream* into the night. It drifted down into the gardens where the jasmine bloomed; it spread sweetly through the treetops, and out into all the air so that whoever breathed it, heard.

Quiet groups began to collect in the streets below. Never in Djerba's history had anything but the muezzin's call to prayer come from the old minaret—and now this intangible, fairy-dance that falls and falls from the dark tower. They were familiar with shrill, nasal, Oriental music. But here was something utterly mystifying and appealing. Houmt Souk had known few violins, and never had it heard one played so skillfully—in the starry darkness, from a source in the high minaret, which they could not see and could not understand.

For a Djerban to have carried his pipes into the mosque would have been sacrilege. Yet no one came to disturb Leon and me. And so in the moonlight, his violin sang on and on, of triumph, and pain, of loneliness, and of yearning. Rimsky-Korsakov's "Song of India" floated away with a dreamy languor that seemed part of this lotus land. He played the "Hymn to the Sun" from *Le Coq d'Or,* and the swelling, radiant "Prize Song" from *Die Meistersinger.* And there was Wagner's gentle, muted "Evening Star" from *Tannhäuser,* and *Prince Igor's* mad ballet. Unconscious of the realms below, he stood with the wind from the sea rumpling his hair; his face and violin lifted toward the pale golden goddess revealing herself in the high altar of the sky.

It was almost midnight before he thought to pause. The lights from street and window had faded one by one, and one by one our audience had faded, too. Leon's fountain of music was running low. There remained, before we left the old minaret alone with the stars, but one more song to sing: Tosti's "Good-By." Lifting his bow one last time, he played the familiar melody, and as he played he spoke the familiar words:

"Hush . . . a voice from far away! . . . 'Listen and learn,' it seems to say. . . . 'All the tomorrows shall be as today . . . all the tomorrows shall be as today.' . . . The cord is frayed . . . the cruse is dry . . . the link must break . . . and the lamp must die . . . Good-by . . . Djerba . . . good-by . . . good-by . . . Good-by . . . Djerba . . . good-by."

Back from across the courtyard of the mosque, there came to us one small, sad echo of "Good-by." Then the last faint whisper of harmony died away, and over the land of the lotus there was silence.

23

The Cyclops' Cave

✴ Ulysses did not entice his lotus-loving men away from Djerba on any such simple pretext as promising to let them return as soon as they got home. Using sterner methods, he "led them back to the ships weeping, sore against their will, and dragged them beneath the benches, and bound them in the hollow barques."

We do not know how many days the ships bore northward seeking again the Ionian Sea and Ithaca. We only know that after having "sailed onward, stricken at heart" they bumped at length into Sicily at its extreme western end just at the point where the modern city of Trapani is built.* About four miles offshore, the Greeks noticed a rugged island called today Favignana, and in one of its harbors Ulysses chose to beach his ships, for the moment, until he could test the safety of the mainland.

Next morning, accompanied only by the men sailing in his own ship, he crossed the straits between Favignana and Sicily. When they came to the

* Some traditions place the Cyclops' cave on the east coast of Sicily, but if this theory is held, Ulysses could not have reached Aeolus' island, his next stop, without going between Scylla and Charybdis.

mainland, they noticed a cave in the face of a cliff near the sea. Choosing from his crew the twelve bravest men to follow him, and leaving the others on guard, Ulysses struck out to see who lived there. He carried not only his sword but also a skin of strong wine with which he was prepared to win the heart of any fierce savage he might meet.

They entered the cave and, finding it to be the dwelling of an absent shepherd, decided to wait and see what he was like. Not till evening did he return, and then Ulysses bitterly regretted his curiosity, for the cave owner proved to be not a man like themselves, but the terrifying, one-eyed cannibal giant, Polyphemus.

To follow Ulysses to the Cyclops' cave, Leon and I had to drag ourselves away from Djerba and its enchantments. A storm, which began the day we left, prevented our chartering the little trading vessel that had brought us from Tunis and striking out boldly for Trapani straight across three hundred miles of open Mediterranean in the exact tracks of Ulysses, for the Tunisian captain did not have the courage to put out to sea in heavy weather. In his disappointment Leon would have kidnaped Abdulla and the orange-sailed sponge boat and crossed to Sicily in this, but we both realized in time that the precious violin would probably never live through it.

The only alternative was to return to Tunis by an un-Homeric motorcar.

We reached the city in time to make a Naples-bound passenger boat stopping at Trapani. In the face of ever-increasing wind, the ship struggled out of the harbor into one of the most savage seas I've ever known. Leon and I thanked our guardian devils that we had not persevered in the sailboat plan. We could not have remained afloat an hour, and if we had we would have been swept hopelessly from our course to end up in Spain or Palestine.

Next morning, as the ship was plunging past the rocky coast of Favignana where Ulysses' ships awaited his return from Polyphemus' cave, we weak and weary passengers emerged from our cabins more than willing to disembark at Trapani.

Here we struck the rain which was now accompanying the wide-spread storm. It fell in torrents. All morning and until early afternoon the blustering downpour beat at our little hotel. This was a fine greeting to the Cyclops' land. Even a large bottle of wine failed to cheer us. It wasn't drunk in vain, however, for it did make us reckless enough to thumb our noses at the elements, leave behind the violin and all our clothes except shirts,

240

shorts and shoes, and, pretending we were ducks, splash out hatless, rain-coatless, umbrella-less into the flooded streets.

A map gave us the general direction of the Cyclops' cave—we were told at the hotel it was about ten miles up the coast. That seemed rather remote from Favignana. The *Odyssey* reads that when Ulysses on leaving this island "came to the land *which was not far off,* he noticed a cave." But it was no doubt just our wine that made us see incongruities.

Before walking ten feet we were drenched. We didn't care; it was such good sport wading in the pools along the streets and building mud dams across the gutter. We hadn't had so much fun in years. It was still summer, and although the storm had brought a falling temperature, we paddled along fast enough in the blinding rain to keep comfortable in our sodden clothes.

The road presently struck the shore and followed close alongside the roaring breakers. On the other side the western slope of Monte San Giuliano, barren of any habitation and half hidden in clouds, rose abruptly above us. Reckoning after an hour's walk that we were about one third the way, we sat down on the rail of a bridge to take the gravel out of our shoes. Looking about at the dripping scenery, we caught sight of a low-browed cavity in the hillside about two hundred yards from the road.

"Let's go over there and wait for the rain to stop," I said to Leon. "I'm beginning to get cold already, and we've still a long way to walk."

He was more than agreeable. As we approached what we thought was only a cavity, we saw that it was a cave, and a rather large one. We heard the bleating of sheep inside, and saw smoke coming from the entrance. Leon hallooed as we came up to it. Two angry dogs ran out to bark at us, and a voice from within called them back. We entered through a gap in a five-foot stone fold, and found ourselves in a wide-spreading grotto fifty feet square, thirty feet high, and packed with sheep driven there to escape the storm. On a ledge, drying his blanket before a charcoal fire, the shepherd himself sat, a piquant-faced, weather-beaten, tousle-haired, barefooted Sicilian boy of about fifteen (a slightly larger edition of Lazarus), puffing solemnly away at a cigarette.

My Italian was mostly French, so Leon, who seemed to speak every language on earth, had to do the saluting and felicitating. The lad's dialect, if difficult, was understandable.

"We'd like to rest here from the rain, if we may."

"Come in, Signors."

The young shepherd received us with an unconcerned air that made him rather likable.

"It's a fine cave. Do you own it?"

"No, nobody owns it. I spend the nights here in summer. The wall there keeps my sheep in."

"Your cave doesn't seem to be marked on my map. Has it a name?"

"Ah, *si, si*. It is *La Grotta di Polifemo!*"

The young Cyclops peered at us quizzically and no doubt wondered what on earth had struck us that we should be jumping up and down so at the mere mention of the cavern's name.

"But, Leon," I said skeptically, "this can't be *the* grotto. The hotel people said sixteen kilometers—that's ten miles—and we've come scarcely four. Maybe they were just frightening us into hiring one of the hotel motors. Still, Polyphemus might have had two grottos. Ask the boy."

The shepherd insisted that this was the only one he knew about. We asked him if his name was Polyphemus Junior. He said no, that it was Rosario.

Not at all disappointed by this unexpected discovery of our destination, Leon and I sat down to rest and to decide what to do next. We decided that the best thing to do was to take off our clammy shirts and shorts, and dry them before the shepherd's fire. It was a slow process, for the fire was only a handful of charcoal, and the air was heavy with moisture. We might have been a bit miserable except for Rosario's cigarettes which he shared with us like a true host.

By the time our clothes were dry, twilight had come, and with it yet more tempestuous winds and heavier downpour. The shepherd milked several of his goats and gave us a full pail to drink along with a portion of his bread and cheese. The night grew darker—the rain, rain, rain, fell incessantly. Presently there was no light left in the cave except the glowing coals, our cigarettes, and the flashes of lightning. The five of us (two men, one boy, and two dogs) were sitting close together for companionship against the storm and the darkness and the weird unfathomable shadows that filled the deep cavern. Whatever natural self-consciousness the boy may have felt on his meeting with two foreign strangers, he had lost by now and talked with less shyness than one might have expected.

"Do you know why your cave is called *La Grotta di Polifemo?*" Leon asked him after he had told us simply and ingenuously about his small world.

"Yes, it is because a giant by that name lived here."

"Do you know the story about him?"

The young Cyclops shook his head.

It seemed a shame that this lad who sat where Polyphemus sat, and milked his goats, and tended his sheep, and trod the same hillside, and lived the same life in the same cave as Polyphemus, should not be aware of his infamous predecessor's history, and that this rude sheepfold where he spent his summer nights was one of the most celebrated corners in literature.

So Leon told the boy the story (with such vivid pantomime that I, knowing it by heart already, followed the narrative as easily as if I'd understood Italian). He explained briefly who Ulysses was, told of his landing on the beach below us and his visit with twelve men to this very cave.

"They came right through this opening," Leon continued, pointing to the passage between the walls of the sheepfold. "The cave doorway was much narrower then. Otherwise everything is just as Ulysses and his men found it. Nobody was here to greet them, for Polyphemus was away in the pastures up above on Monte San Giuliano.

"Ulysses' men begged him not to stay here. They sensed danger. But Ulysses wanted to see what manner of host this cave dweller might be, so he made them stay."

The boy was listening eagerly, for Leon was a master storyteller who re-lived every small incident of the narrative and pointed out in the ghostly cavern every exact spot where events took place. The shepherd no longer was aware of the rain which the gusts of occasional wind blew under the ledge in on us. He ignored the thunder and his bleating sheep. He was such a lonely boy—only his flocks for company—so hungry for human association—and here was someone who had just dropped with the rain from the clouds to talk to him and tell him stories about the very roof above his head. His eyes said eloquently, "Go on!"

"That evening Polyphemus came home, an enormous giant as high as this grotto, and with only one eye in the middle of his forehead. He had a rather quaint way of greeting his guests. He seized two of them in his enormous hands and dashed them onto the floor right here below us, so savagely that their brains flowed forth on the ground. Then he ate them." Leon re-enacted dramatically how hard the helpless Greeks were smashed on the rocks.

"Ulysses realized that unless he acted quickly the ogre would destroy them all. He thought of a desperate plan. The wine they had brought along he knew was very strong. He persuaded Polyphemus to taste it, and it was so good that the Cyclops drank the entire skin—straightway falling into a drunken stupor.

243

"Acting quickly with four of his men, Ulysses thrust a pole into the fire and when it was red-hot, they drove the sharp end of the glowing bar into the prostrate monster's single eye, gave it a heroic twist and ran like mad."

Leon went through all the motions of the terrible thrust, and the leap to safety, indicating the very recess where the brave Greeks sought refuge. We were all so preoccupied with the story no one thought to fan the coals, so that the raconteur was talking in almost total darkness. But one did not need to see Rosario to know that he was listening with painful intentness. When we had again built up the fire, Leon continued:

"With a yell that could be heard for kilometers, Polyphemus sprang to his feet, tearing the stake from his sizzling eye socket and crying out to Neptune, his father, to help him lay hands on his tormentors. He pushed the boulder from the entrance and sat before it stretching forth his hands to grasp the Ithacans if they sought to go out along with the sheep.

"Once more the crafty Ulysses was more than equal to the situation. Noiselessly he secured himself and all his men under the bellies of the rams, and in this way they escaped, for Polyphemus never thought to look *under* his sheep as they ran past.

"Once the Greeks had again put to sea, Ulysses could not resist the temptation to taunt his blinded victim. With a great mocking shout he hurled derision at Polyphemus, still watchfully waiting right here in the cave: 'Here, Cyclops! If any man ask who blinded thee, say that it was the warrior Ulysses who lives in Ithaca.

"Of course you or I couldn't shout that far. Ulysses could, though, because he had a tremendous voice that easily carried from the sea up here.

"When the Cyclops learned that his enemies had escaped, he flew into such a rage that he broke off the top of a hill—I don't know which one, perhaps it was just the great rock that blocked the entrance, because it isn't here any more—and hurled it at the taunting voice. The huge missile missed the ship by only a hair's breadth and sank thunderously into the sea. You know the little island out there, Rosario, called the 'Asinelli'?"

"*Si, si, Signor,*" the shepherd replied with eager understanding. "Is that the rock Polyphemus threw at them?"

"That's the very same rock, Rosario. So you can see how enormous Polyphemus must have been to throw a whole island that far."

"What happened to him then?" The boy's eyes were wide, and so very serious.

"Oh, no one knows. He just disappeared. But I wouldn't be surprised if

244

he came back here someday to visit his old cave. He was the son of Neptune, the sea god, and so he's probably an immortal and still alive. Even Neptune couldn't cure his blindness; so if he comes back to look for his cave, he may have trouble finding it."

"I'll show him the way," Rosario said, a little wistfully.

Faintly the dying embers cast a last red glow upon the cavern walls. The rain, rain, rain, and the wind, and the inky night beat across the cavern face. Outside the world was all hostility and sorrow. Inside there was trust, and security from every harm. Little by little, the five of us sank to sleep on our rocky beds, disturbed only by the shepherd dogs which stirred and whined, whenever the ghosts of the Greeks Polyphemus had eaten drifted forth from the shadows, weeping and yearning for Ithaca.

24

Stromboli–the Island of Aeolus

✳ I wonder why it is that islands charm us so? I suppose it's because we always expect to find romance there—and so often do. Homer was no less affected by their lure than anyone else, and whenever it was possible he made his characters live, or his action take place, on islands. This "blind old man of Scio's rocky isle" was probably an islander himself. The lotus-eaters' island; the islands of Circe and the Sirens; the "Island of the Sun"; Calypso's isle; Scheria, the island home of Princess Nausicaa; and, finally, Ithaca, show how frequently in the *Odyssey* the poet depended on the veil of romance that enshrouds an island to help enchant his audience.

On the most extraordinary island in the Mediterranean, Stromboli—"a floating island, all about which is a wall of bronze unbroken, with the cliff running up sheer from the sea"—Homer enthroned Aeolus, the king of the winds. And thither, after the escape from the Cyclops, he sent Ulysses with his ships.

Had Ulysses followed the southern coast to Sicily, on leaving Favignana, he might have sailed straight to Ithaca without meeting a single obstacle. But that was not his fate. The winds blew him around the northwest corner of Sicily, and then one hundred and sixty miles eastward. If it was fair weather he saw Aeolus' island long before he got there, for it seems to "float" on the

247

horizon, and rises like a smaller Fujiyama in a perfectly-shaped volcanic cone three thousand feet high.

All day it pours out its column of smoke from its crater, the cage of the winds; all night with a thundering roar it tosses up great geysers of sparks and bubbles of flaming lava which burst high in the air and cascade in a burning curtain down "the cliff which runs up sheer from the sea."

The ancients never doubted that this roaring, smoking, "floating" island was the home of Aeolus and his wind cages, nor do I doubt it, nor would anyone else doubt it who had seen from afar the wild weather vane of smoke issuing from its rumbling crater, shifting now to the south, now to the east, as Aeolus unleashes Boreas to churn the seas with icy tempests, or Zephyrus to lull them again with a gentle western breeze.

With his family of six sons and six daughters, Aeolus entertained the weary Greeks for a whole month, and when they sought aid of him for their homeward way, he gave it cheerfully. To Ulysses he gave a sack made from the skin of an ox, and in it he bound all the winds but Zephyrus. Only the West Wind he sent forth to blow them home.

All went well till the Greeks were in sight of Ithaca. Then curiosity as to what was in the leather sack overcame them. They opened it, and out rushed the imprisoned winds which straightway blew the ship back to Father Aeolus, back to the cages in the crater of Stromboli.

But this time the king, who had previously been the most obliging of hosts, drove them away, saying: "Begone! I dare not shelter him whom the gods hate; and hated by them thou surely art."

So Ulysses and his men, despairing, launched their weary ships once more, and sadly sailed away from Stromboli.

Leon and I impatiently sailed toward it. As one sees smoking Vesuvius from across the Bay of Naples when the low-lying fog has hidden its link with earth, or Fujiyama from a hundred miles at sea when only its snowy summit hangs suspended in the heavens, Leon and I saw Aeolus' island, from far, far off. A haze hung over the ocean, but Stromboli, gleaming in the sunset, poked its steep-sloped cone imperiously above the miserable mist, a "floating" island, a regal, earth-shaking volcano, a glorious picture of grace and symmetry, a perfect thing.

Zephyrus was unleashed, for the weather vane of smoke was drifting straight toward the east and Italy. However, we did not need Stromboli's weather vane to tell us the west wind was a-blowing, for in our fishing smack we were being sped forward by it at a spirited rate. We had chartered the boat at Trapani, after the storm had passed, and by heavy bribery prevailed on the captain and his crew (one man) to make the longest voyage in their lives.

Leon united with his violin and knapsack once more, and I with my camera and baggage (which consisted mostly of some eight different translations of the *Odyssey,* and every learned commentary about it I could find, and a toothbrush), we sailed away from Cyclops-land, not without first seeing that the hospitable Rosario was provided with a mandolin, a raincoat and enough cigarettes to last him for six months.

The same wind that blew Ulysses' ship around the northwest cape of Sicily blew us too. The sea was still tossing from the storm; the waves frequently slammed over us, but with bailing and praying and clinging to the shore, we made the seventy-five miles to Palermo in thirty hours. I'd never sailed at night before in a small sailboat in the open sea. It was a vivid, intense adventure. We were right in the path of shipping and had to watch sharp since both freighters and liners passed us every hour on their way to Africa.

Putting in at Palermo for recuperation, we set sail again, and still favored by a bright September sun and the kindly Zephyrus, coasted on east, past the city of the Laestrygones where Ulysses lost eleven of his twelve ships soon after leaving King Aeolus. Reaching the Milazzo peninsula, some hundred miles on down the shore, we turned away from the mainland at right angles and sailed straight for the seven Aeolian Islands (one for Aeolus and for each of his six sons), the outermost of which is Stromboli, the prison of the winds.

Just as it had called to Ulysses an entire day before he reached it, the mountain called to us, challengingly from afar: "Turn your eyes and your helm to me, mariners. Behold my purple symmetry blocking out the sky. Come climb, climb my roaring, shaking, untrodden slopes; stand at the rim of my thundering crater and watch all the elements of hell hurled into the air. Hear the winds burst from my subterranean cages and fly away in clouds of smoke to Aeolus' bidding. Dodge my rain of sizzling stones, breathe my poisonous sulphur breath, flounder in my dense ash banks. Climb me if you dare, you insignificant little worms. But be warned: I shall fight you, and flay you, and if I can, destroy you, for I am a tyrant; I am the merciless master of the storms—I, I, am Stromboli."

The challenge was a visual challenge from the distance; it was a spoken challenge as we approached—a roar—a concussion—a shaking of land and sea. Close beneath the cliff down which the burning rocks and lava tumble, we drove our little boat. The deep, muffled thunder never ceased. Five times an hour with mechanical regularity the Old Faithful of volcanoes roared like a thousand angry lions and, shooting its shower of blazing infernals a thousand feet into the air, literally "blew up."

One of these explosions greeted us as we beached our boat just at darkness on the shore along which the little town of San Vincenzo struggles, shrinking as far away as possible from the bellowing crater; another rattled the windowpanes as we entered the small and ancient hostelry, and all through the night sleep was murdered, for Leon and I did nothing but lie awake with taut nerves, waiting for the next earthquake, which always made us uncomfortable enough when it came, and twice as uncomfortable when it didn't.

Unable to sleep, we got our clothes back on, roused our grumbling "crew," launched our smack in the darkness, and with sail and oars circuited the shore till we could stand just off the two-thousand-foot terrace down which the volcanic discharge tumbles.

When we reached this point, the "crew" stopped grumbling, and so did our captain. Neither of them had ever seen anything so spectacular, and never had Leon, and never had I. Every twelve minutes the white-hot bubbling lava was shot upward into the black night amid great fountains of sparks that illuminated heaven and earth with their blazing. Then the flaming geyser would fall back onto the slope, and in waves upon waves of molten rock ripple glitteringly two thousand feet down to the hissing sea. The more solid masses not rolled, but leaped, in a few wild bouncing plunges, leaving a trail of skyrockets and little meteors behind them, and fell thundering into the water. The crater boomed unceasingly—the terrace flashed and flamed. For ten eruptions—two hours—we sat in our boat, a hundred yards offshore, and marveled each time the more at this brilliant, blazing waterfall of fire.

Next morning dense clouds of smoke hid Stromboli's crest, and the natives insisted it was exceedingly dangerous to attempt the ascent in these circumstances. There was absolutely no trail, and the whole top of the mountain was a mass of chasms and old craters and treacherous ash banks which one could not see for the dense black fog. No one ever climbed the volcano anyway, even in windy weather when the smoke was carried aside. Now, there was not enough wind to remove it; and the thundering devil was roaring and spouting more savagely lately than it had in years. Weren't we close enough to the awful noise here in San Vincenzo? If we went up there the falling rocks would surely crack our heads; the sulphur fumes would suffocate us. Another deluge of lava over the whole island might be expected

The volcano of Stromboli

any hour; we couldn't choose a worse time to visit the crest, and if we *would* go we were just plain crazy and they washed their hands of us.

But we *would* go. What could be better fortune than to have the volcano perform all its wildest tricks now that we had come so far to see it? The more blood-curdling the San Vincentians (not five of whom had ever climbed the irascible mountain they lived on) painted the terrors of the top, the more alluring it became. However, their warning was *so* dire, Leon and I decided to wait one more day in hope that the summit atmosphere would clarify. At two o'clock that very afternoon we glanced toward the peak—and the cloud had gone. While it was too late to ascend now, tomorrow morning we would be ready.

Tomorrow morning found the sulphur blanket hanging thicker than ever over the crater, only to drift aside at two o'clock again.

"It's like that at this season," said the old lady in whose house we were lodged. "At two o'clock the fog generally lifts."

On the third morning we decided to take a chance on the weather prophecy, and trust to luck that at the same hour the breeze would drive the cloud aside.

By heavy bribery we persuaded one of the stouter hearts to go along (not that he had ever been before) to act as beast of burden. Then—having followed the shore to the slope right alongside the escarpment down which the volcanic discharge flowed, we started up—up through the exuberant underbrush. Halfway we struck the barren slopes of ash and sank into it over our ankles, struggling forward, sliding back. The smoke had drifted halfway down—dense, suffocating, sulphuric smoke. The roar of each eruption grew more fearful. The rumble of the fiery chunks of lava bounding down the great cascade close beside us grew more disconcerting, especially as we couldn't see it. Each convulsion above left us deafened, and faint inside. The trembling of the mountain caused a sickening feeling of helplessness, and the heavy smoke screen only added to our insecurity.

Our native escort began to climb with less and less enthusiasm, until finally, when the volcano gave a superterrifying bellow that shook our very teeth, the lifelong resident on Stromboli's slopes cried out like a suddenly frightened child, and, with all our water and provisions, fled back down the slope, heedless of the mockery we shouted after him.

The mockery was purely to bolster up our own faintheartedness. Had either of us been alone, Leon or I would probably have retreated too. But together we had developed a common courage that steadied our knees when the Aeolian thunder broke over our heads.

252

It was soon necessary to make a mask of our bandannas, for the sulphur fumes and fine, flying ashes were suffocating. Crawling on upward with utmost caution, we gained the level of the wild furnace, still invisible. The soldiers at the Marne could not have suffered a more terrific cannonading than we when the hellhole "blew off" at this close proximity. It was enough to give one shell shock.

Hurrying on as fast as we dared in order to get as high above the monster as possible before it bellowed again, we presently noticed that the slope had flattened out—we must be on the crater rim. Now precaution was trebly imperative. We had absolutely no idea of the summit topography, but that there were crevices and cliffs and chasms, and somewhere perilously nearby a great yawning crater six hundred feet deep at the bottom of which were several lava-spouting entrances to the infernal regions, we knew, though we could not see ten feet ahead.

I looked through the sulphur smoke at Leon's half-masked face. Though it was blackened with lava dust, his ash-rimmed eyes were still twinkling.

"Oh, this lovely mountain air!" he coughed out. "If Aeolus and his six sons and six daughters had their palace up here, I'll bet they all died of galloping tuberculosis."

"They certainly would have had to spend their lives in a bathtub unless they wanted to look as Nubian as you do, Leon. Maybe they were black already and didn't mind. I'm not surprised Ulysses wailed the way he did when the winds drove him back to this ashpile."

"Wish I had a drink of water," Leon said abruptly through his bandanna, expressing the thought that was dominating both our minds.

"Why be so plebeian? I'd much rather have a mint julep, or champagne in a bucket of ice. They're just as easy to wish for as water. *My* wish is that Aeolus would chase this cursed cloud away. We're going to step off into some roaring crater and down in a puddle of lava, if he doesn't."

"You make your wishes very timely," said Leon, looking at his watch. "It's almost two o'clock. I suggest we sit tight and wait. The weather is exactly as it was yesterday."

We had not been seated very long when the earnestly hoped for, and fully expected, relief came. Gradually the smoke began to drift aside. Eurus had been sent to our rescue. Thinner and thinner grew the sulphur fog. We could see twenty feet away—fifty—a hundred—until presently, though the cloud was never entirely dispersed nor our vision entirely clear, since there was a continual discharge from below, the great crater of Stromboli, deep, savage, awesome, hideously scarred by fire and battle, yawned wide open beneath our feet.

And as it opened it began to roar its earth-shaking roar, first deep down below the sea, an ugly, ominous rumble; nearer and nearer it came, fiercer and fiercer. Then with a concussion that almost knocked us over, from six hundred feet above it, we saw the eruption explode through a huge beehive, hurl its bursting, flaming lava bubbles up, up, up toward us as we looked down on it, nor spend its force till the high-flung rocks were level with our eyes. The dense thousand-foot column of black smoke that followed floated on skyward and westward to form the weather vane we had first seen sixty miles away, and the lava fell back on the slope to tumble down to the sea in the waterfall of fire we had watched the previous night.

Startled and frightened by these sudden, simultaneous dramatics, we caught our breath. All the configuration of the mountain that had puzzled us so in the smoke was now completely revealed. The wall of the great crater was only three-fourths there. One entire quarter section had been blown out eons ago, and through the outer edge of its jagged stump, right at the surface of the mountain, the beehive which caused the frightful thunder and poured its eruption down the slope, had broken out. There were a dozen other minor craters in the big crater floor. Each one boiled and bellowed, but it was only the beehive through which all the suppressed steam and smoke of all the earth's interior seemed to find its deafening escape.

For an hour we stood on the rim of this amazing spectacle, with the sea shimmering in a perfect circle, three thousand feet below, dotted with the six islands that belonged to Aeolus' six sons. Only Mount Etna, seventy miles away, broke the hazy horizon. Five times, while we rested, the beehive "blew off." Leon and I were suffering terribly from thirst, but the fascination of watching the geysers of lava, hurled up from below almost, yet not quite, into our laps, was so great that we just sat and endured and gloried in the wildness and brutality of the sight.

The roaring, the bursting, the flames, the inspired feeling of height and mastery over land and sea, made an insane something in my brain struggle for expression—a shrill, savage intoxication—a kind of delirium such as whole armies have in blind, murderous, hand-to-hand fighting, when killing becomes a lust and a joy. I wanted to shout back at this roaring thing; I wanted to fling rocks at the rocks it flung at me; I wanted wings with which to leap into the abyss and jeer at the devils as they snatched at me through these doors to hell. I knew exactly how Nero felt when he burned Rome for musical inspiration. How gloriously and wildly he must have played, gone mad and drunk on the fire below him! Wild music, that was what I wanted—music as wild and drunk and savage as this roaring, evil monster.

"Leon, Leon," I exclaimed with arms flung dramatically out over the chasm, "why didn't you bring your violin? I want music—*music,* while Stromboli burns."

Leon answered me with a mock exaggerated calmness such as one uses on a maniac when trying to get him quietly back into his strait-jacket without his killing anybody.

"There, there, now, Dickie. Don't you get excited. I'll go back and fetch you the fiddle. And of course you would need accompaniment—that would make it sound much louder—so I'll bring along a grand piano. I'll tell you what! You come, too, and help me. I'm sure it would be easier to carry if you gave me a hand."

Leon took me coaxingly by the arms, fearing that if he used force it would make me suspicious and rebellious, and I followed happily and submissively at this delightful idiot's heels, all the way home.

25

Circe the Enchantress

✳ Her name was Rosa, and her eyes were black as midnight. We called her Circe because she lived on Circe's island—and was an enchantress. Ulysses spent an entire year here with the original goddess; Leon . . . but I'm getting ahead of my story. . . .

Ulysses did not attain Circe's island without suffering the most harrowing difficulties. On leaving Stromboli, the twelve ships of the unhappy Greeks, cast forth by King Aeolus, struck Sicily again at the harbor of Cefalu,* the city of the Laestrygones, some thirty-five miles east of Palermo. Here the inhabitants, who turned out to be cannibal giants worse than Polyphemus, cast great stones at every ship that had entered the harbor, so that all but the ship of Ulysses, which had warily remained outside, was destroyed, and their crews speared for food.

All alone, the single remaining vessel fled to the northward, one hundred, two hundred, two hundred and fifty miles before they again came to land. This time it was the island of Circe (though at first they did not know it), called today Monte Circeo, and located on the west coast of Italy halfway between Rome and Naples. Since the Roman era it has been a rocky promontory rising seventeen hundred feet above the sand flats that connect it with

* Students disagree about the location of Laestrygones' home. Samuel Butler and the city's topography argue eloquently for Cefalu.

Monte Circeo

the mainland. In Homeric times it stood alone in the sea, ten miles from the shore.

Ulysses, having rested on the narrow beach with his demoralized companions, climbed to the top of the steep-sloped mountain to look about. On the opposite side he saw smoke rising from some habitation.

To learn who lived there, one of his lieutenants took twenty-two of the men and found a palace in the woods. On approaching they heard a woman inside, singing with a sweet voice, and plying the loom. Presently, radiant as a goddess, she came out and, seeing the Greeks, invited them to enter her dwelling, showed the wonderful web she was weaving and gave them wine to drink.

It was fatal refreshment, for their hostess was the enchantress, Circe, and the wine contained mighty drugs which so changed the Greeks that when she touched them with her wand they were instantly changed to pigs. Ulysses would have suffered the same fate himself when he came to investigate, had he not been protected by a certain herb given him by Hermes to render him immune from Circe's magic. When her charms failed to work on Ulysses, Circe realized he was aided by the Olympian gods, and, in alarm, not only turned the pigs back to men but royally entertained the entire company for a year.

Necromancy did not die with Circe, for, just as the goddess made pigs out of the Greeks, her black-eyed descendant and disciple, Rosa, made monkeys out of Leon and me.

We had tarried at San Vincenzo after our conquest of Stromboli just long enough to get clean—two days. Then, launching our fishing smack, we sailed once more beneath the lava cliff, away from Aeolus' roaring island. As it had bellowed a greeting to us, it bellowed a farewell and with unexpected generosity turned its smoking weather vane to the south, unleashing a breeze that blew us past the other islands that belonged to Aeolus' sons and safely into the snug harbor of the Laestrygones.

Ulysses didn't tarry long at Cefalu, and neither did we, though we had none of the reasons for a precipitate departure he had. *We* found the Cefalutes most cordial. In fact, after Leon, in a café, played "Glory, Glory, Hallelujah" on his violin for the assembled multitudes (a hymn he had never heard before I brought it into his life, and which became such a favorite with him that I began to regret my contribution after I'd heard it seven thousand times), a dozen or more of the younger Laestrygones escorted us all the way to the railroad station.

We had discharged our fishing smack and crew in the harbor, for though Leon and I were willing to risk the long voyage in it across open seas to Circe's island, the captain refused to sail any farther away from his base at Trapani. It was just as well, because had he agreed to go on, this one more time, we'd probably have persuaded him to continue all the way back to Ithaca, and then on home by way of Suez, Singapore, Samoa, and San Francisco.

The train took us to Palermo, a ship to Naples, and more trains to Terracina, seventy-five miles up the coast, and the point on the mainland where one takes a vehicle to reach San Felice, the village on the "island" of Circe, ten miles away across the marshes.

San Felice boasts no hotel. No visitors ever come there except crazy archeologists. But Leon and I meant to stay, if not a year like Ulysses, at least several days, and we needed shelter. Leon by now was stony broke; so, not being too fastidious, we walked around the small ill-kept town looking for hospitality.

Passing beneath a balcony where the windows were wide open, we heard a woman "singing in a sweet voice." It was more than a sweet voice: it was a haunting voice. We stopped to listen. She was singing carelessly to herself as she sat in a chair by the window darning socks.

"There she is," Leon said with a tone of finality.

"There who is?"

"Circe, my child."

"She certainly sings like it."

"And she's weaving a magic web."

"And look, Leon! *There are pigs all around!*"

Hearing conversation below, in a strange tongue, the singer—she was not more than twenty—leaned over the balcony to investigate. We saw her then, clearly, and marveled that so handsome a face and so rich a voice should be found in this savage little village. I suppose Leon and I both stared at her, because she stared back, and smiled, from amusement no doubt at Leon's bare knees. Anyway, her smile was divine, as were her hair and her pale skin, and, as I have said, her eyes were black as midnight.

"Good afternoon, Signorina," Leon said to her in Italian. "We were listening to your singing. It's lovely. Please sing some more."

She laughed shyly, and remained on the balcony.

"We are strangers here, looking for a place to sleep," he continued easily

260

(and I envied him his facile tongue). "There doesn't seem to be any hotel. Do *you* accept lodgers?" he asked with sudden inspiration.

"No-o. But I might."

With a flash of white teeth, and a flash of black eyes, she disappeared with her sock, and returned with her father, a real man of the soil. Leon repeated his request. There was low consultation between the two, daughter urging father to oblige us. No one could have denied such eyes anything. So we were invited in.

"My name is Leon. His is Riccardo." My talkative companion believed in getting acquainted at the start. "What's yours?"

"Rosa."

Rosa! It fitted superbly. She *was* a rose, not of the frail hothouse variety, but the sturdy bright-cheeked kind. There was an air of strength combined with gentleness about her as she busied around her own room which was being prepared for us, talking a little timidly to Leon, who gaily talked back. Several times she tried to ask me a question but I was perfectly dumb in the face of her rapid Italian. It was exasperating. I ached to speak her language—she was so vital, so good-looking, despite—or because of—her peasant dress and peasant surroundings. If I didn't do something quickly to overcome this confusion of tongues, Leon would usurp her entire interest. She was spreading fresh covers on a bed—I leaped to help her. She went out to the cistern to draw water for our washstand—I went along and carried the bucket by one side handle as she carried it by the other. The laughter we enjoyed over our struggles to get it up the steps made us such good friends that when I again faced Leon I gave him a very patronizing look.

At supper—for Leon, backed by Circe's smiling plea, had talked papa into providing us with meals too—I managed to sit next to the enchantress, and we got along famously. Whatever progress I made there, however, was more than counterbalanced after supper by my rival when he took up his violin, and, sitting in the open window, played "Glory, Glory, Hallelujah" with variations.

Rosa loved music. It was Leon's chief passion. He could follow a song, unknown to him, once, and then play it. Some of Rosa's songs he already knew. A bit self-conscious at first, she softly hummed when the violin struck a familiar melody. Little by little she gained courage, and before our first concert was over was singing with all the abandon of a nightingale—untaught—unnoticed—unaware of the beauty and rich sympathy of her voice. In the lamplit room, what peasant ruggedness her face might have had was softened away. She sat in the shadows, a picture of pure loveliness. But as she sang she looked at Leon with gentle eyes, and I felt my own cause slipping.

Slipping, yes, but not lost. Next morning I rushed into the battle with a new and telling stroke. I was wearing woolen golf stockings, and they were in a shocking state of disrepair. The first time we saw Rosa she was darning socks; so I knew she would know how to darn mine. I reasoned that if I could persuade her to do this for me, all the mother instinct which such an honest-hearted peasant girl as Rosa had in abundance, would be brought out as she saw me standing around helplessly while she darned my stockings. It worked magnificently. She fretted over the disgraceful rips and holes, and while she darned she called me "poor bird" and "poor child." Then and there, I resolved to use Penelope's trick and unravel the darning every night so that it would have to be done again the next day.

On Sunday the three of us went to the ancient cathedral, Rosa dressed in black, Leon with his knees well laundered, and I attired as foppishly as my wardrobe would permit. After church we decided to explore the mountain, take Rosa with us as guide, and carry along a picnic basket. Only by subtle maneuvering could I persuade Leon to leave behind his deadly violin.

There was a good path up the back of the mountain to the signal station atop the lower peak. We would have taken this had there not been a fine breeze blowing that day which persuaded us to choose the steeper, pathless, seaward slope, in order to watch the waves dash against the rocks and to visit the grottoes where the Homeric Circe had urged Ulysses to "bestow his goods and all the gear."

Rosa knew every inch of the mountain. It had been her playground as a little girl, so that she had a reverence and affection for it. She knew where the trails were, and the springs, and the ruins. Physical exertion she accepted as a matter of course. She had climbed and toiled like a man, and alongside men, all her twenty years. Monte Circeo offered no difficulties for a girl who had pitched hay and driven oxen. She climbed with as little fatigue as Alpinist Leon himself.

The signal station was attained—twelve hundred feet. It was to this point, probably, that Ulysses came on his reconnoitering expedition, and from here that he noticed the smoke rising from Circe's palace. For us this was not enough. A second peak rose five hundred feet higher, and on top of this were the ruins of Circe's Temple. We decided to spread our picnic lunch

262

on its utmost rock; so, undaunted by the prospect of a yet steeper climb, Rosa found the new trail and led us to the assault.

Such scrambling, such slipping, such shouts of laughter from Rosa! Leon and I both would have been ready to win favor by giving her elaborate assistance, had she not scorned our aid all the way up. On the barren-domed summit, the three of us flung ourselves down and let the strong wind cool our faces.

Oh, what a view!—the rolling Mediterranean at our feet on three sides; the mainland of Italy across the marshes; and smoking Vesuvius eighty miles away, beyond the Gulf of Gaeta; and all the rocky islands that are strung along this part of the Italian coast: Ponza and Ischia and Capri. In clearer weather than we enjoyed, the sixty-mile-distant dome of St. Peter's itself was visible. While we couldn't see it for the haze, neither could Ulysses.

We used a big stone from the scanty remains of Circe's Temple for a table and made way with the bread and cheese and oranges and wine we had brought along.

Leon told Rosa he thought she was the best sport he had ever seen. I should have had some fine compliments of my own to give her had my Italian not been so elemental. At least, Leon didn't have his violin. I'd seen to *that*. The weak point in this little triumph was he really didn't need it, not with his glib tongue and easy sunburned smile. That combination plus the violin was becoming more and more formidable, and I was beginning to be worse than discouraged over the outlook. There they were, sitting side by side, with their legs swinging over the cliff, chattering away like two magpies, utterly happy and at ease together. Perhaps I'd better do the magnanimous thing, since my case was lost already—resign in favor of my better-equipped rival and reserve my romancing until I either learned to speak more fluent Italian or met someone who spoke English.

Then—just in time—my guardian devil whispered a diabolic suggestion in my ear:

"Remember, all's fair in love and war. Leon has his violin and his Italian, but he's stony broke—and *you*—have the money."

"What good will that do, if she likes him better?" I asked hopelessly.

"What good will that do! Don't be such a dunce! Isn't she a woman and doesn't she want pretty clothes and junk from the jewelry store? Use your head, son!"

"But I haven't got a lot of money, guardian. I can't give her diamond stomachers."

"Diamond stomachers! Minerva's Owl! All it will take is a string of glass beads to conquer Leon's violin—and a pair of silk stockings will speak far more eloquently of love than Italian. You'll see!"

Next day the shops were open, and I set out to buy my way into Rosa's heart. The glass beads I found easily—bright red ones, and the silk stockings also, to match her Sunday dress.

That evening when we went to the cistern in the courtyard for water, I clasped the beads about her neck and had the satisfaction of seeing a perfectly radiant young woman. She danced up the steps with such elation that half the water from the side handle bucket was spilled back on me. Had it drowned me, I shouldn't have cared.

At supper I was king. Rosa helped me to the biggest piece of fish and the biggest turnip. Leon seemed very quiet and, the moment our meal was over, pounced on his violin. This was his irresistible weapon which he wielded against the girl's music-loving nature with a devastating effect he fully appreciated.

He played that night with intense feeling, straight into Rosa's heart. And she sang her lullabies and forgot the red glass beads.

But the silk stockings, so dear to a woman's heart, recaptured my lost prestige. They were the first silk stockings she had ever possessed; and a gift of the Italian crown jewels could not have made her happier. She tried to tell me, by speaking emphatically and with pantomime, how much she thanked me. While I understood the idea, Leon (very bored) had to interpret most of the words.

He met the stocking blow with masterful tactics, taking advantage of his ability as a raconteur and holding Rosa spellbound by telling her of his ski jumping in the Alps, of the exciting bobsled races and the midwinter mountain climbing—things that this child of sunny Italy had never dreamed of. She listened as eagerly and admiringly as had the young Rosario in the Cyclops' cave, and her opinion of Leon as a sportsman and a hero soared. I had tales to thrill her too—tales of the Himalayas, and the jungles of India and Malay, tales of Spain and Siberia, and of the wonders of America, but not one small adventure could I relate to Rosa in order to win a part of the admiration she was heaping on Leon. And Leon knew that my pride would not let me use him as an interpreter to match his tales of prowess, just as his own pride haughtily refused to borrow money from me with which to combat my bribery methods. No, each of us had chosen weapons he could wield best in the circumstances, and we felt it dishonorable to steal the other man's thunder.

So, as Ulysses in the palace of Circe, on this beautiful mountain isle, lived on for a year charmed by the enchantress' voice, her graciousness, her lavish hospitality, Leon and I put aside all thoughts of leaving our own Circe's singing and alluring black eyes. Like Ulysses, we were deaf to the call of Ithaca.

The days passed, and the battle raged. I found for Rosa a pretty box in a notion shop and filled it with all the moth-eaten confections the town offered—and Leon on the starlit balcony played to her "The Last Rose of Summer." One afternoon she danced into our room to show us how beautiful she looked in a black lace piece I had given her to wear on her head —and Leon straightway broke her heart with Mendelssohn's "Cradle Song." After supper that night I slipped away to buy for my Rosa a privately-owned coral breastpin that the jewelry-shop keeper had told me was for sale. But when I brought it home for her I found that she and Leon had gone down to the beach, with the violin—and they didn't come back for hours.

When Leon tiptoed into our room, close to midnight, and undressed in the dark, I was still awake and spoke to him.

"Hello, Leon. Did you have a good time on the beach?"

"Dick! Are you awake? Yes, it was beautiful. Where did you disappear to after supper? We waited half an hour. You didn't come, so we went ahead. Rosa sang and sang. I'm learning to play her songs rather well. If we continue, we'll have to go on a concert tour with you as manager."

"I've a better suggestion than that, Leon." An idea had come to me as I lay in the darkness waiting for my friends to return. Deep down in my own heart I realized that I was going to be beaten, that my guardian devil was wrong for once—partly wrong, at least. With all Rosa's naïve susceptibility to pretty baubles, she still loved Leon's music more—and I knew it. So I magnanimously suggested to Leon that together tomorrow morning we go away from Circe's island.

For a full three minutes he didn't answer. And then he said: "I'll go."

Next morning we broke the news to Rosa. It was very obvious she was sincerely distressed. As a parting gift, I gave her the really fine piece of old Neapolitan coral, bought for her the night before, while she and Leon were singing on the beach. The tears streamed down her cheeks, and she shed a few of them on my coat. Leon was like stone. He didn't say a word of

265

good-by—just took her hand, and looked at her with his clear, blue eyes.

Our inconsiderable board bill paid to papa, we climbed in the dilapidated motorbus, and were bumped across the square. Rosa ran behind until we passed through the ancient tower gate. Then she stood there waving and smiling and weeping, until a turn in the road took us out of sight.

Leon and I knew that the departure from Circe meant our parting from each other. Our voyage northward from Sicily was part of his return journey home to Switzerland. I must go south again to face the Sirens Ulysses had faced, with hope that the gods would see me safely back to Ithaca before the winter came along. At Terracina, on the "mainland," I bought Leon a ticket to Rome (since he was utterly without funds) and one for myself to Naples. He would accept nothing more than the ticket. He was a "wandering minstrel." From Rome he would win his own way with his violin. We parted with heavy hearts. I have never had a more engaging companion; I have never known a more loyal friend.

A week later at Naples his first letter came to me. It was not from Rome; it was not from Switzerland. *It was from San Felice!*

I opened it with a burning face:

"Odysseus Dick, *Salute!* You probably fell dead when you saw the postmark on this envelope; so I really needn't write any letter at all. But I'll take a chance that you *did* survive. As you see there's more on Circe's island than a post-marker. I'm here too—and so is Circe. I'm reoccupying our old room, and writing at the open window before the balcony. Circe is singing in a sweet voice and weaving another magic web. And it's *my* sock this time. I knew I was coming back the minute I agreed to go away, but Rosa didn't know it. I swear that to you. I went to Rome and wired home for money. It came next morning, and that night I was back at San Felice, playing "Glory, Hallelujah" beneath Rosa's balcony. Did she rush out to see me? She did not. She just sat still in the window and sang to my accompaniment. Then we went down to the beach and had a concert.

"I've learned to appreciate your bribery methods, Dick, and brought her a coral necklace from Rome to match your breast-pin. But she still loves the red glass beads the best and wears them all the time.

"Tomorrow I'm taking Rosa to Milan. I think she has the finest untrained voice I ever heard, and the teachers there will make a real songbird out of her. With those eyes, and that smile, and that sympathy of heart, we may

266

someday see our little Rosa queen of La Scala. Then I'm going to write an opera for her and call it *Circe the Enchantress.*"

I found myself sitting in a chair gasping from surprise, and hot from confusion. Those fat rascals! How completely and how rightly Leon had won the war! Oh well, I didn't care—much. I'd find another—and another, for I knew that

> Love, like Ulysses,
> Is a wanderer;
> For new fields always
> And new faces yearning . . .

And I knew too that I may as well put by any waiting for Rosa, put by my weaving, for

> Unlike Ulysses,
> Love is unreturning.

26

Siren Isles

✳ Despite this sage philosophy, deep inside I felt dejected and hurt and cheated. I felt that, after all, nobody loved me, and decided in this blue mood to go off to the National Museum and eat worms. Maybe I could find a nice ossified one from Pompeii. Anyway, the well-known bust of Homer was there, and I thought probably he might like to meet me.

I never did find Homer, but I met Jimmy who was much nearer my age and understood English, which the Greek poet would no doubt have considered a very barbaric tongue. "Jimmy" wasn't her name. I called her Jimmy because her real name was such a preposterous one, and this just suited her.

The Bay of Naples tossed in the October wind as only the Bay of Naples can. Our small steamer, bound for Sorrento and Capri, alternated between nose dives and tail spins in the most seasickening manner. Jimmy and I regretted, as our deck chairs slid about among the prostrate passengers, that we had chosen to seek Sorrento by water instead of by motor. It was really the only thing to do, however. We had no idea how long we would be gone, or what we were going for, except that we were looking for Sirens; and on such a dangerous expedition we felt it best to be rid of such useless impedimenta as Mrs. Rolls-Royce.

The Bay of Naples

We had two destinations in mind: the little Galli islands off the south coast of the Sorrento Peninsula, and the Blue Grotto at Capri. Legend insists the Sirens sang their fatal songs from the cliffs of Li Galli, but anyone who has seen the Blue Grotto will champion its claims to the honor.

The nearest coastal town to Li Galli, where we might hope to find a boat, was Positano on the Amalfi road, eight miles from Sorrento. Having planned for a heavy schedule that day, to save time we took a motor to cover the distance. Reaching the summit of an intervening ridge, we could see the blue Gulf of Naples dominated by Vesuvius, glitter in the sun on one side, and the just-as-blue Gulf of Salerno spread itself out for our admiration on the other. And there, in the latter bay, two miles out, apparently barren of any vegetation or habitation, we first saw the black, bleak rocks past which Ulysses sailed, struggling to break the ropes that prevented his answering the Sirens' call.

On the beach at Positano we found a number of large rowboats drawn well up on the sand, for the heavy wind, after two days' duration, was driving tremendous breakers against the shore. It was Sunday morning, and many of the fishermen were idling at the café which faced the harbor.

Between Jimmy's Italian and my own, we explained that we wanted to be rowed out to Li Galli. Our request was met with smiles and shoulder shrugs: the weather was too rough—the waves would capsize our boat before we could get it launched—it would be very dangerous for the lady—perhaps tomorrow or the next day the wind would subside and allow us to go in safety.

One look at the roaring breakers was sufficient to convince us that they were right. We remembered what these same waves had done to our steamer crossing the bay. I was all ready to abandon the idea and come back later. But not Jimmy.

"Oh, nonsense!" she exclaimed. "I want to go now. I shouldn't care if we did turn over; can't imagine anything more agreeable than a swim after that dusty ride over the ridge. This weather isn't likely to subside for days. If we don't go now we never shall. Maybe if we offer them a hundred lire they won't think the trip quite so dangerous."

It was worth trying, anyway.

"Will you go for one hundred lire?" I asked one of the boat owners.

"No, Signor."

"One hundred fifty?"

"No, Signor. It is too rough."

"Two hundred?" That was about ten dollars and well worth getting drowned for.

"*Si*, Signor. I'll go."

This did not settle the matter. We had to recruit three other men to help row, a rower for each of the four oars. It was only after I had offered a fifty-lire gratuity as a prize that we could get volunteers from the large crowd that had gathered around to watch the strange foreign couple perform.

Ten obliging friends of our crew pushed the boat over the skids toward the water. Jimmy and I climbed aboard as a great breaker came roaring in. Our manpower jumped after us just as the wave ebbed, and the accommodating launchers, in water up to their knees, with a shout gave the boat a heroic shove.

Ulysses' rowers never fought harder to get clear of the rock-hurling Cyclops than ours did to get clear of the Positano beach. Ulysses escaped; we didn't. The succeeding wave caught us too quickly, lifted us like a chip and flung us sideways back at the land, throwing all six of us into a scrambled mass in the bottom of the boat and burying everything under a roaring mountain of cold water. A flying nine-foot oar gave me a blow on the head. I saw a thousand stars. It all happened in a flash. Jimmy! Where was Jimmy? There she was, struggling to her feet with half the Gulf of Salerno streaming from her tailored coat suit, but still clinging to her gold vanity case and trying to laugh.

Never have I been so indignant at the ocean. My enthusiasm for the Galli Islands had been only halfhearted before. Now, by all the gods, I'd get there if I had to swim! The four boatmen, gasping from shock and cold water, gasped yet more when, the dory having been dragged away from the lashing waves, I got back in and ordered another attempt. The half-drowned boat owner and I had a heated argument. He wouldn't go back in that surf for *twice* two hundred lire.

His resistance only aroused my stubbornness the more. I had six hundred lire in cash with me, and I was willing to expend every centime of it, for I was *going to Li Galli!*

Still in my waterlogged clothes, I stood up in the dripping boat, waved equally wet bank notes in the air at the crowd that had drawn close to enjoy the details of this unexpected Sunday entertainment, and offered them to the three men who would risk another launching; I'd take the fourth oar myself.

Ten dollars apiece! The temptation was too much. Three lads about seventeen years of age accepted my bribe. Changing to another boat, we again started the embarkation.

Jimmy begged to go again, and had she possessed a dry outfit—why not? —since she swam like a fish. But a dry outfit she did not have. It would have been worse than foolhardy for her to sit two or three hours in her sodden clothes, in an open boat and in the October wind. She finally realized that herself and, deeply disappointed, agreed to accept the shelter of a hospitable matron's home until I returned.

Then the four of us got ready for a possible second drenching. We took off our shoes and coats and shirts and left them behind. One of the boys, named Giovanni, took a harmonica out of his trousers pocket and was about to place it for safekeeping with his coat, when I asked him to bring the mouth organ along in case the Sirens wanted us to join their glee club.

A second time, standing up to our oars, we were pushed out with an ebbing wave, and this time by fast rowing and good luck, we got away. There was a loud cheer from the crowd on the beach. Jimmy, whose light blonde hair always made her distinguishable, waved *bon voyage* with her wet, red felt hat.

Now that we were safe in the open sea, we decided to enjoy our little adventure. My companions were bright-faced, merry lads, greatly elated, despite the continued shower bath we were getting from the flying spray, over the prospect of soon possessing so much money. Two hundred lire apiece! They'd go to Naples that very night and paint the town. Giovanni was so happy over the idea he began to sing "Funiculi, Funicula," fortissimo, and the others joined in. While I didn't know the words, I knew the music and could tra-la-la as loud as they.

Tossing and plunging, we skirted the coast, a sheer thousand-foot precipice, for three miles (Li Galli are not opposite Positano but three miles up the coast and two miles out), keeping about two hundred yards offshore, safely out of reach of the great rollers that raged against the adamantine cliffs. Reaching the point directly facing Li Galli we turned our boat and "Funiculi, Funicula-ed" straight for the seat of the Sirens.

Though the wind bore down with fresh fury, away from the shore, we stubbornly held our course with long, slow, steady strokes, until we came within the shadow of these inhospitable isles. There are three of them in a triangle; two are just great chimneys of rock, and the third, while quite as rocky, is sufficiently level in spots to permit a little vegetation. These three islets are scarcely a hundred feet apart. The waves surge through the nar-

273

row straits and clash and boil and boom. How easy it was to see what havoc the Sirens with their magic voices could have brought about, once they lured mariners into this sinister triangle of rocks and their lashing, snarling waters!

On the leeward side of the largest isle was a small cove extending some twenty feet into the cliff, with a convenient ledge at one side. I wanted to get ashore if possible, and here was the only hope. Catching an incoming roller, we rode it with a crash into this little gap in the rocks, using the oars as fenders. At the psychological moment I made a leap for the ledge and gained it, as the boat was dragged back by the ebb. Waiting for the next roller, the boat again tumbled into the cove, and, as Giovanni leaped, tumbled out again to stand by, manned by the two remaining men till we came back.

The young Italian and I climbed up the steep rock bank and sought the top of the highest cliff we could find overlooking the bursting breakers. Here, surely, the Sirens sat and sang. It was disappointing to find them departed after all our trouble. We wanted to join them in a music fest. Oh well, if we couldn't sing with them, we could sing without them. So we sat down on their rocky throne, our bare wet legs swinging over the edge, and while Giovanni accompanied me with irresistible allure on his harmonica, I sang "Funiculi, Funicula" at the top of my lungs.

We might have continued to improve on the Sirens for hours, had we not feared that the hypnotic call of our music might enchant the other two rowers and cause them to wreck our boat and drown, which would prevent our getting back to Positana for supper.

We had a hard enough time getting back as it was. But my guardian devil was on hand to see that Giovanni and I leaped and landed in our craft as it rode a breaker into the cove, and to see that it didn't capsize even when another roller lifted us high on the Positano beach.

Jimmy was awaiting our return, quite dry, neatly pressed, chic as ever, with her impudent nose generously powdered, and her bobbed blonde hair blowing in the wind.

"You stayed so long I was afraid the Sirens had you," was her greeting.

"They almost did," I replied. "Especially the redheaded one. She had the most beautiful freckles—just like yours, Jimmy. Only one thing saved us: Giovanni's harmonica. Just when all was lost, he played 'Funiculi, Funicula' so ravishingly the Sirens dropped their lyres to listen. That broke the spell and we rowed away like mad. They were awfully put out. Have you got my shirt? I'm dripping wet."

Jimmy had already telephoned to Sorrento for a motor to come after us. It was a touring car, and as there was plenty of room we waited till my well-paid young rowers had arrayed themselves in their Sunday clothes, and gave them a ride to Sorrento where they could take the boat to Naples and squander their two hundred lire in riotous living.

Early that afternoon Jimmy and I crossed to Capri, for while all the guide-books insisted that the Sirens had lived at Li Galli, I had not found a trace of them, and thought that the Blue Grotto might offer evidence of their having lived here.

Our very good intentions to visit the celebrated cave at once were doomed to disappointment. The stormy weather showed no signs of abatement as the day advanced, and we found, soon after landing, that only in calm seas was the low, tortuous grotto-entrance accessible.

Jimmy was loath to remain at Capri overnight since she had planned to be absent from her hotel in Naples for the day only, and had come away —as had I—without even so much as a toothbrush. But I was equally loath to leave without a visit to the grotto, for it was unlikely we would have a chance to come again.

While we were arguing the matter, the last boat that afternoon back to the mainland took advantage of our diverted attention and sneaked off without us. Now we *had* to stay.

Embarrassed by her lack of baggage, Jimmy refused to register at a hotel. A cabman came to our rescue and directed us to a small family pension where the proprietress, sympathizing with my companion's predicament, took her in and provided her, as she had been provided once before that day, with every requirement.

Jimmy was exceedingly impatient with me for having allowed the last boat to escape. Her surf-bathed costume, despite the application of hot irons at Positano, was still far from comfortable, so that the prospect of being away from her wardrobe another twenty-four hours was anything but an agreeable one. In a somewhat angry mood, she even accused me—more justly than she guessed—of missing the boat on purpose, and to punish me maintained an icy aloofness as we sought the pension.

But her lodging turned out to be so snug and so picturesque, and our dinner that night in a garden beneath the stars was so excellent, she forgave me my sins sufficiently to say good night with the old twinkle in her eyes, when, utterly weary from the day's adventures, I departed for my own hotel.

Although another entire day passed before the waves subsided, Jimmy became resigned to the delay, and managed, by supplementary purchases at the local shops plus continual encouragement from me, to maintain herself at the pension. A modern girl no longer needs a maid and seven trunks to keep presentable. With only one small piece of laundry soap, a basin of water, a fragile handkerchief and her vanity case, Jimmy worked miracles on her appearance. No girl in Capri was fresher-looking or better groomed than Jimmy.

The delay, unwelcome as it was, gave us a chance to prowl about the island, up this mountain and down that, never tiring of the dramatic pictures seen from the high places: Vesuvius to the north, Li Galli to the south, sea and sky and autumn air all about us; mountains and islands, colorful villas and terraced vineyards. Ulysses, though he may have passed right by the Blue Grotto on his way south from Circe's island to Sicily, did not land at Capri. It's just as well, for if he had he never *would* have got home.

Next day the wind and the thrashing waves died down, and scouts reported that access to the Blue Grotto was possible. Renting one of the frail little grotto skiffs at Marina Grande, the port of Capri, Jimmy and I embarked once more to look for Sirens. Our equipment consisted of one lunch box, two bathing suits and a Turkish towel.

Modestly supplied with all the swimming requirements, we bounced along the mile and half of beautiful precipitous coast to the obscure crack in the rocks that leads to the far-famed "Grotto Azzurra." We had chosen the noon hour for our expedition. The morning boatload of tourists from Naples had come and gone; the swarms of skiffs that conducted them into the sea cave had disbanded, and there wouldn't be another deluge of tourists till afternoon. We should have the Blue Grotto all to ourselves. As I rowed toward the entrance, I thought it best to enlighten my ungeological companion in regard to its history.

"Jimmy, if you'll stop telling me how to row this boat, I'll tell you some things you ought to know about our grotto."

"I don't trust you, Dick, after the information you gave me about art at the Naples Museum. You'll probably say the grotto was once a stable for sea horses, or that a baptism in its waters will cure delirium tremens—and freckles."

"No, Jimmy," I said, deeply hurt. "I'll tell you only the gospel truth. I read it in a book while you were out buying bathing suits."

"All right, but don't you wander."

"Well, the book said that up till 1826—you weren't even born then—the cave had a very uncanny reputation. Fearful legends hung about it. It

Inside the Blue Grotto

was said to be haunted by evil spirits, and nobody dared go inside. Every islander rowed rapidly past the opening in the cliff—tell me when we get there—half expecting to see some terrible monster come forth. One day a fisherman saw what he thought was a big fish swimming out of the cave. He threw his harpoon and struck it. Instead of a fish, a bleeding man rose to the surface, shook his fist——"

"Now, Dickie——"

"But it's true, Jimmy. It's in the book. The fisherman fainted, was washed ashore in his boat and died in a week. And that isn't all. The book says some of the Capri fishermen still insist that every night after the German and American sightseers have all gone home to bed, the Sirens sing sweetly there. So you see I wasn't wrong about the Sirens. They did and do live in this cave.

"Two German painters finally dared to investigate the dreadful place, and they found—oh well, what they found we'll find, because there's the entrance."

Through a narrow cleft in the cliff only three feet high, where the water from the sea flows in and out, one must seek the cavern. The cleft isn't even high enough to permit one to sit upright. Waiting for an inrushing wave, I seized the cable strung along the tunnel and, lying flat in the boat to keep from bumping my head, gave it a jerk which propelled us through the keyhole.

We sat up and looked about—and caught our breath, for we found ourselves floating no longer on water, but on sky—iridescent, diaphanous, azure sky, shot with blue-burning fire. Blue-blue-blue, silvery, shimmering, fairy blue danced upon the walls, electrified the quivering lake of jewels, turned the stalactite ceiling to great soft sapphires and touched the very air with supernatural spirits, overwhelming us with its radiant, magical, glorious, blue beauty.

"Dick! We've died and gone to Heaven." Jimmy at last found words to speak.

But it wasn't Heaven. It was real—a caprice of nature such as the fairies with all their witchery could never have created. Some literal scientist has come along and analyzed its loveliness, explained its harmony, dissected its enchantment. He tells us the Blue Grotto is not the Spirit of Beauty imprisoned in a cave, but the result of sunshine entering through a submerged window in the sea wall of the cavern, which causes the white light to be refracted, absorbing all the color rays except the blue, which is allowed

278

to penetrate the interior and tinge everything with its own pure, translucent hue. Close the submerged window, and you have only a dark hole in the rocks, where the Sirens, deprived of their eerie illumination, would no longer have the heart to sing.

One of the amazing features of the Grotto is the magic effect its water has on anything dipped beneath it. An oar, a hand, is turned to flaming silver, leaving ripples of fire in its wake. We had come to swim in this phantom blue, and we must hasten while the Grotto was all our own.

"Dick, we didn't bring along a bathhouse. Where am I going to undress?"

"Oh, use the boat. I'll close my eyes, count sheep and whistle."

"No, sir! I won't change in this seashell. It's too rockety. I want to preserve my coatsuit from any more salt-water bathing. It's still in very poor health after Positano."

"Then we can use Tiberius' landing-place there on the side. It leads to a gallery fifty yards deep that once connected the cave with the emperor's villa above. I read that in the book, too. You put your Mother Hubbard on in the passage and I'll stand guard outside to keep the mermen away."

Jimmy disappeared into the gallery, saying something caustic about mer*maids*. When she reappeared presently, in a bathing suit, I was in mine, and together we dived into the cold, bottomless, blue incandescence. Ten million burning bubbles rose to the surface. We were transformed to great silvery fish that stirred the sapphire sky we swam upon with sapphire flames. Remembering my quest for sponges at lotus land, I pushed my way deep down and, opening my eyes, found myself in a glassy sea of limpid azure light. It was not water; it was light, light, we drifted in.

As I watched, Jimmy dived from the ledge and plunging downward became a fiery comet with a nebulous tail of sparks. The agitated water cast phosphorescent reflections all about us, and the whole grotto danced and glittered.

Then I would dive and Jimmy watch. Then Jimmy was a porpoise and I a seal. We splashed and shouted and reveled in this airy fairy world. Every sound reverberated against the gleaming walls, and, as reluctantly I put my earthly vest and pantaloons back on, I made the celestial grotto ring with the magnificent strains of "Funiculi, Funicula."

That evening, while all Capri was asleep, Jimmy and I tramped across the island, following the trail that led at length to the ruins of the Roman villa directly over the cavern we had swum in that noon. Steep rock-hewn steps led down the cliff face to the grotto's entrance. Not a soul was near. Even the wind had deserted this haunted spot, and only the subdued waves broke the stillness.

As we looked with dreamy eyes out over the starlit ocean, from within the cavern faint music came to us softly through the darkness. Prosaic people would have said it was the sound of water lapping on the grotto walls. But we knew that was not true. We knew it was the sweet, soft voice of Ulysses' Sirens—singing.

27

Between Scylla and Charybdis

✳ Back in Naples we found Mignon, Jimmy's equally English traveling companion, in a state of great excitement. She had returned from Rome unexpectedly to find Jimmy gone and to learn from the hotel clerks that her friend had departed several days before with "the American." Mignon had never heard of "the American"—certainly no one that Jimmy might do the disappearing act with. The motorcar was still safe in the garage, so evidently she had not "eloped with the chauffeur." That was some consolation.

In preparation for our reception—if we ever *did* come back—Mignon had prepared a long moral lecture full of big words she was going to deliver to her wayward comrade, but when the bubbling, breezy, unrepentant Jimmy came bursting into their hotel, Mignon saw the hopelessness of trying to reform such an irrepressibly happy soul and, instead, listened with honest envy to the enthralling description of our crimes.

Mignon was a perfect complement to Jimmy. With her dark eyes and hair she was handsomer than Jimmy but not so gay. She was an angel; Jimmy an imp. There was an air of dignity about her. No one ever called her "Min"—till I did. I had to do something reckless to win her favor after having absconded with the only companion she had—and this worked.

That night the three of us dined sumptuously together and discussed the next act.

"Didn't Ulysses have some interesting adventure with two nice girls, on his travels in this part of the world?" Min asked.

"He probably didn't know any nice girls, if he was anything like a lot of his Greek descendants I saw in Athens," Jimmy interjected.

I flew to my hero's defense. "You're all wrong there, Jimmy. Ulysses was always a gentleman. He was gone from his wife *twenty years*, and in all that time only two women ever broke down his fidelity to Penelope—Circe and Calypso—and they were both goddesses, so he couldn't help it. Ulysses' character was entirely *too* irreproachable.

"But we're off the subject. No, Min, unfortunately, Ulysses didn't have any more adventures in Italy after he left the Sirens behind, except with Scylla—and she was anything but a 'nice girl,' considering the way she ate six of Ulysses' men for breakfast without even cooking them."

"Oh, that reminds me," exclaimed Jimmy. "You never did finish telling me what happened to Ulysses when he passed between Scylla and Charybdis. You were just about to, on top of Vesuvius, when you grew tired of talking and wanted to hold hands. Remember?"

"Yes, I remember. Well, it's a sad story. Ulysses sailed on down the west coast with a heavy heart. He didn't dare tell his men what terrors lay ahead of them for fear they'd refuse to go on. That is, he didn't tell them about Scylla. There was no keeping Charybdis a secret. As they approached the narrow straits, they saw a cloud of vapor and heard a mighty roar and dropped their oars in terror. Ulysses pleaded with them to take courage. Of course, he knew there was really no hope for some of them, for any moment Scylla might seize the very men he was trying to encourage. But though he lost twice six of his comrades, they must keep as far away as possible from the sucking, roaring whirlpool on the other side. So he ordered his helmsman to steer the ship close beneath Scylla's rock. Then arming himself, he stood at the prow anxiously waiting for whatever might happen.

"Closer and closer they came to the hungry Charybdis. The maelstrom was sucking in the water with a dreadful noise, and with eddies so deep one could see the sand on the bottom. Everyone, with his heart in his mouth, gazed in terror at the whirlpool, expecting each moment to be his last—when swoop!—Scylla with a hideous cry suddenly reached her six long arms out of her cave and snatched up six of Ulysses' men. Writhing in their death struggles and screaming for their leader, they were lifted high into the cave and devoured gluttonously by the savage Scylla. In

282

after days Ulysses said this was the most sickening sight he saw throughout all his voyages.

"Fortunately, at this heavy price, they escaped Charybdis, and getting through the straits, sailed safely on down the Sicilian coast to anchor at the harbor of Taormina."

"Not Taormina!" Min exclaimed. "Why that's the place we've been intending to go to for weeks. I hear it's the most beautiful town in Sicily. Everybody I've ever seen who has been there simply raves about it. It seems the town has Mount Etna for a background and the ocean for a foreground, and is filled with flowers and artists and invalids and Englishmen. Of course you're going if Ulysses did."

"Certainly I am—I must. I've got to go to Messina first though, and see if Scylla is as bad as Homer paints her. I understand the Charybdis whirlpools are still there—actually."

"When are you going, Dickie?" Jimmy asked. I tried to detect some note of alarm in her inquiry, but I couldn't.

"Pretty soon now. I want to swim the straits. I've wanted to ever since I got across the Hellespont. Wouldn't it be great sport to swim from Scylla to Charybdis? I'm told it's never been done—probably because nobody ever thought of it but me. I must hurry, because tomorrow is the twenty-seventh of October. The water's getting awfully cold. Don't you remember how cold it was in the Blue Grotto?"

"Why not let's all go?" suggested Min. "The only reason Jimmy and I have hesitated this long is because it means taking the Rolls-Royce so far from a service station. We'll feel safer if you're along. You can fix punctures and wiggle things when the engine goes dead."

"All right. But remember, lady, I'm a union man, and if you don't like the way I wiggle things, don't you try to hire anybody else. I'll have my rights."

Fortified with their pledge to observe union rules—whatever they were— I secured road maps next morning, and by afternoon Min and Jimmy and I, all on the front seat, our baggage in the rear, were whirling southward—through Resina (with a new spare tire and radiator cap), past Sorrento, and over the familiar road to Positano. Li Galli had not moved since Giovanni and I had concertized upon the Sirens' throne. We tarried at Positano to say hello to our young mouth-organist friend and inquire about his riotous excursion to Naples, but found that, although a week had elapsed since his departure, he was still rioting.

We stopped for the night at the famous Capuchin Monastery high up above the harbor of Amalfi, and next day, having visited the stately Greek temples at Paestum, sped on down the coast some hundred and fifty miles more. The next afternoon, despite twisting mountain roads, we approached the Straits of Messina.

About five miles before reaching the ferryboat, we came to the picturesque little town of Scilla (modern Italian spelling), built partly on a high, naked promontory of rock that thrusts itself boldly into the sea. This great rock was the home of the voracious Scylla. There is a local legend that up to the eighteenth century a cavern opened into the sea, but that repeated earthquakes have destroyed all signs of what was possibly Scylla's cave. Raising its shining head two hundred feet sheer from the water, and dominating the entrance to the straits, Scylla could not have chosen a more strategic watchtower for observing any ship that dared choose the Italian coast in favor of the whirlpool of Sicily.

From the battlements of the medieval castle on top of the cliff, one clearly sees the extreme northeast corner of Sicily. It was disappointing to find the straits so wide here, for though the channel is only two and one half miles across from this point of Sicily to the place directly opposite on the Italian shore, Scylla, located two miles higher up the coast, is four miles away from the point.

It took small imagination to look over the brink of this rock and picture Ulysses' ship coasting fearfully along its base to avoid the roaring Charybdis—or to picture the consternation among the crew when the six-armed monster fell like a thunderbolt upon them and horribly devoured six writhing Greeks before Ulysses' very eyes.

I was so intent on picturing the dreadful tragedy that I had no desire to climb down from my Scyllan clouds and return to earth. But Min and Jimmy could be such prosaic young women at times. They insisted that sitting on a hard rock one whole hour was enough for anybody, and pulled me back to the road. We raced to the ferry station, ran the motorcar onto a ferryboat and crossed the fabulous straits to Sicily.

It was a sparkling, late October afternoon as the boat pushed away for Messina, and for me, a sparkling moment. Here was the channel famed in song and story—notoriously treacherous and violent. Here Ulysses, reeling from the ghastly encounter with Scylla, five miles back, had sailed with his unhappy Greeks, fleeing into open water again, with the screams of his comrades and the bellowing of Charybdis still ringing in his ears.

Except at Troy, and Ithaca itself, I have never felt so close to Ulysses as in this channel. Never had he seemed so real, so tangible. Here was one great anchor of historic fact to which I could cling in trying to reconstruct his travels, for there is no possible doubt that the Straits of Messina flow between the Rock of Scylla and the Whirlpool of Charybdis.

In the city of Messina I deserted Min and Jimmy. While this place was all-important to me, there was nothing of interest to hold them here. So I sped my friends on their way to Taormina, thirty miles farther down the coast. Jimmy insisted that if I were going to swim the channel she wanted to be alongside in a boat, but I knew that several days of preliminary reconnaissance would be necessary before the final attempt, and that even then I might abandon the idea. And so, though it would have been great fun to have her along, I insisted they go on ahead without me.

Immediately I began to investigate distances, currents, etc., and found that unless the whirlpool had changed its position since Homer's time, the poet had been slightly misinformed in regard to the topography of the straits, for Charybdis, instead of being directly opposite Scylla's Rock, lies eight miles to the south, just outside the sicklelike peninsula that protects the harbor of Messina.

From the top of the lighthouse that rises above the sickle, one enjoys a splendid view of the whirlpool only a hundred yards offshore. It is called in Italian *garofano* (carnation), for, with its rapidly-curling, choppy, white-topped waves, it resembles nothing so much as this flower. The whirling pool is a gigantic eddy caused by the powerful rush of the tides past the obstructing peninsula. With them it waxes and wanes. I looked down on it at the height of its disturbance, 11:00 A.M., and realized that while a modern steamer would pass through it unharmed, a comparatively small sailboat such as Ulysses had would be completely helpless in its clutches.

This is by no means the only whirlpool. There are several others, much smaller and far less dangerous, farther up the channel, but it was in all probability upon sailors' tales of the *garofano* itself that Homer built his terrible Charybdis. While the smaller pools are not powerful enough to endanger even the fishing boats, they certainly can wreck a swimmer. I'll vouch for *that*.

If I had any secret hopes of actually plunging into Charybdis and swimming through it across to Scylla, eight miles away, they were quickly shattered after one glance at the tidal currents that gallop through this bottleneck channel alternately back and forth every six hours. The

285

Hellespont adventure had only proved to me that I was far from being a sea lion—especially far in currents. Certainly I couldn't last out eight miles of such obstreperous wintry water. The currents would land me under Jimmy's nose at the Taormina beach, or up at Stromboli, before I got across, depending on which way the tides were moving.

However, there were other *garofanos* and other possibilities. At the tip of Sicily, the straits, as I have said, are only two and one-half miles wide, and though Scylla is four miles away from the tip, this distance across to the Rock was less than my Hellespont swim. I believed that if I could catch the north-rushing tide I might be able to gain Scylla, as I had gained Abydos, before the current carried me past. At least there was no harm in trying everything once. And if I failed, what of it? It would have been a fine gesture.

The trolley took me up the coast to the Point. Here there is another great lighthouse, and a small fishing village. Innumerable fishing boats were lined up along the beach, and I believed that I could hire one of them with rowers to accompany me across.

The moment I approached a boatman and made my request, the news spread that a crazy foreigner was going to swim to Scylla. Fifty people gathered round to inspect the curiosity and tell me that at this hour the tide was flowing furiously south—I'd be carried back to Messina—better come again tomorrow morning. I did, and this time the tide was flowing just as furiously north. I thought this would be ideal, but the fishermen insisted we'd all be swept out into the open sea. Better wait till noon when the currents were changing and comparatively quiet. Even then, they insisted no one had ever swum from their village to Scylla, and no one ever would. Just look at the little whirlpools all along the shore, and the way the water was swirling now forward, now backward, now across, in a perfect bedlam of currents. And they swore the channel was infested with sharks which collected in the Messina vicinity to feed on the refuse. If I was determined to go I would have to wear a rope around my waist by which they could drag me in if need be.

Noon came, and the changing tides. The water seemed rougher than ever. In midstream the frothing whitecaps were dancing south; nearer land they were rushing north, and close to the shore the little *garofanos* were whirling stronger than ever. I looked across to the great beckoning Rock of Scylla with a sinking heart—so close, and yet so far.

There was none of the old Hellespont spirit surging within, as I ordered

286

the men to launch the boat. There was no Leander and no Lord Byron to have blasted a path. There was no bright burning sunshine here, and no bright sapphire sea. The sky had that day become overcast; it was a November sky, glowering and dark. The straits looked cold and gray. There was no faithful Roderic to encourage me. (Why, oh why, had I let Jimmy go?) There was no precedent, no lifelong dream, no romantic inspiration, to spur me on. I loved every wave in the poetic old Hellespont, but these ominous swirls and whirlpools reminded me of angry snakes. I entered the Hellespont with a song in my heart; I entered the Straits of Messina with clenched teeth and grim determination.

The entire village lined up on the shore to see us off. I disappointed two hundred people by not putting on a red bathing suit and plunging dramatically into the largest whirlpool. If I had, that would have been just as far as I should have gone. It was necessary to proceed beyond the *garofanos* strung along the shore, if I hoped to have any life left in me for the remaining four miles. So I climbed in the boat and was rowed beyond them.

As at Positano, a man stood up to each one of the four oars. We pushed away and fought across the intervening eddies to be driven a hundred yards along the shore before we were a hundred yards away from it. The whirlpools behind us, I stripped and was about to dive overboard when the boat owner caught me by the arm and wanted to fasten the anti-shark rope about my waist. It was the anchor rope and half an inch thick. I stormed with impatience at such a preposterous idea—I'd rather be eaten by sharks than try to swim with such an impediment. He expostulated and gesticulated—pantomiming the shark's terrific jaws clamping upon my leg and dragging me down if I didn't have the safeguard of the rope; and his pulling me nimbly alongside and giving the big fish a punch in the nose, if I did. I was *still* obdurate and once more was about to leap, when the fisherman became threatening and vowed that if I refused to use the rope, he'd refuse to accept the responsibility, row straight back to shore and abandon the whole enterprise.

With a mixture of rage and despair, I submitted to the harness, and, attached to the rowers by fifteen feet of tether, at last dived in.

God! What cold water! I came to the surface gasping from shock, and struck out furiously. Before I'd gone a hundred feet the hemp hawser was tangled up in my legs and dragging me down by its weight. I tried to sneak out of it in the water where that devil holding the other end couldn't

287

see what I was doing till too late. The old fox's eyes, however, were too sharp for me. Before I had more than started to untie the knot, he began to haul me in to the accompaniment of more dire threats. *Why* wasn't Jimmy here! *She'd* have some sense. And to think it was I who had sent her on ahead. Fool!

I glanced back to shore, and the people standing there looked half a mile away already. This was only because we were being swept parallel to the shore so rapidly, and not because I'd swum any great distance from it. I must redouble my efforts if I intended to reach Scylla before I froze to death.

Longer, slower strokes began to get me somewhere, though the ten-ton cable reduced my efficiency by at least a third. In about half an hour I had crossed the northbound current and reached the southbound, having been spun about and battledored and shuttlecocked by the whirlpools at the dividing line.

Just as I had been driven north for over half a mile, I now began to sail southward. In half an hour more I found myself back in line with the fishing station, and no more than a mile out. One mile nearer Scylla in one hour! And I was already getting numb. The Hellespont cold was hell-fire and brimstone compared to this. The rope swelled and was tightening around my waist. The hatred I expended on the rope exhausted me much more than the swim.

The mid-channel southbound current seemed endlessly broad. Every time I looked toward Scylla it was farther north. In another half-hour I was beginning to despair of ever getting there when an especially entangling alliance with the hemp boa constrictor broke the last straw of my resolution. I had the boatmen drag me in and remove the hated shackles. I acknowledged myself hopelessly beaten. But as no one else, so far as I can ascertain, has ever swum the straits either, I need not have felt so bad about it.

We were now halfway across the channel and one-third the way to Scylla. If I couldn't swim the rest of the distance, I'd sail it! So I ordered the boat-men to raise their canvas and get me to Italy.

To my surprise they refused—they must return to Sicily—I was so slow a swimmer the tide had changed and all the water in the channel would soon be sweeping south—they might not be able to get back for six hours—it would be night then. No, by all the saints they weren't going another foot toward Italy.

This was all that was necessary to bring to a climax my smoldering anger against the boatmen and the rope and the water and the currents and the world in general. I vowed by all the saints they *were* going. No Scylla—no lire! They understood that all right, and stopped to reconsider, since it was a fat rate I had offered them for their services—at least five times what a native would have paid. With a sly leer they agreed to complete the crossing if I'd double their promised reward. Such banditry added fuel to my flames of indigation. Even then I was so determined to land upon Scylla's Rock I would have submitted to the pirates had I had the extra money. I didn't have it; I had left my surplus funds behind in Messina, in the hotel safe, bringing along only the amount of lire I thought I'd need.

Money or no money, I was not going to permit their unscrupulousness to wreck an idea I had pursued for three days and already wasted so much time on. I pretended to subside, and agreed to meet their demands. Satisfied, and smiling at my gullibility, they raised the sail and presently beached on the sand below the rock. Here I gave them the overlarge fee agreed upon in Sicily, and no more. It was all I had except five lire for transportation to Messina.

One could have heard their howls in Naples, and it was music to my ears. I made them a low and sweeping bow and strode off toward the town.

But that by no means ended it. They were right at my heels, and had it been dark enough, would have given me a good murdering for my remaining five lire.

A gendarme, hearing the boatmen's groans of agony, came up. On being told the story of my default, he arrested me and conducted us all to the tumble-down police station. The Chief was not on hand. To his assistant the four scoundrelly fishermen vowed I had refused to pay them more than half the guaranteed fee, which they swore was one fifth the amount I had actually put into their hands. The police lieutenant, with sufficient panto-mime for me to understand, ordered me to meet my obligations or be locked up till the Chief returned tomorrow. I refused. I didn't have the amount of "my obligations,"and if I had had, even though the situation was becoming unendurably humiliating, I should still have refused.

The police then searched me and found only the five lire. I didn't have even a passport. It too had been left in Messina. I had nothing but my cold word that I had filled the agreement made in Sicily and paid *ten times* over the amount the boatmen had acknowledged receiving. In the face of their hysterical denials my word was naturally discredited.

Seeing that I really had no more money, my persecutors dropped their demands, and insisting they must get back across the channel "before the tide got too strong," were dismissed.

The lieutenant by no means dismissed *me*. My supposed refusal to understand his Italian, my lack of passport and money, my utterly demented attempt to swim the straits, my absurd knee-length knickerbockers, and this deliberate, criminal acceptance of a service from poor, simple, downtrodden peasants, for which I knew I could not pay, all stamped me as a suspicious and dangerous rogue. In fact I was probably a spy. To jail with me!

I spent the night locked up in an empty anteroom of the police station. For supper the lieutenant gave me a glass of water and a dish of cold, pasty spaghetti, which, ravenous as I was from the long frigid battle with the straits, I could not swallow. The rage and humiliation that had been boiling hotter and hotter all afternoon must have scorched the miserable cot I had to lie on, thinking up diabolic tortures for the police lieutenant. Undoubtedly he was one of Scylla's own brood.

The night dragged itself sleeplessly, sullenly, along. It wasn't the shame of imprisonment I minded so much. I'd been in before—at Gibraltar. There, however, I had an honest trial for the honest crime of taking forbidden photographs. There the whole thing was a romantic adventure, a real genuine drama, shot full of good humor, and handled with dignity and courtesy by army majors and English judges.

But this was only despicableness and discomfort. How had I ever allowed myself to sink into such an ignoble predicament? I wondered if I'd tell Jimmy, and if I did tell her, what she'd say—most likely laugh for ten minutes. Jimmy found humor in everything. She'd probably think the cold spaghetti *especially* funny.

Next morning I was marched before the Chief. I told him, with the assistance of a townsman who had been to America and spoke a little English, that if he'd telephone my hotel in Messina, the manager who had my passport and checkbook would verify my story. This he had the extraordinarily good sense to do, and though he still felt sure, along with his assistant, that anyone who wore such funny pants as mine and tried to swim the straits in November was a sinister character; he gave me back my five lire and reluctantly set me free—without any breakfast.

Five lire! Five miles to the ferry! Should I purchase food and walk or go hungry and ride? I went hungry—as far as the first restaurant that served fruit and eggs and chocolate.

Thus fortified against any further outrages, I started to walk along the same highway Min and Jimmy and I had motored over in our million-dollar Rolls-Royce four days previously. Reaching a point on the coast elevated well above the straits where the road turns a sharp corner and shuts the scene of all this action from view, I looked back and made faces at the city of Scylla and its damned Rock. Then asking Heaven with every step to bless the good kind Italians, I tramped majestically on through the dust.

28

City of the Sun God

✳   That afternoon at the crowded Taormina railroad station I looked about anxiously for Jimmy's bright red hat. I had wired her in advance of my arrival, and believed she would meet me. But there was not a red hat to be seen! My disappointment was painful. I had missed her so keenly—and she evidently didn't care whether I came or not. I stood on the platform as the other passengers moved away, feeling, and probably looking, thoroughly glum. I had thought——

"Dick!"

I whirled about. It was Jimmy's voice. It was *Jimmy*. She had been standing near by all the time and I hadn't recognized her. And no wonder! She wasn't wearing her red sport hat; she wasn't wearing her leather motor coat or the well-known blue coat suit; she wasn't even wearing her brogue shoes. Instead, a floppy black hat hid her merry eyes, and a smart black dress, that I had not seen before, completed the disguise.

"You look as if you had just found a hole in your new red-top boots," she laughed as I leaped joyfully to greet her.

"I thought you hadn't come, Jimmy. I was looking everywhere for freckled noses and small red hats. I never thought to look for you under a big black one. Isn't it new?—and the *swell* black dress?"

"Why, Dick! you *noticed* it! I never even hoped you would. Your wire

293

came this noon, and I hated to meet you in the old red ruin. So I made Mignon give me this one. She bought it in Rome, and was saving it until she met the king. Why didn't you come *much* sooner?"

"I came as soon as I could. The police had me till this morning."

"So that's where you've been! I'm not surprised. Mignon and I both knew you'd get into trouble the moment we left."

"I know it, Jimmy. I lost all of my luck soon as you went away. I tried to swim the cursed straits, and the currents made fun of me, and there wasn't any sun, and I almost froze to death, and my boatmen made me wear a rope, and halfway across I began to die and had to give up. Then I had a squabble with the boatmen, and I was arrested at Scylla and put in the police station for all of last night, and made to sleep on an awful cot, and fed cold, clammy spaghetti; and then I didn't have any money and had to walk home. Oh, and a lot more! It's just what happens whenever you desert me—I can't even keep out of jail!"

Jimmy had not brought the motorcar to meet me. The town of Taormina lies six hundred feet above the harbor and station, and the communicating road is such a steep, tortuous one that a cab is the best means of traveling it.

At the hotel we had a gay reunion with Min and, as it was time for tea, had it served on the hotel balcony overlooking the sea and the rose garden. There they told me about their safe, escortless journey from Messina, and I gave them all the gory details of my encounter with Scylla and Charybdis.

We didn't drink much tea. It got cold while we watched the sun set against the snow-clad summit of Mount Etna.

This glorious volcano dominates Taormina with majestic tyranny. It is a graceful, skyscraping background for every landscape. It blocks the vista down each ancient street. One sees it through the almond trees; one watches it glow and fade as the seasons and the sunlight paint its slopes; one greets it each morning when one wakes, and looking out the window sees this queenly mountain rising from the sea almost eleven thousand feet, framed in the purple clematis that climbs about one's balcony.

For two magic weeks Min and Jimmy and I clung to Taormina. We climbed up the venerable villages perched dramatically on neighboring mountaintops; we met all the "artists and invalids and Englishmen." Though it was November in the unhappy world without, in the hotel gardens here the walls were covered with roses, and the orange trees bent low with their bright fruit.

If I felt that I should look about for some good excuse to defend this long

Mt. Etna from Taormina

relaxation from my pursuit of Ulysses, I was not long finding it in the fact that Ulysses himself tarried here for a month or more. True, our reasons for delaying the journey on to Ithaca were not the same. Ulysses' departure was held up by contrary winds; mine, by the hypnotic charm of Taormina's sky and sea and flowers and colorful society, and by the lure of Min's and Jimmy's comradeship.

Enchanting as it was, Ulysses did not wish to land at Taormina, for the Sun God's cattle grazed here and Teiresias, in Hades, had warned him that, should his followers even by chance harm one, it would bring about the destruction of the ship and its crew. So he instructed the rowers to head away from such a dangerous place.

But for once Ulysses' wishes were not followed by his men. They had rowed four hundred miles from Monte Circeo and now demanded that they be given a rest on shore.

Fearful of this move, but unable to oppose his entire company, he granted their request, and exhorting them not to touch the cattle, beached the ship. Their landing place was undoubtedly in the harbor of what is now Taormina, for here the first break in the long straight shore line south of Charybdis offers a refuge for ships.

That night the Greeks slept on the sand and, because of contrary winds, for the thirty nights that followed. Their provisions supplied by Circe became exhausted. Hunger began to press them seriously. Even Ulysses was forced to forage as best he could for food.

One day during his absence the Greeks became desperate and, deciding they would rather die instantly from the Sun God's wrath than by inches from starvation, slaughtered several of the inviolate cattle.

Furious at this sacrilege, the Sun God sought Jupiter on Mount Olympus and threatened to cease shining unless the father of the gods punished the guilty Greeks. Punishment was promised—quick, deadly punishment; and so Helios went back into the firmament, content.

Yet for six days the doomed Greeks feasted on. The seventh day, the wind changed to the west, and they set sail once more, toward Ithaca. It was to be their last voyage.

From the Greek Theater, built into the end of a high promontory that overshadows the harbor, one can look down and see the probable beach from which Ulysses' ship sailed away to meet the judgment of Jupiter.

The panorama from the rim of this theater, with the ancient castles perched high above, the mountains of Italy across the narrowing straits, and the vision of glittering Etna soaring gracefully out of the boundless blue, is truly one of the great sights of Sicily. No day was ever complete for Jimmy and Min and me, regardless of how filled with color and happy adventure it may have been, until we climbed from the orchestra to the topmost gallery of this theater and felt our spirits soar within us as we looked back beyond the ancient stage, across the ocean and the purple valleys, to the great white poem in the clouds.

One morning when the early sun was tinging Etna's snows with rainbow lights, Mignon put into words a feeling about the mountain that Jimmy and I likewise felt.

"Etna doesn't seem like other mountains to me. It's more like a human being that has a great magnetic personality. I can't keep my eyes off it. It's the last thing I look for at night, and the first thing in the morning. I can just sit and stare at it all day."

"I feel the same way, Min," I said. "I feel myself being pulled toward it. I wonder if anybody ever climbs the old thing?"

"Of course they do," exclaimed Jimmy. "I'll climb it if you will; and you, Mignon, even though Ulysses didn't do it. We three would have a great time."

"But, my children," warned the more cautious Min, "it's almost the middle of November. It will be frightfully cold on top."

"Good!" said Jimmy. "I've wanted to be an Eskimo ever since I can remember. Here's my chance."

"Me, too," I agreed. "If you two mountain goats will get the motor out I'll have the hotel fix us a basket of blubber, or walrus oil, or whatever it is Eskimos live on."

In an hour we were off for Mount Etna, supplied with what proper clothes and heavy shoes we could scrape together. Our climbing equipment consisted mostly of a huge lunch basket, six pint bottles of champagne, and an Alice-blue Rolls-Royce. The hotel manager told us to go to Nicolosi, about forty miles away and well up the slope of the mountain facing the sea. The road that far was good. We could get guides there to conduct us to the summit, twelve miles beyond.

We reached Nicolosi without mishap and engaged an experienced guide. He tried to discourage us: the summit was already deep in snow; the winds blew violently; it would be exceedingly cold; we should have woolen helmets; the observatory building near the top where we would have to spend the night was not suitable for ladies.

Jimmy's reply to all this was only to ask what time we started.

"Tomorrow morning at five o'clock if you are determined to go, Signorina."

And at five, with one horse to carry the "blubber," we were in motion, walking upward, upward, through the chestnut groves that grew luxuriantly in the deep lava ash. The base of Etna is ninety miles in circumference, and this entire great area at one time or another has been flooded with lava, for Etna, though its eruptions are irregular, is one of the liveliest volcanoes in the world.

At eight thousand feet we struck the snow and the wind. Already, we regretted the silly impetuosity with which we had tumbled into this climb. We were wearing the heaviest shoes we possessed, but the snow seeped through, and the cold wind bit to the very marrow.

There was no grumbling. Though Mignon was not so athletically inclined as Jimmy, she was just as cheerful a sport. We had danced into this mountain climb in a larking spirit, and we were determined that it was going to be a lark even if we froze to death and were buried on top. So we made light of our frosty feet, helped one another up the dangerous places and laughed at the increasingly savage opposition of the wind. A flask of brandy I had thoughtfully brought along helped make the laughing easier.

As we approached the observatory building at nine thousand seven hundred feet, where a room is reserved for climbers, Jimmy hesitated to enter.

"If I go near a fire now," she shouted above the young blizzard, "I'll thaw too quickly and spoil."

"Oh, it's only a handful of charcoals," I shouted back encouragingly. "You'll be safe."

We pushed through the door and closed it with a bang. Two tiers of board bunks piled high with blankets almost filled the room. Antonio, our guide, got the pot of charcoal to burning. Min and Jimmy filled the kettle with snow and put it over the coals to make tea. I emptied my pockets of the chestnuts I had stuffed them with on the way up and, amid loud praise from my companions for this noble idea, I got them—along with our shoes—to roasting.

The crater rim was yet another thousand feet above, and, realizing how ill-prepared we were to face the summit blasts more than once, we decided to postpone the final dash till early next morning when we could watch the sun rise from the rim.

Through the fast-gathering twilight Min and Jimmy and Antonio and

298

I, all wrapped in blankets, huddled about the coals and dined on the "walrus oil" and two of the bottles of champagne. At eight o'clock, Antonio ordered us to sleep—an order which, with blankets piled about us, and a twelve-mile climb behind us, and ninety-seven hundred feet below us, we found very easy to obey.

Long before sunup, our brutal conductor dragged us out again. With pieces of rope we each draped a blanket about head and shoulders to serve as a topcoat. Under this etheral headdress Min, with her dark expressive eyes, made a perfect Madonna. Jimmy said that at last my Eskimo dream had come true—I looked just like one.

Whirrrr! The wind all but swept us off our feet as we left the shelter of the building and braved the elements again. It was a clear night, for the full moon, which had not yet set, shone upon our high peak of snow like day. Fighting every foot against the freezing blast, we clung to our blankets with one hand, and dug our walking sticks into the snow with the other. There was no time to laugh now during this last, steep, slick thousand feet. It demanded care and every ounce of effort to keep the wind from lashing us down the other side of the iceberg. We were so intent on our climb we scarcely noticed that the breaking dawn was giving us increasing light.

With one last effort, we gained the rim and, feeling that we were on the top of the world, peered over into the terrifying abyss. It was a mass of whirling smoke and steam and clouds driven savagely about by the wind. The crater floor, eight hundred feet below, was hidden, and the opposite walls, one-third of a mile away, were only a blur. The gravel and ashes and bits of ice and snow, that were fired at us from out of the great seething chasm, stung like needles. It would have been suicide, with our insufficient clothing, to expose ourselves here more than a few brief moments. It wasn't that we could not have stood the cold had we been wearing enough sweaters and mittens and helmets. I had been on top of the Matterhorn in October and Fujiyama in January and stood it well enough, but in neither case was I chiefly dependent for protection, as here, on the warmth afforded by the bright blueness of my shirt and cravat (which matched the shirt most elegantly), and a blanket flapping hysterically about my ears.

We had not timed our final ascent accurately with the sunrise, for we were back at the observatory before the first sparks began to fly over the east. Using the small stone building as a windshield and resorting to the brandy to lessen our rigors, we stood shivering and watched one of the sublime pictures of the world unfold.

Hovering close to earth, an ocean of soft white clouds obliterated everything from sight except the highest peaks in the toe of Italy, and familiar Stromboli, seventy miles away, which appeared like a purple island in the snowy sea. Huge and glowing, the red disk rose above the white blanket, spangling it with showers of gold. Then the Sun God, pleased with us because we had not harmed his cattle at Taormina, dismissed the clouds as if by magic order and gradually spread all Sicily before our grateful eyes— Scylla and Charybdis, all of Aeolus' seven islands, and the north seacoast beneath which Cefalu, the city of the Laestrygones, lay hidden. Mignon had Antonio show her exactly where Taormina was. She wanted to look back into her window from which she watched this immaculate peak we stood on turn to rose and silver in the early sun.

In packing for our descent, we discovered that we still had four of the six pint bottles of champagne brought all the way from home. What carelessness! It would be bad luck to carry them back again. So I opened all four and gave one to each of our quartet with the suggestion that we race to see which of us could drink up his bottle first.

Antonio won without trying. I took second honors, while Jimmy and Min were merely "also ran's." This generous and sudden quaff at the thin altitude of nine thousand seven hundred feet had an amazing effect on Madonna-faced Min. She spread her blanket on the observatory floor and did the most surprising Oriental dance on it. On the way down the mountain she said that, by looking intently to the east, she could see the swaying minarets of Istanbul quite plainly. I told her I believed it because, by looking to the west, I could see Pike's Peak. Jimmy said that no matter how intently she looked, all she could see was stars.

Back in Nicolosi we found that our motorcar, this time, was intact. Before abandoning it, we had removed all the removable parts and locked them in the hotel safe.

On the return to Taormina I faced the inevitable—some immediate decision in regard to my next move. This long, unanticipated delay in Sicily had thrown me weeks behind my schedule. November was half gone, and Ulysses, facing the judgment of Zeus, in his doomed ship was still far from home. If I hoped to complete my Odyssean expedition before Christmas, I must be off, and at once.

29

Fifi Plays Calypso

✳ The chariot of Jupiter rumbled in the far heavens. Black clouds loomed on the horizon, and a sudden cool wind swelled the sails of Ulysses' flying ship. Though Etna was hardly out of sight, another storm was at hand. Jupiter had promised Helios to avenge the slaughtered cattle and had passed a sentence of death on every guilty Greek. Thundering down on the doomed vessel he rent it in pieces; and the thirty-one Ithacans, all that remained of the original hundred who had set sail in this same ship thirteen years before, perished in the waves.

Only Ulysses was spared, for he had taken no part in the destruction of Helios' cattle. Clinging to the floating keel, he was borne away by the currents and carried back up the Sicilian coast straight into the roaring Charybdis. By another one of those rather convenient miracles, Homer preserves his hero from the whirlpool, and sends him south again on the changing tides.

Past Taormina, past Etna, past Syracuse and the southern end of Sicily he was carried, still clinging to his raft. For nine days he was tossed by the wind and wave. On the tenth the pitying gods stranded him, more dead than alive, upon the beach of Ogygia, the island now called Gozo, close to

Malta, where Calypso, the goddess of mortal speech, rescued and revived him.*

And on this island, in the cave dwelling of Calypso, Ulysses was kept an unwilling prisoner by the amorous goddess who had fallen in love with this handsome, heaven-sent Greek, and who, for seven long hateful years, was deaf to all his pleas that she send him on to his yearned-for Ithaca.

Seven years! What a long time to have to live with a goddess. It is no wonder Ulysses was so disconsolate. Goddesses have absolutely no sense of humor. They never laugh delightfully. In fact, I never heard of one laughing at all. They are usually big healthy women who go around wearing bronze helmets and carrying spears—and that would get on any man's nerves. Of course, Venus was a welcome exception to all this. She had curly hair, and a beautiful complexion, and feminine allure. If *she* had been in Calypso's place, Ulysses probably wouldn't have grumbled so much. But including even Venus, I think goddesses would be deadly bores after a week or two. I'd prefer Jimmy any day.

And *especially* on the day I left Taormina. The train took me down the Sicilian coast to Syracuse, passing en route along the familiar slopes of Etna, slopes which reminded me every time I looked up at them of Min and Jimmy, and the jolly chilly hours we had spent on top.

I had allowed Ulysses to return to Charybdis without my following him. One encounter with that strip of cold, swirling water had been so much more than sufficient for me that had I found myself being carried back for a second visit I should have been just as alarmed as he was. I was on my way to Malta with Ulysses' whirlpool episode scrupulously left out.

As I had stuck to "blubber" and champagne at Taormina and left Helios' precious cattle strictly alone, the Sun God had no reason to be wroth with me, nor Jupiter to use my Malta-bound ship as a target for lightning practice. In consequence, the voyage was utterly dull—so dull in fact, I was sorry I had been so virtuous.

Comfortably lodged in Valetta, the chief port of Malta and one of the great British naval stations, I set out in quest of information concerning Gozo and Calypso's cave. Overtaking an intelligent and courteous-looking gentleman, I stopped to ask for directions to the American consulate where such information might be found.

---

* While there has been serious disagreement among students as to the geographical location of Ogygia, sacred local tradition, backed by the fact that Gozo is in the path of currents flowing south from Charybdis, should give this island first claim to the honor.

302

"I'll show you the way," he said pleasantly. "I happen to be going there myself. It's only a block."

"Do you know the consul?" I inquired as we walked along. "I've a lot of foolish questions to ask him; so I hope he'll be in a good humor."

"Oh yes, I know him quite well." He laughed. "You're lucky if he's even civil to you today. His disposition is dreadful on Thursdays."

"Is it better on Fridays? I might wait and come back tomorrow."

"Oh, I wouldn't humor him that way. He's spoiled enough already."

"How awful to have grouchy people for consuls!" I said. "He'll probably make me wait all morning."

"And there's nothing for you to read in the waiting room but economic statistics and the *Pipe and Valve Review,*" he lamented. "And the chairs are enough to give one spinal meningitis."

As we got to the door I held back.

"Honestly, you've frightened me so I don't dare go in."

"Oh, come along," he urged. "I'll see that the ogre doesn't eat you."

In the reception room a secretary bowed to the floor as we entered.

"What fine secretaries!" I thought to myself.

My companion led me straight into the consul's office, and sat in the consul's chair behind the consul's desk, and offered me one of the consul's cigarettes.

"Now, sir," he said with mock pompousness, "the American consul is at your service."

And then and there we laughed our way into a fast friendship. His disposition on Thursdays was charming. He took me to lunch that very noon in an exquisite club built in the sixteenth century as quarters for one of the orders of the celebrated Knights of Malta. We dined and we tramped; we talked without ceasing; and there was not an inch of road over the curious, colorful, historic little island that our motor did not traverse.

Several days after my arrival, a friend of the consul gave me a tea party and asked every American in sight. They were a variegated lot: commercial agents, the officers of a passing ship, a family or two residing in Malta for the winter, and a few wandering tourists.

Of this last group was Fifi. Fifi wasn't a day under sixty-five, but that didn't keep us from falling in love at first sight. If her smartly bobbed hair had turned gray, nobody was ever going to know it; and if she couldn't dance the Charleston it wasn't because she didn't try hard enough. Her seven grandchildren were all safely at boarding schools; her third husband had been worn out trying to keep up with this indefatigable globe-trotter, and left behind somewhere to recuperate. She was a freed woman at last, and certainly took advantage of it.

After the first cocktail we were so well acquainted I was smoking her cigarettes and she was fishing for the olive in my glass. Two cocktails, and Fifi had confided in me that she had been a great and good actress, and could play Ophelia in pink gauze *right now*. Three cocktails and I was urging her to do it.

Fifi's presence in Malta took less explaining than mine. Her boat on the way from Africa to Italy had anchored for a day at Valetta, and she was so interested in the picturesque harbor that she had got off all alone, and stayed. That was two weeks before. I told her about my Odyssey and my quest at the time being for Calypso's cave. I was just about to add that I wasn't overly eager to visit the cave as I was sure there wouldn't be any Calypso there for me to play with even if I did find it—when the inspiration came to substitute Fifi for the missing character.

"Oh, madame," I exclaimed, "if you'd consider returning to the drama I've a superb role for you—a *goddess!* That's much more your type than addlepated Ophelias."

"I'd love to," she replied, "only don't call me 'madame'—that sounds so matronly. But I'm afraid I can't accept the part. I'd planned to leave Malta tomorrow. I've a fussy old husband in Naples threatening to divorce me on the grounds of desertion unless I hurry up and join him."

"Aren't you rather accustomed to that by now?" I said unchivalrously.

"Yes—that's true. I am. And it would be fun to play a goddess, wouldn't it? As you say, that *is* my type. Which goddess would I honor?"

"I'll explain. In reliving the *Odyssey* I like to break it up into acts and scenes according to Homer's chapters, with myself as the stock hero and usually most of the cast. Act nineteen is laid in Gozo—a little island four miles to the west of Malta. Scene one is in a cave overlooking the sea. I want you to be the goddess Calypso who lives there. It's not a difficult role. All you have to do is rescue me from the waves, fall passionately in love with me, and drag me unresistingly into your grotto. Of course there won't be any audience."

"*Well*—I'm glad of *that!*" said Fifi.

"And there won't be any salary."

"Naturally not! We must keep the drama on a high moral plane."

304

"The only description of Calypso Homer gives us is that she had 'braided tresses,' was 'of mortal speech'—and *very* ardent."

"You're right, Dick. I *will* make an ideal Calypso—that is, so far as the talking and the ardor go. I can't very well braid my boyish bob. I'll emphasize the ardor. Then you won't notice my un-Homeric coiffure. I'll wire George right away that I've returned to the stage for a few days, and not to expect me in Naples till Sunday."

"Good! We'll visit the cave tomorrow morning. You'll have to go in a dizzy little tugboat. You won't mind, Fifi?"

"I won't mind anything if I'm to be a goddess. Only don't forget the ambrosia—and the nicotine."

Well supplied with both, plus a de luxe basket luncheon, next day Fifi and I boarded the tugboat. The consul wanted to go along as wardrobe mistress and noises-off-stage, but Fifi wouldn't let him because the script didn't call for changes of costume or departing hoofbeats. I suggested we add a few nymphs to our cast to attend the goddess. Straightway Calypso had a temperamental outburst, and insisted that such a suggestion plainly showed that already I had inclination toward infidelity. In fact, she objected so strongly to the nymph idea I didn't dare even look at the *Queen Elizabeth* when this great British battleship got in our way as we chugged out of Valetta harbor.

Once we landed at Gozo, it was not far to Calypso's cave. The cabman knew it well, and drove us from the dock over the flat, treeless little island to the abrupt headland where the grotto was located.

We arrived at the cavern, still called by the name of the goddess, penetrating a great cliff, one hundred feet above the ocean. Measuring some thirty feet square by ten feet high, it was hung with beautifully-shaped stalactites, and formed a room where the lady must have found a snug and happy home. Obviously, it had been repeatedly used as a dwelling from the most distant age. Signs of the chisel were everywhere. A convenient shelf extended from the door, like a porch, out over the beach. This shelf made an ideal point of observation, so we sat down on it to rest. Fifi took off her jaunty little toque, and let the wind blow through her close-cropped hair—while I tried to picture Ulysses and his raft washing ashore on a curve of sand below, and Calypso, with a cry of "A man! A man!" hurrying down the path to rescue him.

It was a dreamy day. In the open, the December chill was penetrating, but here on the protected sunny ledge one would never have realized that winter—such as it is—was close at hand. The cave and the sea and the solitude brought back memories of a similar (if more turbulent) situation two months before—memories of the Cyclops' land where Leon in the Grotto of Polyphemus related to Rosario, our shepherd-boy host, the tale of Ulysses' encounter with the one-eyed giant. Leon—and his music . . . What had become of him? His letter from Monte Circeo was the last word I had received. Was he back in Switzerland? Or was he at Milan—with Rosa? . . . Rosa . . . Such great dark eyes she had, this simple peasant girl. Had he really taken her away from the "island"? He might well have—or he might still be there himself, on the beach, accompanying her sweet singing with his violin. What a comic little drama that was at San Felice—our solemn contest between beads and Beethoven, silk stockings and Tschaikovsky—and the noble triumph of music over money. Suddenly I laughed aloud.

Fifi looked at me quizzically.

"What *do* you see, Dick, that's so funny?"

"I see an Italian peasant girl scorning my vast riches and my knightly love for a barelegged Swiss minstrel."

"And you laugh? Her husband must have put poison in your rival's spaghetti."

Before I had finished explaining that this wasn't the case, I had told her the entire story of Rosa. In fact, there wasn't much I didn't tell her during the hours we loitered before the cave. Fifi had a subtle yet irresistible way of wheedling out of me all my past she thought might be worth hearing. Self-possessed older women can always do that with younger men they are fond of. Whenever I began to regret my expansiveness, she shattered all resistance by reminding me that she had a grandson my age, and that she was just a sympathetic old lady who had been sent by heaven for me to confide in.

At twenty-six, I hadn't had an *especially* crimson record to confess. However, I wasn't going to disappoint her by admitting it. Fifi never listened to a more profligate autobiography than the one I made up and related to her on the porch of Calypso's cave. Of course she was far too sophisticated to believe me entirely. It gave her a great thrill nevertheless—as it gave me— to hear the heart-wrung revelations of my scarlet years.

She learned that my life had been just one long series of passionate episodes. And, oh, how I had suffered! I had flung myself into my present expedition in a desperate effort to overcome the melancholia to which a recently broken heart had driven me. I'd never heard myself so eloquent.

"What a beastly thing love is!" I exclaimed, inspired by her rapt attention. "How wretchedly, deliberately perverse! Look at Circe and Calypso and Ulysses. Circe, who tried to turn him into a pig, he loved completely. He lived a year in her palace, was the father of her son, and was made to leave her only under pressure. But Calypso—who saved his life when he was cast by the sea on the beach down there, who brought him up here to the shelter of her cave, nursed him back to life, loved him with all her heart, and promised him eternal youth if he would only forget Penelope and live with her forever—Calypso, he scorned. Why is it that those we hunger for never love us, and those that do, leave us cold as ice? Why must people live and love in profile? Why must each one turn away his eyes from the one that loves him to someone ahead who, instead of looking back squarely, only yearns for the next in line? Profile—profile! Oh, Fifi, is there no full-faced love?"

Fifi was simply palpitating when lack of breath made me conclude my outburst. Never with all her three husbands had she heard such a *cri du cœur*. It was just too marvelous. She insisted on my telling her more about love, but that was all I knew about it, so I tried to sidetrack the subject.

"Fifi, you're not playing your role of the Goddess Calypso ardently enough. You're letting your Ulysses jabber away by the hour without a thought for his comfort. It's two o'clock, and you've not even fed him lunch—much less ambrosia."

"Well, it's your own fault. How do you expect me to think about bread and beans when you are ensnaring beautiful women? I *have* been neglectful, though. Here's the ambrosia," she said, rummaging in the basket, "and here's a cup. Now put this coat under your head, Ulysses, and Calypso will feed thee."

The basket proved to contain a banquet which the original owner of the cave with all her magic could not have improved on: caramel cake, and apple tarts, and chocolate bars, and ginger cookies, and tangerines, and olives, and *lots* of ambrosia. We never even got to our stuffed eggs and peanut-butter sandwiches.

I proved especially destructive to ginger cookies. Still clinging to an uneaten fistful, I leaned back in the warm sunshine against the cavern wall, with a feeling of benign contentment.

"You know, Goddess," I said, "I think Ulysses was a dub to have left

Calypso, if she treated him as well as you treat me. This certainly is the life! What do you say we improve on Homer, and instead of sending me off on a raft, and leaving you here all alone and everything, we sail away together and form a traveling theatrical company? You could play all the Homeric heroines to my Ulysses. There's Princess Nausicaa at Scheria where we'd go straight from here, and there's Queen Penelope at Ithaca. You admit you've never been happy since you left the theater. Here's a chance to come back, and combine your art with your travels. Secretly, I've always wanted to be an actor myself. I'm never so happy as when I'm speaking a piece. Of course people might misinterpret our purely professional association. But you wouldn't mind if it caused a little scandal in Malta, would you?"

"Mind it! I'd be *proud* of it at my age, Dickie. Only tell me—before I sign the contract—where is this Scheria place? I can't go to the Arctic, or the Indies—not if you're traveling on that raft you mentioned. I've got to go to Naples, if I'm ever going to meet my husband."

"That's perfect! Scheria is the island of Corfu, and it's only a few hours from the heel of Italy. It's not much out of your way—that is, not much if you want to go."

"I do want to go, Dick. I'd love to keep on playing Homer—it's so dignified; and I've always wanted to see Corfu. The island must be beautiful from what I hear. If only it weren't for George—he's been sending me more and more disagreeable wires every day. I was supposed to reach Naples a week ago. He's probably already excommunicated me for the wire I sent him yesterday postponing my sailing once more."

"But, Fifi, you'll never have this chance to act again. George is no doubt as mad already as he can get, so a few more days' delay won't make him any madder. If you'll join my company I'll co-star you. Just think, that might even lead to the movies!"

"I know it. But, Dick, I'm almost broke, and in the circumstances George would *never* send me any money for a trip to any place except Naples—especially if he thought I was running off with an actor."

Driven to it by her stubbornness, I played the card I had been holding back in case she refused to respond to reason:

"Fifi, if you'll go on to Corfu with me like a good girl, and play Nausicaa, I'll tell you some things about my love life that are just so *terrible* I couldn't even mention them today."

"Oh, I'll go! I'll go!" Fifi exclaimed hurriedly.

30

The Princess

✳   And what's more, Fifi *did* go. George continued to wait in Naples while his gallivanting wife continued her relapse into the drama. He waited while we embarked at Malta, shortly after our visit to Gozo, on a liner bound for Trieste; and he waited while we changed boats at Brindisi in order to cross the Adriatic from Italy to Corfu.

The second boat was a dreadful little tub. Fifi's stateroom proved so stuffy I sat up with her on deck most of the one night we had to endure the voyage, and in the cold starlight, to keep her from regretting our escapade, further analyzed the intricacies of love.

"You remember, Fifi, what I said at Gozo about people always loving in profile?—and about the Circe-Ulysses-Calypso triangle? Well, the usual thing happened at Corfu, when Ulysses arrived there and met Princess Nausicaa."

"Who got pursued then?"

"Ulysses, again. She was mad about him, and so, of course, he was bored with her. 'Nausicaa' is a fine dramatic role. Your interpretation of a goddess showed such talent I'm expecting great things of you as the young Greek princess."

"Must I always be cast as the disappointed woman?" Fifi asked.

"But that's the only part in this act worthy of your genius—unless you want to be an attendant maiden, or the princess' middle-aged mother. If you'll go on to Ithaca I'll cast you as Penelope. Think of my sensational home-coming—with all my demonstrations of faithfulness to you after twenty years' absence! That should compensate for the disappointments at Gozo and Corfu."

"All right, I'll play; only I wish you'd tell me more about this princess part—and the plot. Must I have braided tresses again, and be of mortal speech?"

"Not any more. This time you are a pure maiden about eighteen. You must be able to drive a team of mules well, play ball, and do the family wash."

"Ye gods, Dickie! While I'm at first base scrubbing shirts, what are you doing?"

"Why, I've come on a raft from the cave of Calypso. Jupiter persuaded her to send me home to Ithaca. On the way there, Neptune raises a storm and destroys my raft, and I have to swim two days before the waves fling me up on the west coast of Corfu. You see, I'd blinded his son, Polyphemus, nine years before, and he had a long memory. I crawl ashore covered with beard and brine, and stumble into a thicket of trees to sleep.

"Now here's where *you* enter—driving a mule wagon piled high with soiled linen, and surrounded by court maidens. You and the other girls launder everything in the little stream that flows into the bay there, and while the clothes are drying, several of you play with a golden ball on the beach. One of the less skillful pitchers throws it into the sea, and everybody screams and shouts.

"In my grove of trees I am awakened by the noise, and walk forth to find out what it's all about. I'm so wild-looking, and so undressed, the maidens fly in terror down the beach—except you."

"But Dick, shouldn't I fly too—to be—er—modest?"

"Of course not. You're a princess, and very brave. Nothing disconcerts you."

"Do you think this act will get by the Board of Censors?"

"Why shouldn't it? Didn't Homer write it? And isn't it a classic?"

"Well, go on. What happens next?"

"Nausicaa sees that Ulysses is a helpless, suffering castaway, and takes pity on him. She gives him a tunic—or whatever it is Greeks wore—and has him follow the wagon to her father's palace. There she falls in love with the stranger. No harm comes of it, though. Ulysses reveals himself to the king, tells Nausicaa he'll be a brother to her, is given a regular bust-up of a banquet, and escorted home in a private yacht. *Now*—how do you like your part?"

"It's improving. Think I'll go back to my stateroom with my stockings right away and rehearse the great laundry scene."

Realizing at Corfu City what objects of gossip theatrical people are at all times, Fifi and I decided to allow the breath of scandal no chance to enter our newly-formed company. She found quarters in a delightful hotel with a garden, while I went decorously to a pension three blocks away.

For several days we were so occupied with Corfu's poetic setting and color-ful people we didn't take Homer too seriously. When, at last, the spirit moved, we secured a 1920 model Ford—shades of an Alice-blue Rolls-Royce—and rode across the island under the endless olive groves to the west shore where Ulysses, coming from Malta, must have landed.

There we found glorious scenery—great five-hundred-foot cliffs stretching out of sight all along the coast, with a single brief interval where the walls relented and made room for a small bay fringed with beach. Being the only beach on the west coast, this had to be Ulysses'.

"Here's the theater, Princess," I said as we climbed out of our motor and reached the sand.

The theater proved rather bare of properties. We couldn't find a stream where Fifi could do the washing—so we had to leave that out. I had brought along a lemon for the golden ball, but there were no court maidens to throw it at—so that was left out too. December was well advanced, and the water like ice, so I decided to leave out the part where our hero is cast ashore on a wave. Nor were they any trees for me to come leaping from adorned in beard and brine; and even if I had leaped, my whiskers, carefully unbarbered since last Wednesday, were still not nearly ferocious enough to cause young maidens to go fleeing down the beach, screaming.

In fact, the only part of the Homeric parallel we could perform was my acceptance of Nausicaa's invitation to follow her Ford mule wagon to the palace. Even this wasn't altogether authentic, since in shameless contradic-tion to Homer, I not only made the princess let me ride on the front seat, but also took over the driving of the team myself when my benefactress proved inept at keeping the reins clear of the mules' tails.

Whatever liberties we may have taken in eliminating action from the first

Royal Greek Embassy Press & Information Service

Corfu

scene of the act, we more than made up for in the scene at the palace where King Alcinous, Nausicaa's father, gives Ulysses the lavish banquet. True, we didn't have a king, so, to get around this discrepancy, I had the princess give the banquet.

And how well she gave it! Homer would have been more than satisfied with the abandon and the dramatic genius we put into our acting in the dining hall. Fifi stopped at nothing to make her party sumptuous and expensive. She certainly did succeed. I had indigestion for days afterward.

Toward midnight, when the pheasant from Albania and the champagne from France had been exhausted, and we were feeling rather reckless, I secured a skiff, and rowed Fifi out to the islet in the harbor known as "Ulysses' Ship." Tradition declares that Neptune was so vexed with the Scherian sailors for having escorted Ulysses safely back to Ithaca, he struck the returning vessel with a thunderbolt as it entered the home port, and turned it, and all its mariners, to rock. The islet is on the opposite side of Corfu from the Homeric city, but let's not notice such a little inconsistency; the story is too sacred, and the island, beneath its ancient cypresses, too lovely.

Fifi and I bumped ashore, and, moving cautiously through the dense dark grove, found the chapel built on the island's "fo'castle." Here, beneath the chapel walls, we rested. The night, and the stars, and the wind through the cypresses, and the shadow of the ghostly little shrine, all made me feel so religious I obeyed the impulse to confess to Fifi whatever of my sins she had not extracted before. I was under obligation to her anyway for the banquet, and when she reminded me that she was just a "sympathetic old lady sent by heaven to comfort my distresses," I realized that a confessional was a highly acceptable way to pay my debt. With appropriate sighs and tears I recited the last two chapters from my past that had been tenaciously withheld before—the story of the girl in Argentina who shot herself when I skipped the country—and the awful scandal that had caused me to be expelled from Oxford. Of course, I'd never been near either place, but that only gave my imagination added freedom, for there were no realities to inhibit me. My conscience had not enjoyed such a thorough cleansing in years. It was three o'clock in the morning before the corpse was buried, and I felt sufficiently consoled and absolved by High Priestess Fifi to lead her stumblingly back to the skiff.

As I rowed away toward home, Fifi sank wearily onto the bottom of our boat. All day long I had ignored the fact that with all her sporting spirits, she was not the girl she used to be forty years ago, and I had dragged her about mercilessly since early morning. And yet, even then, as she rested her head on the gunwale, and the wind fluttered through her hair, and the dim starlight softened her features, she did not appear to be half her age.

"Fifi," I said, "I understand now how well you must have played Ophelia. In that position you look just like her."

"Ophelia. My God!" she exclaimed with a groan of utter exhaustion. "You mean King Lear!"

31

Ulysses Returns

❋ On the day Fifi and I had glorified the drama on the Corfu beach, I had climbed to the top of a headland and looked south, down the rocky coast toward Ithaca, only a hundred miles away. And as I looked I caught something of Ulysses' own spirit of impatience. Ithaca! Ithaca! For six months I had been on my way to Ithaca, and now at last it was just beyond the horizon. My pulse beat a bit faster at the thought, for I knew at this point what Ulysses did not know—that the greatest test of his courage and resourcefulness was to be his own castle. Standing on the cliff above the bay, I could see the harbor where Nausicaa's city had stood, and could picture Ulysses in a swift Scherian ship sailing forth from it, speeding southward through the night, and landing at Ithaca at dawn.

I must go on—and alone, for the next morning after our visit to "Ulysses' Ship," an ultimatumish cablegram came from George (instead of the thousand lire Fifi had wired for) demanding that his peregrinating wife abandon the drama and return to private life. As unreasonable as his cable was, Fifi realized his patience was quite exhausted, and that she had best not tax it further by going on with me beyond Corfu. It was a sad decision. Never would she play Penelope now. She must say farewell to Homer and go back to George.

Ithaca, home island of Odysseus

Somewhat annoyed with Ulysses for his willingness to leave behind such agreeable company as Nausicaa's, I sailed away from Scheria and sped southward through the night, just as my great example had done. At dawn I looked from a porthole. There was my island, mountainous, gray, immortal. "I live on clear-seen Ithaca, wherein is a mountain, Neriton," Ulysses had told King Alcinous. And there was Neriton, rising majestically above me.

I go ashore in the Bay of Vathy—the very shore where Ulysses was landed by the Scherian sailors. I deposit my baggage at the little hotel. Burdened with only a large map of Ithaca and my faithful pocket *Odyssey,* I strike out down the beach to the place where Athena, Ulysses' best friend among the gods, comes to aid him. She is aware of the fact that a swarm of insolent suitors of Penelope are living wantonly in his castle, and that he must approach cautiously and incognito.

Disguising Ulysses as an aged beggar, Athena assists him to store his Scherian gifts in a cave overlooking the bay, and then tells him to go to the Rock of Korax, to seek his old swineherd, Eumaeus, who is still faithful.

I find the cave—exactly as it is described in the *Odyssey.* From there, on the pages of my book, I see the transformed Ulysses start toward Eumaeus' hut.

I am right behind him. By means of a mountain path we reach the Rock of Korax, "a place of wide prospect." From it I can see the coast of Greece, twenty miles to the east, and there, far away, and high, gleams the snowy summit of Parnassus rising above the clouds. Parnassus!—where I had prayed to Apollo, months before, to guide and encourage his humble supplicant in order that I might reach Ithaca in safety. Considering everything, I think Apollo did very well by me. In fact, I promised him right there on the Rock of Korax that if he would only see to it that this book, in which he was going to be frequently mentioned, turned out to be a readable and a worthy book, I'd build a temple to him in Central Park.

As the old beggar approaches the hut of Eumaeus, several huge dogs rush out on him. Ulysses wisely sits down on the ground and drops his staff. As I approach the hut of a modern swineherd on the same plateau, several huge dogs rush out at me. Imitating Ulysses, I sit down on the ground and drop my walking stick until the yelping animals are called off.

By the swineherd's hearth, Ulysses meets Telemachus, now grown to manhood, and reveals himself to his son. Then he learns that Penelope's suitors are not ten, nor twenty, but over a hundred, all living like leeches on the absent king's estate, and refusing to disband till Penelope has chosen one to be her husband.

317

Father and son, vowing that these invaders must pay for their crimes with their lives, depart for the palace. With one eye on my book, and one on the path, I follow Ulysses once more.

It is a nine-mile walk to the Homeric city—up and over the narrow isthmus which connects the two sections of the island. The site of the royal home is on a flat hilltop overlooking the little Bay of Polis from which the twelve Ithacan ships and twelve hundred men had sailed away to Troy.

At the door of the court Ulysses encounters an aged dog, Argus, whom in the old days he had reared with his own hands. Argus must have been just a pup when Ulysses went away, for twenty years had intervened; but even so, the faithful animal had not forgotten the man who had been kind to him.

When the beggar speaks, Argus knows the voice. Twenty years he had waited. And now his master has come home at last. He tries to raise his head and crawl toward him, but he has not the strength. Feebly he wags his tail, and drops his ears, and whines pitifully, and dies at Ulysses' feet.

Then—so reads my *Odyssey*—the beggar enters the great hall. It is filled with a hundred roistering men. There is loud drunken laughter, and smoke from the open fires, and motion and uproar everywhere. The king of Ithaca who had left his home so well ordered, so happy, returns to this wanton scene, and to the wreckage of his household.

In my fancy I slip into the hall and climb into a balcony where I can sit and watch the growing drama. All through the evening the suitors continue their revels, and at midnight reel out to find their quarters.

Meanwhile, Penelope, in her apartment, has given way to despair. Ulysses would never come. Tomorrow she would agree to marry any one of the suitors who, with Ulysses' bow, best shot an arrow at the mark.

And next day she sets about to make good her resolution. As my pages turn I see her enter the hall with the bow and quiver. I see the bow go the rounds—unbent, until the beggar asks for a trial. There is a storm of indignation. Penelope insists the old man's request be granted. I hold my breath. I know what is coming. Penelope leaves the hall at Telemachus' insistence. My eyes are racing down the page.

Ulysses puts an arrow on the string, and sends it flying at the mark. The suitors, with a cry of astonishment, leap to their feet . . . and in my balcony I see myself leap to mine. I see Ulysses, standing at the end of the hall, tearing off his rags. Like an enraged lion he glares at his enemies. I see

318

Antinous, the arrogant leader of the band, with a bowl of wine raised to his lips. Ulysses seizes a second arrow. Away goes the shaft—at the human mark. It drives straight through his neck. The blood gushes from his nostrils; the silver cup dashes to the floor; and Antinous plunges on top of it. There is a roar from the suitors ... with a pounding heart I clutch my little book, and read furiously. . . .

"Dogs!" shouts Ulysses. "Did ye think I should not come back from Troy!"

In consternation, the suitors look to the walls for the weapons that have always hung there. Telemachus has removed them all. They run to the doors. Every exit has been tied fast from the outside. Blocked and defenseless, they rush at Ulysses with knives. Telemachus strikes them down. The arrows are flying, flying, and slaughtering. The bare dirt floor is red with blood. There are cries of rage and agony. Grim and desperate, father and son face the multitude. A shower of missiles is flung at Ulysses. Athena turns them all away. Then the suitors know that they are doomed, for the gods are fighting on the other side. Like maddened cattle they try to escape. There is no escape. Splashed crimson, Ulysses piles the dead on the dying. The banquet hall becomes a shambles of butchery and death. I see myself grow sick and faint from the holocaust below. Nothing stays Ulysses' vengeance, not while one cursed suitor lives. Gasping, gory, crazed with blood lust, he stands in the middle of the carnage.

Still clinging, in my fancy, to my balcony, I see Ulysses' servants rehabilitating the slaughterhouse. The bodies are dragged out; the benches purified. Cleansed of his bloody rags, but still disguised, Ulysses awaits Penelope. Someone has gone to tell her that the King of Ithaca has returned.

Incredulous, hesitating, Penelope comes into the hall. Can this beggar be her husband? Is it not one more groundless rumor? And then Athena, in this last need of her favorite, lays her hand on his head, and before my very eyes, the disguise falls away. The Ulysses that I have been pursuing these many weeks, the Ulysses that Penelope has been waiting for these twenty years, young, strong, heroic, stands before us. In tears, Penelope melts into her husband's arms, and he holds her there, tenderly.

The last scene of Homer's epic poem has been played, the last page read. I close the book regretfully, and turn my eyes from the precious little volume to the sunset which, viewed through the shining olive trees on Ulysses' castle site, is enflaming the western sea. Never had I known a sky to be so radiant, so gold—a glorious end of a glorious day and of an immortal story. On such a scarlet sky as this, three thousnd years ago, Ulysses and Penelope, reunited, had watched the darkness creep.

And now, once more, the darkness creeps on Ithaca—and me. The scarlet fades. The evening stars come out. Peacefully falls the curtain of my play. I pocket my faithful little book and leave the twilit stage. My Odyssey— is ended.